SEEKING
GOD
EVERY
DAY

**A 365-Day Journey to a More Powerful
and Purposeful Life of Faith**

Introduction

"The lions may grow weak and hungry, but those who seek the LORD lack no good thing" (Psalm 34:10). When I see a lion, I think of strength. The proud papa lion with his bursting mane looks back at my scrawny figure from the other side of the protective zoo glass. The mama lion stretches out her stride as she bounds after her family's dinner on an episode of *Planet Earth*. There is a reason that professional sports teams love to use the image of a lion on their logos. Because we all want to be strong.

Yet, according to this passage, you can be even stronger than a lion. When you and I direct our daily attention toward the Lord, his character and his promises, we find a kind of strength that would turn a lion's golden mane green with jealousy.

How exactly do you seek the Lord? Good news— the answer is in your hands.

When we meditate on the Word of God, reading and rereading the Scriptures, wrestling with their meaning and application to our lives, we are seeking God himself. And when we do that, we find everything our hearts truly need—forgiveness for our sins, the love of a perfect Father, a place in the community of the saved, and purpose for our daily lives.

So I hope that you enjoy these daily devotions. I pray that they would fill up your heart with God's love and let you stride out into your week with strength.

Like a lion.

January

There is surely a future hope for you,
and your hope will not be cut off.

Proverbs 23:18

Tap into your willpower
New Year's Day
Pastor Matt Ewart

"Habits eat willpower for breakfast."—John Ortberg

I was 33 years old when I completely gave up on the concept of New Year's resolutions. I remember someone asking me that January if I had made any resolutions for the year. I just gave them a blank stare and said, "Nope." That was that.

I'm guessing you've experienced the sting of a resolution that failed. Here you had identified something in your life that wasn't right. At the very least you found something that could've been better. Even though you gave it a good shot, you just couldn't stick with it.

Whether it's a resolution we want to implement or a temptation that we want to resist, the thing that will determine our success is willpower. Willpower is like a battery. You only get so much of it every day, and then it's gone.

You don't have the willpower to do something difficult indefinitely. You can't depend on your willpower to resist temptation. It's only a matter of time until you fail the resolution or fall into the temptation.

So instead of relying so much on your own willpower to defeat temptation, use that willpower to tap into a greater power. Use your willpower to establish the habit of praying at a certain time. Spend that willpower on building the habit of personal Bible reading. Your power is limited. God's power isn't.

"My grace is sufficient for you, for my power is made perfect in weakness" (2 Corinthians 12:9).

Jesus & self-esteem

Pastor Mike Novotny

I studied under a Christian scholar who reads three hundred books a year and presents the Christian message to audiences of all ages, backgrounds, and beliefs. With all that experience, this professor told us the hardest biblical teaching for modern people to believe—that they are sinners. Many of them refuse to buy that age-old church teaching of original sin, that we're born bad.

It seems rather depressing to look at yourself in the mirror every day and admit, "By nature, I'm not a good person." Much more appealing are the self-esteem mantras of the modern age: "I'm wonderful, worthy, and good."

Jesus, however, offers something even better than "good." He offers sinners, humbled by their own struggles to love God and others, the best gift of all—perfection. **"If we claim to be without sin, we deceive ourselves and the truth is not in us. If we confess our sins, he is faithful and just and will forgive us our sins and purify us from all unrighteousness"** (1 John 1:8,9).

We can't lie and claim to be sinless, spectacular people. Yet the truth of our sinfulness doesn't have to crush us if we end up with Jesus. We can confess to him, trusting that he will always be faithful and forgive us. We can walk away completely pure, rid of the shame of anything unrighteous we've done.

Those teachings—our sin and his salvation—keep us humble and happy. Who doesn't want to end up like that?

Be ready

Pastor Clark Schultz

A friend had his car broken into the night before his wedding rehearsal. Among the items stolen was his briefcase. Inside it were 1) his marriage license, 2) his and his fiancée's passports for the trip they were going on out of country, and 3) the wedding rings. There's a feeling of vulnerability when someone steals something from you. Cybercrimes and identity theft are on the rise.

It should be no surprise that the last days are compared to a thief in the night. Most robberies don't happen in the daylight but under the cloud of darkness. We don't know when judgment day will come—we need to be ready.

"But understand this: If the owner of the house had known at what time of night the thief was coming, he would have kept watch and would not have let his house be broken into" (Matthew 24:43).

God encourages us to be ready, vigilant, to have our hearts in tune with God and the security his Word provides. His Word is a lamp for us in these dark days of the world. Put on the armor of God that allows you to get through the struggles you face.

Security systems and car alarms are designed by humans and have flaws. God knows when judgment day is coming. With him there is no vulnerability. Just 100 percent assurance!

Humble & happy

Pastor Mike Novotny

Have I ever told you about my note cards? One of the few stories I repeat often in my teaching is the research I did about the names that God calls Christians in the New Testament. Years ago, I skimmed through all 27 books, from Matthew to Revelation, and wrote down all the positive names (child of God, bride of Christ, etc.) and all the negative names (wretched man, sinner, etc.). When the tally was complete, I counted 682 total names—70 were negative and 612 were positive! A 9 to 1 positive ratio! In fact, 15 of the books had 0 negative names for Christians (proving that Jesus is really good at his job)!

Those numbers can save you from two terrible places—pride and despair. Pride, the belief that you're better than "those people," makes you defensive, unforgiving, and extremely impatient with the sinners around you. Despair, the belief that you're too bad to be loved by God, forgiven by God, or pleasing to God, will rip away the joy Jesus offers your soul. But these New Testament names can save you from both.

The writer to the Hebrews captures this so well: **"For by one sacrifice he has made perfect forever those who are being made holy"** (10:14). We are still "being made holy," still fighting against sin and needing forgiveness. Yet we are already "made perfect," already secure as loved and cherished children of God.

That, brothers and sisters, is the biblical formula that can keep you humble and happy.

Thank heaven for young women
Jason Nelson

The Equal Rights Amendment says, "Equality of rights under the law shall not be denied or abridged by the United States or by any State on account of sex." The idea was introduced to public debate in the 1920s and was passed by congress in the early '70s. But it isn't an amendment to our constitution because the required 38 states didn't ratify it. Just 35 did. It remains controversial. Nevertheless, much of its inherent fairness has percolated into American life. Just visit a major medical center and pay attention to the young women who work there. Their competence, intelligence, and professionalism are gifts from God, just as they are. My wife's primary care physician is a young woman. So are her oncological surgeon, her medical oncologist, her genetic counselor, her radiation oncologist, and her nurses. They work together seamlessly to save my equal partner in life. I thank God for them.

Saving people through young women is nothing new to God. He picked a very special young woman to give birth to his only Son. He didn't drop baby Jesus on some unsuspecting guy's doorstep. He delivered him to us all through a virgin meek, mild, and introspective. Blessed is she among young women (Luke 1:42).

My daughters and granddaughters are young women too. I don't need an amendment to support their right to fulfill their God-given destinies: to learn and grow, to lead and serve, to save something or someone whom God wants saved.

I want to be this tree!
Andrea Delwiche

A leafy tree casting its summer shade over a tranquil lake or meandering stream is my favorite heart-image—a picture that's taken root in my heart. This imagined scene helps me envision who I want to be as a follower of Christ. It comes from Psalm 1:

"Blessed is the one who does not walk in step with the wicked or stand in the way that sinners take or sit in the company of mockers, but whose delight is in the law of the Lord, and who meditates on his law day and night. That person is like a tree planted by streams of water, which yields its fruit in season and whose leaf does not wither—whatever they do prospers" (verses 1-3).

I mull those words over, and the Holy Spirit works in my heart. I'm filled with yearnings and questions. I want to be this tree! How do I delight in and meditate on the Lord's teachings so that I have a fruitful life? Nearly everything conspires to tear me away from these tranquil, life-giving waters.

Silence comes to mind—space for the Lord and me to talk. Prayer comes to mind. I can ask the Lord to keep my roots wet and my leaves green. Memorization also comes to mind. Daunting? Perhaps, but so helpful. When I truly *know* these words, I carry this picture with me. Love for the Lord and his ways fills my heart. I begin to "prosper in whatever I do."

Lord, let your life flow through me. Keep my leaves green. Make my heartwood new. Amen.

Stop comparing

Pastor Jared Oldenburg

I was reading a book the other day, and I stole this question: "Would you rather have $70,000 today or $70,000 in 1900?" You might choose $70,000 in 1900 for one obvious reason—you would be filthy rich. Keep in mind, though, that you wouldn't have a car, commercial airline flights, or penicillin. And the average lifespan would be about 42 years. That option doesn't sound so great anymore, does it?

This backs up the results of a study that concluded that only about 10 percent of our happiness is linked to our possessions. In fact, most of our happiness comes from being better off than the people around us. Here's the kicker. Someone is always better—smarter, prettier, richer, funnier, and better at school.

There's lots of conjecture about how we can be so depressed as a nation even though we live relatively (historically and globally) amazing lives. One cause? Comparison, specifically comparison on social media. In a world of constant information, there's basically no break to just be you. At any given moment, you see the best of your friends' lives and the worst of yours. That doesn't feel so good.

What does feel good is seeing who we are in Jesus. John tells us, **"See what great love the Father has lavished on us, that we should be called children of God! And that is what we are!"** (1 John 3:1).

Maybe it's time to stop comparing ourselves and start knowing who we really are in Christ. We're God's children, lavished in love.

Dismiss or discuss?

Pastor Mike Novotny

As a teenager who read the Bible cover to cover, I had lots of questions about God. *What does that mean? But how could a loving God do that?* My unanswered questions filled a notebook; until one day, I brought that notebook to my pastor.

In that moment, he had to make a very important decision. It's a decision that you'll have to make someday as a friend, as a parent, and/or as a Christian leader. The decision is—Do you dismiss it? Or do you discuss it? Do you tell the person to stop asking so many questions and "just believe"? Or do you take the necessary time to discuss the tougher objections to the Bible?

Thankfully, my pastor chose the path of the apostle Paul: **"So [Paul] *reasoned* in the synagogue with both Jews and God-fearing Greeks, as well as in the marketplace day by day with those who happened to be there"** (Acts 17:17). Paul reasoned with people. He explained the evidence. He listed all the points that pointed him to Jesus.

I hope you can do the same. Yes, there are many questions that can't be answered in this life. But the Bible is filled with good reasons to believe that God exists and that Jesus, our Savior, is risen from the dead. So don't dismiss tough questions. Ask the Holy Spirit for guidance and discuss them. A skeptical soul will one day thank you for your time.

Are you lonely?

Pastor Matt Ewart

People are lonelier now than ever.

Even though loneliness is often portrayed as a weakness, what happened in the beginning suggests otherwise. On the sixth day of creation, just before God rested the power of his universe-creating voice, he spoke about one final detail that still needed attention: **"It is not good for the man to be alone"** (Genesis 2:18).

I often joke that the reason for this observation was because Adam couldn't properly dress himself, but the truth is that community was and still is an essential component of our humanity.

God is love, and Adam was created in God's image. But Adam could not show love when he was alone.

In other words, Adam was lonely, not because there was something wrong with him. He was lonely because he was perfect.

When you feel lonely, that means something is *right* with you. Not only did God design you to crave community, but God personally redeemed you through Christ to reflect his love to others.

Today I'm praying for the people reading this devotion who are struggling with loneliness. May the same voice that brought joy to Adam bring hope to you today: **"Surely I am with you always, to the very end of the age"** (Matthew 28:10).

Jesus declares that though you feel alone, you are never by yourself. Though you feel isolated, you are never abandoned. Surely he is with you today just as his Word declares.

Be bold!

Ann Jahns

When it comes to common phobias, what do you think ranks toward the top? . . . It's the fear of public speaking.

Speaking in front of a group—and the vulnerability it entails—is truly terrifying for so many of us. Are your palms sweating just envisioning it? But what about as a believer? What is your greatest fear? Perhaps it's this: speaking to others about your faith. What if you don't know what to say? What if you say something that's just plain wrong? What if you're ridiculed or even harmed for speaking about your hope in Christ?

Even Moses, one of the pillars of faith in the Old Testament and God's chosen spokesperson, didn't feel qualified to speak to others on God's behalf. In Exodus 4:10, Moses lamented to God: **"Pardon your servant, Lord. I have never been eloquent. . . . I am slow of speech and tongue."** But God gently rebuked him, **"Who gave human beings their mouths? . . . Is it not I, the LORD? Now go; I will help you speak and will teach you what to say"** (verses 11,12).

So, be bold! You're God's instrument on this earth— his chosen spokesperson. You and I can share the hope that we have in Christ, even if it scares us. God will help us speak. And remember: we don't have the responsibility—or the power—to create faith in someone. That's God's work through the Holy Spirit. But it is our responsibility to share the hope that we have in Christ.

Follow Jesus as your priority
Pastor Jeremy Mattek

When I was in high school, a friend of mine was driving us to a school event. At one point, he reached over to the radio to change the station. As he reached over, he accidentally turned the steering wheel so quickly and sharply that the car swerved off the road, rolled over three times, and landed upside down in the bottom of a ditch. Remarkably, everyone was okay. My friend didn't break any laws by trying to change the radio station. It's a good thing to listen to the radio—except when it gets in the way of safe driving.

There are any number of good things on which we might focus our attention in life—our families, friends, jobs, and hobbies. It's good to focus on these things—except when we give more attention to them then we do to Jesus.

"[Jesus] **said to another man, 'Follow me'**" (Luke 9:59). When Jesus calls individuals to "Follow *me*," he isn't suggesting that he is one of many good things in this world to which we might pay attention. He is expecting to be our highest priority. Why?

Because only Jesus keeps us safe for eternity.

Because our family, friends, jobs, and hobbies are all gifts from him.

Because when we realize how inattentive we have been to his Word and will, Jesus always treats us with grace.

Because when we look at the cross of Jesus, we see that his greatest priority will always be to love us.

Mind width
Jason Nelson

America doesn't have enough digital bandwidth to carry all of the data that could educate us, entertain us, or help us do our jobs. I know because I live in a rural dead zone that barely gets signals. We also don't have enough mind width to seize the opportunities before us. Under President Bush 41, the 90s were designated "the decade of the brain." Government and philanthropists funded ten years of research. Imaging and lab work allowed scientists to map the brain and the human genome. They discovered that we're not born with all of the brain we need. The brain itself adds to its own mind width by directing us to have broad experiences so it can grow more nerves and make new connections. Lo and behold, cell growth is greater after intense training, after facing difficult challenges, and after rigorous education even well into old age.

This is a miracle. The righteous God **"who probes minds and hearts"** (Psalm 7:9) has given us the capacity to probe our own minds and grow our own mind width. We know more about what sticks in our memories and our place in the world because 30 years ago we saw how glial cells and grid cells go to work in our brains. Brain research is helping those with Alzheimer's. Gene therapies are treating other tough disorders, proving once again that those who hope in the Lord not only renew their strength; they also expand their minds.

Stand out!

Ann Jahns

Anyone who lived through the 1980s can attest to the fact that we'll do just about anything to fit in. Not to stand out. To look like everyone else. How else can you explain a whole decade of hair that big? Believe me; I'm not pointing fingers. I'm just as guilty, and I have the high school yearbooks to prove it.

There's something in us that wants to fit in, and that's what the world wants us to do too. It wants us to talk, look, and think a certain way. Satan, the father of lies, tells us we need to conform to the attitudes and values of this world.

But Jesus calls us to stand out from the world: **"You are the light of the world. A town built on a hill cannot be hidden. . . . Let your light shine before others, that they may see your good deeds and glorify your Father in heaven"** (Matthew 5:14,16).

What does this look like? Perhaps it's guarding our tongues when we're tempted to gossip. Perhaps it's being a diligent worker, even if we don't necessarily love our jobs. Or perhaps it's just being different in how we respond to our circumstances—so when those around us notice and ask us why, we can share the hope that we have in Jesus.

Those of us who love Christ, who follow him, are called to be different. We're the light of the world, so shine on, believer. Stand out!

Joy vs. happiness
Pastor Jared Oldenburg

What would make you happy, like really happy? If you were asked and you didn't have to admit it out loud, what would you say? Would you be happy if you had a little more money? What about a full head of hair? Would you finally be happy if you got a promotion or if your grandkids called you more often?

For most of us, happiness is a concept that's off in the distance. We're here. It's way out there. To find happiness, we try out different bridges to reach it. Have you ever tried a diet or gone shopping or even drowned your sorrows in a glass? Yeah, me too. It may take awhile, but soon enough we figure out that these things don't really work.

As believers, you and I know our real goal in life is not happiness, but rather joy. Paul says it this way: **"Rejoice in the Lord always"** (Philippians 4:4).

Happiness comes and goes with circumstances. Joy, on the other hand, is quite different. Joy is finding contentment where you are right now. No more bridges, just contentment.

So are you still looking for happiness? I'm not sure you'll find it. What I do know is that in Christ you already have everything you need to rejoice!

One-sided coins
Jason Nelson

There are teachings in the Bible that are one-sided coins. **"Those whom he predestined he also called, and those whom he called he also justified, and those whom he justified he also glorified"** (Romans 8:30 ESV). You have faith in Jesus because God wanted you to have faith, he called you to faith, and he will raise you in glory. God flipped a one-sided coin, and you came up heads. Grace is a one-sided coin.

We're more familiar with two-sided coins and how to flip them. "Heads I win. Tails you lose." We think that's how God flips coins too. We assume he picks winners and losers. So we make judgments about people based on the faith we recognize in ourselves but can't discern in others. We're quick to flip a coin with a label on each side. We have the habit of sorting people into "believers and unbelievers." Those categories exist, but only God knows who is in them at any moment in time. We have to be very cautious when we try to referee in God's behalf.

But we can always tell the good news of a one-sided coin. The Word became flesh. He dwelt among us. We have seen his glory. **"For from his fullness we have all received, *grace upon grace*"** (John 1:16 ESV). Grace upon grace is the coin God flips for all mankind. That's how we're called. That's how we're justified. And that's why we will be glorified.

Trust God's advice

Pastor Clark Schultz

I love shopping on Amazon, but I also like to seek advice before buying something. I ask friends who already have the product. I scour through the many reviews of the product, looking for the five-star positives and wondering what made someone give a product only one or two stars.

God gives us advice. He tells us to love him first. But often there are other things that creep into our hearts and become more important than God. He says to love others like we love ourselves. But gossiping and bullying and teasing to make ourselves look better become our norm.

It's been said that a true friend will stab you in the front, not in the back. Meaning they may tell you something you don't want to hear but need to hear.

God stabbed his own Son in the side and jammed nails into his wrists and feet for you! He knows how we fall short, but he also knows how he can help us.

As the apostle Paul reminds us, **"Who has known the mind of the Lord? Or who has been his counselor?"** (Romans 11:34). True, it may not make sense to our brains, but trust God's advice when he says, "I have plans for you, plans to prosper you."

Hear his counsel when he says, "Come to me you who are weary and burdened." And remember that no matter what, nothing can separate you from his love—a love more precious than any five-star rating on the internet.

Praise the Lord for his amazing victory
Pastor Jeremy Mattek

Sometimes you might think you'll never see or feel anything good again. The pain of losing a loved one can be difficult to recover from. So can the struggles that come with addiction. Maybe you've gone through a stretch where you've lost so much and haven't gained anything.

But with God, good things can happen even when we think they can't.

Moses and the Israelites sang a song of praise to God for opening a way to freedom that they never saw coming: **"The Lord is my strength and my defense; he has become my salvation. He is my God, and I will praise him, my father's God, and I will exalt him. The Lord is a warrior; the Lord is his name. Pharoah's chariots and his army he has hurled into the sea"** (Exodus 15:2-4).

God showed them he was fighting for them when he divided the waters of the Red Sea, allowing them to walk to safety before bringing the waters together again to destroy the enemy that was pursing them.

You may never be caught between an army and a large body of water, but the same God who delivered Israel has already provided a way to a greater Promised Land. Through Jesus, God has guaranteed that your enemies of sin and death won't keep you from him in heaven.

Maybe you have days when it doesn't feel like you're on your way there, but that doesn't mean you're not. In fact, because of Jesus, you are.

january 18

Church family

Pastor Matt Ewart

If I was prepared for ministry the way Jesus prepared his disciples for ministry, I'm not sure I would have made it.

While a lot of people would be grateful for the disciples, what they probably didn't expect is that some people would end up dead because of their work.

"Brother will betray brother to death, and a father his child; children will rebel against their parents and have them put to death" (Matthew 10:21).

Without getting into all the historical details, some families were broken up because one of its members followed Jesus. The households loyal to Jewish laws and traditions would consider a relative who followed Jesus guilty of blasphemy, punishable by death. Eventually, households loyal to Rome would consider a relative who followed Jesus an insurrectionist. Their fate would be the Coliseum.

It was no accident, then, that the New Testament letters refer to the church using family terms such as *brothers* and *sisters*. Many of those first-century Christians were abandoned by their families of origin and had nowhere to go except to one another.

What they found is what we continue to find to this day. While the church on earth never will be perfect, the Spirit adopted us into a family that runs much deeper than genetics. This is a family where unconditional love is proclaimed and practiced. This is a family that doesn't live under the threat of death, but rather under the promise of life.

Thank God for the family he gives you in his church!

Call on God
Pastor Clark Schultz

Alexander Graham Bell, inventor of the telephone, made the first call on March 10, 1876, to his assistant, Thomas Watson. What were the first words ever spoken on the telephone? "Mr. Watson—come here—I want to see you."

Fast-forward to 2017. About 15,220,700 texts were sent every minute of every day worldwide. This doesn't include Snaps. Add that number, and it almost triples. On average, how many of those statistics do you contribute too?

This is not meant to cause guilt, but how many of those calls are to God? God encourages us to call on him: **"Call on me in the day of trouble; I will deliver you, and you will honor me"** (Psalm 50:15).

One of my favorite conversations to overhear is when people talk trash to each other about cell phone providers. "Oh, you have X; they stink. I have . . ." Or "I have X, and I'm always dropping calls."

God has the best network there is. Think of this: You can go anywhere in the world, and you will never have a dropped call. He hears and he listens.

He answers all our prayers. Yes, there may be times when we're put on hold, but the answers God gives are better than what we could imagine. Let your next call to God be this: "God—come here and be near me—I want to see you."

Friends, call on God!

Put reason in the right place

Pastor Mike Novotny

Human reason and logic are stunning gifts from a generous God. Without reason, you wouldn't be able to apply God's love for the world (John 3:16) to your 21st-century self. Thankfully, via the laws of logic, you and I trust that the words "the world" apply to us too.

But reason lovers like me need to be careful. Because the Scriptures are clear that human reason has its limits. I might be able to construct airtight arguments for the existence of God (Romans 1:20) or the resurrection of Jesus (1 Corinthians 15:6), but human reason is unable to do the most important job of all—change the human heart. Only the Holy Spirit, working through the power of the gospel, can change an unbelieving heart into a trusting one. Only that message of Jesus, crucified in our place, can make faith take the place of unbelief. **"Faith comes,"** not from courtroom arguments, said Paul, but from **"hearing the word about Christ"** (Romans 10:17).

What does that mean for us? It's a reminder that reasoning with skeptical family and friends is good but sharing the simple message of Jesus is better. Give the unbelievers in your life plenty of reasons to believe; but make sure that, at the top of the list, is the unreasonable promise that God loves the world, which, according to reason, means God loves them too.

Collectivity

Jason Nelson

Swiss psychologist Carl Jung (1875–1961) made important contributions to the field of psychology. He laid a foundation for understanding different personality types by classifying people as either introverts or extroverts. He also observed that people seem to share a "collective unconscious" mind. He suggested that we inherit an understanding of some fundamental concepts. For instance, everyone knows a good mom when he or she sees one. Likewise, **"When outsiders who have never heard of God's law follow it more or less by instinct, they confirm its truth by their obedience. They show that God's law is not something alien, imposed on us from without, but woven into the very fabric of our creation"** (Romans 2:14,15 MSG).

I've noticed collectivity every time I open one of these Grace Moments books. We writers don't work in adjacent cubicles. We don't have meetings. We don't chat with each other over lunch. But we often write about similar things. Sometimes I think, "Doggone it. Linda used the passage I was going to use." Or "Pastor Mike addressed an issue I wanted to write about." That happens because in our collective Christian minds, we have the same concerns.

That's an encouraging phenomenon. Sometimes we feel like we're the only ones who are frustrated with current events or fearful things are spinning out of control. But around the world other people are thinking the same thing we are because **"there is something deep within them that echoes God's yes and no"** (Romans 2:15 MSG).

january 22

Everyone has a place
Pastor Clark Schultz

How do you feel when you see someone else make the winning basket and you're stuck on the bench? Or how do you feel when the person in the next cubicle gets the new, shiny car and you still drive the minivan with Cheerios on the floor?

Are you happy, jealous, or just insecure?

John the Baptist's disciples were jealous that Jesus was baptizing and getting more fame than their master. Less shine on John's star meant less shine for the disciples. So like a bunch of second graders, they ran to John. John didn't answer with, "I'll show you, Jesus!" or, "Who is this Jesus to steal my thunder!?" Quite the contrary, he let his disciples know that everyone has his or her place. **"He must become greater; I must become less"** (John 3:20).

In other words, everyone has different gifts and talents given by God. John humbly accepted his role as the forerunner to the Savior and trusted God's plan that Jesus was the real Savior people should follow.

God creates each of us with different roles and different talents. Instead of jealousy, why not turn to the God who loves you, died for you, and has made you unique like a snowflake.

Yes, there may be people more talented than you in some areas, but that doesn't make you inferior or less in God's eyes.

Our God is not into petty games of jealousy. He is 100 percent into you and wants you to fulfill the purpose he has for you in this life.

A different government?
Andrea Delwiche

How many governmental promises have been uttered in the U.S. since the beginning of our democracy? How many of these promises have you or I bought into? How's that working out?

The failure of human governments is nothing new. **"Why do the nations conspire and the peoples plot in vain? The kings of the earth rise up and the rulers band together against the Lord and against his anointed, saying, 'Let us break their chains and throw off their shackles'"** (Psalm 2:1-3).

We long for a system where wrongs can be made right. We feel powerless to effect change when we sense our government is complicit with evil. The powers that be seem too big: "They ruin everything." Yet we also turn and scoff and say, "They can't do anything." Even as we ridicule the system, anger and despair show that we place our trust in them.

I might say, "God's in charge." But my fear, anger, and sense of hopelessness show that my heart actually sees human institutions as holding the power in this world. I profess something with my mouth and *think* I believe it in my heart, yet how I *act* ultimately shows what I truly believe in.

What if we put our trust in a different government and our allegiance rested with a different Ruler? You probably know where I'm going with this. God laughs at the rulers of the earth: **"I have installed *my* king on Zion, my holy mountain. . . . Blessed are all who take refuge in him"** (Psalm 2:6,12). Reign in my heart, King Jesus.

Why believe the Bible?

Pastor Mike Novotny

"Why do you believe the Bible?" the skeptic asks. "Because it's God's Word," the Christian replies. "Says who?" the skeptic responds. "Says the Bible," the Christian answers.

Hmm . . . You can see why the logic that Christians love might not persuade a skeptical friend. The reasoning seems as unpersuasive as the parent who responds to their kid's question with, "Because I said so!"

Thankfully, there are powerful arguments to back up our belief in the Bible. One of my favorites is how the Old Testament prophets knew what the New Testament apostles saw. Take Isaiah, for example. Isaiah knew that God's chosen Messiah would be born of a virgin (Isaiah 7). He knew that the Christ would come from the family of King David (Isaiah 11). He knew that the Savior would be pierced for sins, suffer silently, be buried with the rich, and see the light of life again (Isaiah 53). How in the world did Isaiah, living seven hundred years before the birth of Jesus, know all that?

The apostle Peter has a reason: **"For prophecy never had its origin in the human will, but prophets, though human, spoke from God as they were carried along by the Holy Spirit"** (2 Peter 1:21). The Old Testament prophecies were indeed written by humans. But those humans had help. The Holy Spirit. That's how they knew things no human could know. The prophets' knowledge, given by the Holy Spirit, is one of the persuasive reasons that we Christians believe in the "Holy" Bible.

We're depressed . . .

Pastor Jared Oldenburg

Everything I read says that depression is through the roof—men, women, the elderly, and even kids. Logically, a person would assume that people in the worst circumstances would be the most depressed. Here's an example of some of the worst circumstances from the life of the apostle Paul:

"[I have] **been in prison more frequently, been flogged more severely, and been exposed to death again and again. Five times I received from the Jews the forty lashes minus one. Three times I was beaten with rods, once I was pelted with stones, three times I was shipwrecked, I spent a night and a day in the open sea"** (2 Corinthians 11:23-25). The list, as you can imagine, goes on.

I used to think that the devil worked in suffering. I figured that in suffering we are the most susceptible to his temptations. However, in my experience, the people who've found contentment, the ones who find joy in God, are often the ones who are suffering. It seems that when people have everything, it's hard to distinguish what actually matters. In this sense, suffering is a gift because it strips away everything and anything that doesn't really matter.

Are you suffering right now? If so, know this, sometimes the door you walk through to find joy is suffering. Or how did the writer of Hebrews describe Jesus' ministry? **"For the joy set before him, he endured the cross"** (12:2).

Accepting

Jason Nelson

I have an acceptance disorder. It's because I buy into the idea that **"everything is possible for one who believes"** (Mark 9:23). That creates tension between God and me. Sometimes I just don't like what he won't allow. I can't make peace with it. I plop down next to Job and **"give free rein to my complaint"** (Job 10:1). I'm frustrated. I'm curdling like cheese inside because I can't accept that this is how it is and there isn't anything I can do about it. I grit my teeth and let out a primal scream. Job glances my way and says, "Brother, tell me about it." Then I poke my head around and see Jesus sitting on the other side of Job politely expressing his complaint: **"My Father, if it is possible, may this cup be taken from me"** (Matthew 26:39).

Sometimes God lets us be miracle workers. Amazing that sinners can solve problems! We can overcome evil with good. Those are Emmanuel moments. God is with us. But accepting that some difficult things won't change is also a challenge we face. After decades of experience wrestling with this dilemma, we still don't have it figured out. If we accept a bad situation too soon, we could miss out on the next big miracle. If we don't accept it at all, we could wear ourselves out pushing against God's resistance. That's why we not only pray, "God's will be done." We also try to do it.

God & transgender—Part 1

Pastor Mike Novotny

How should Christians approach their transgender questions? When we (or someone we love) feel a disconnect between our brains and our biological bodies, what does God want us to do? Let's tackle those questions in a series of devotions over the next few days.

The best place to start with questions about transgender is the book of Genesis. **"So God created mankind in his own image, in the image of God he created them; male and female he created them. God blessed them and said to them, 'Be fruitful and increase in number'"** (1:27,28). In these words, God connects gender and biological sex, a truth Jesus later referred to in his famous words about marriage (Matthew 19:4). A male and a female, by God's definition, are two people who are able to "be fruitful and increase in number." Biological sex was not assigned at birth by a doctor but assigned by God, with gender intimately connected to it. And when our Father looked at his binary children, male and female, he said, "That's so good!" (Genesis 1:31).

So, why isn't it always good? Why do we deal with nonbinary feelings, unique situations (like intersex people), infertility, and countless other struggles with our bodies? If God made us male and female (and if God doesn't make mistakes), why do God-fearing people feel such a disconnect between the desires of their minds and the design of Genesis chapter 1?

We'll tackle those questions in tomorrow's devotion.

God & transgender—Part 2

Pastor Mike Novotny

If God created us "male and female" and declared that our genders are "very good" (Genesis 1:27,31), why do so many people—even God-fearing, Spirit-filled followers of Jesus—struggle so much with gender?

The answer comes in Genesis chapter 3 when the first male and female fell into sin and gender forever fell apart in the process. The apostle Paul later lamented, **"We ourselves, who have the firstfruits of the Spirit, groan inwardly as we wait eagerly for our adoption to sonship, the redemption of our bodies"** (Romans 8:23). We groan as we wait for Jesus to come back and make our bodies better. Transgender people feel this reality all too often. One young woman told me she felt like she wanted to crawl out of her skin in search of a new body.

But that struggle isn't exclusive to the transgender community. Have you ever battled anxiety? or depression? or addictive behavior? or a heart that suffers from obsessive comparison disorder? or anorexic thoughts that tell you things about your body that aren't true? Why are those feelings so natural? Why are we born that way? Because after Adam and Eve fell into sin, everything fell apart, our brains and bodies included.

Thankfully, Jesus is coming back to redeem our bodies. He'll fix us as thoroughly as he forgave us on the cross. Until then, we wait in faith, trusting that our struggles are not worth comparing to the glory that is about to be revealed to us (Romans 8:18).

Tomorrow learn more about the hope that Jesus gives us.

God & transgender—Part 3
Pastor Mike Novotny

Do you think Jesus experienced the same temptation that many transgender people face? Jesus is God—all-powerful, eternal, present everywhere—but two thousand years ago, when he took on flesh, Jesus humbled himself and experienced the weaknesses of the human body. He got hungry, thirsty, tired, exhausted, sad, sorrowful, and overwhelmed. Look how Paul puts it in Philippians 2:8: **"And being found in appearance as a man, he humbled himself by becoming obedient to death—even death on a cross!"** Jesus knows what it's like to suffer in a body. Before his resurrection, his body was humble, inglorious, and weak. But the God who saw our broken bodies chose to be broken so we could be whole. And one day, just like Jesus who gloriously rose from the grave (with a body!), our bodies will be made wonderfully new.

The first person to open my eyes to that idea was a young Christian who was dealing with gender dysphoria (the disconnect between the gender she felt and the biological sex God gave to her). It gave her great comfort to know that her Savior knew what she was going through. Even more, she held on to the promise that Jesus is coming back soon to make her new.

Until then, it's essential that we love one another in the midst of the struggle. We'll turn to that subject in tomorrow's devotion.

january 30

God & transgender—Part 4
Pastor Mike Novotny

I came across a sobering statistic from the American Academy of Pediatrics. It reported that 42 percent of transgender teens have attempted suicide. 42 percent! That's three times the rate of the average American teenager.

I need that statistic to soak into your soul. Too often, Christians are insensitive and dismissive of the struggles that others have with their gender identity. Tragically, our thoughtless comments are being heard and read online by friends and family who are dealing with transgender struggles. Our lack of compassion might scare them into keeping their struggles a secret, which can lead many to a fatal choice.

This is why, even as we remember that God created us as male and female, we must not forget his call to love one another deeply. Paul wrote, **"If I have a faith that can move mountains, but do not have love, I am nothing"** (1 Corinthians 13:2). In our modern age, when sexuality and gender are being radically redefined, let's remember to love *everyone* with our words, actions, and social media posts. That matters to Jesus as much as a mountain-moving faith.

Why would we? Because Jesus first loved us. When we were dead in sin, blinded by sin, hostile because of sin, lost in sin, and pursuing sin, Jesus loved us (Romans 5:8). That unconditional, before-we-got-everything-right love is what compels us to love all people, even those struggling with gender identity.

Where does that leave us? We'll wrap up tomorrow by answering that vital question for Jesus' church.

God & transgender—Part 5

Pastor Mike Novotny

God gave us a gender (male or female); sin broke our bodies (including our sense of gender); Jesus' body was broken to give us hope; and all Christians are called to love one another, even if the temptations we face are unique.

Now what? While specialized counseling or support groups have their place, the church of Jesus doesn't require special groups for transgender people (or adulterers or porn addicts or the anxious or the proud or any type of sin). We just need to do life together. We need to talk about what feels so good to us but isn't good according to God. We need to share the grace of Jesus with one another. We need to pray for the Spirit to give us the self-control we need to do the will of God. Paul encourages us, **"Carry each other's burdens, and in this way you will fulfill the law of Christ"** (Galatians 6:2). There's no need to rank burdens or feel embarrassed by the temptation that I face and you don't. Instead, we love each other well when we fix one another's eyes on Jesus—his grace, his faithfulness.

Recently, a Christian from our church confessed her gender identity struggles to her small group Bible study. How did they react? With love. They embraced her, encouraged her, and prayed for her. They treated her like any other Christian—someone who faces daily temptation but whose identity is secure because of the blood of Jesus.

That's how we carry each other's burdens. That's how we love people the way Jesus first loved us.

February

Dear friends, since God so loved us,
we also ought to love one another.

1 John 4:11

Embracing trouble
Ann Jahns

I don't know about you, but I'm not a big fan of pain. When I was pregnant with my first child, I vowed, *"I'm going to power through childbirth the natural way!"* Hours into labor, nothing was more welcome than the absurdly long needle administering pain relief. Sometimes even a microscopic paper cut can throw off my day. We humans aren't wired to want to be in pain or go through hardship. And so often, we do everything we can to avoid it. We ignore. We self-medicate. But Jesus assures us: **"In this world you will have trouble"** (John 16:33).

When Jesus spoke these words, he was beginning his walk to the cross, taking a final opportunity to encourage and prepare his disciples for the life-changing events to come. He wanted them to be aware of the troubles they would endure as bold Christ followers.

So why would we want to embrace trouble? It sounds crazy and counterintuitive. But trouble turns us to God. It helps us recognize—and treasure—his blessings. Only after we've endured the valleys can we truly appreciate the sweet joy of the mountaintops. Living through hardships also helps us help others. Having someone walk alongside us in times of pain, someone who has been there, is one of the greatest byproducts of hardship.

Yes, Jesus tells us we'll have trouble. But that's not the end of the story. He concludes with this: **"But take heart! I have overcome the world."** Hang in there, friend. This world is hard. But Jesus has conquered it.

februarry 2

My worst enemy and my best friend
Pastor Mike Novotny

Back in 2001, pop star P!nk released a hit song entitled, "Don't Let Me Get Me." She sang about the daily war she fought against her own desires and lack of self-control. She admitted she couldn't stand the sight of the person staring back at her from the mirror. She concluded that she was her own worst enemy.

Have you ever felt that way? Even as followers of Jesus, we know all about the war against our own desires for comfort/pleasure/the last word. We can relate to that lack of self-control with our words, our assumptions, and our dinner portions. We agree that our greatest spiritual enemies just might be ourselves. You've felt the same regret that I have, haven't you?

Thankfully, we Christians don't just stare at a mirror. We stare at a cross. The cross of Jesus is where our spiritual war was won, where our sinful desires were defeated, and where God gives us a whole new look. He clothes us with Christ, in all of his love, holiness, and spiritual beauty. **"In Christ Jesus you are all children of God through faith, for all of you who were baptized into Christ have clothed yourselves with Christ"** (Galatians 3:26,27).

What stunning words! We're clothed with Jesus, wrapped in his grace, and promised a place in our Father's family. Our last thought before bed and our first thought in the morning don't have to be about ourselves. They can be about Jesus, the Savior who makes us good with God.

Follow Jesus no matter the cost

Pastor Jeremy Mattek

Some people live in what are called "tiny homes." Some are only slightly larger than a backyard shed. Though the living space is small, these homes are skillfully constructed to include most anything its residents might find in a larger house. They've become the home of choice for many people who are glad to live with less compared to their neighbors.

But anyone living in a tiny home owns more property than Jesus did as he was looking for disciples. **"A man said to [Jesus], 'I will follow you wherever you go.' Jesus replied, 'Foxes have dens and birds have nests, but the Son of Man has no place to lay his head'"** (Luke 9:57,58). Jesus was really asking the man a question: "Would you be willing to follow me even if it means losing all your earthly possessions, including your home?"

There are many Christians today who are forced to answer that question. And there are many who choose to lose their homes rather than forsake Jesus. Why?

Because in the Word of God they've found a cross on which Jesus clearly shows his determination to love and forgive us, no matter the cost.

Because Jesus' empty tomb on Easter morning gives us a better home to look forward to in heaven than even the largest and most extravagant home on earth.

Maybe you'll never have to give up your earthly home to follow Jesus. But it would be worth it to follow the One who gave up his life for you.

Thankful for what you have

Pastor Jared Oldenburg

Let me ask you a question. Are you happy? No one's listening. No one's writing this down. I'm not asking you about your kids or your boss. I'm asking about you. Are you happy on a scale of 1 to 10?

I want to be clear here. I'm not asking if you *should* be happy. Theoretically, we should all be happy. We live in one of the richest nations in the world. Most of us have at least one car and a job. Many people have a house, have healthy kids, and are married to someone who loves them back.

Even if theoretically your life is pretty tough, I guarantee I can find someone who has it worse off than you. Try this: Next time you get a rash, just google "severe skin rash" and see if you aren't thankful for the rash you do have! What just happened there? In an instant, you became thankful for what you do have rather than what you don't.

Have you ever thought about what you have as a believer? Isaiah reminds us, **"Though your sins are like scarlet, they shall be as white as snow"** (Isaiah 1:18). You have something special. If you were the only one on this planet, God would have come to save you. Through Christ your sins are wiped clean. You're a child of the risen God: forgiven, accepted, and loved. God has given you a purpose, and no one, not even the devil himself, can bring you down. That's not theory; that's the truth.

Are you a good person?

Pastor Mike Novotny

Are you a good person? The apostle Paul used to think so. But then he became a Christian and came to believe that, by nature, he was spiritually dead, blind to the truth, and hostile to the authority of God (Ephesians 2, 1 Corinthians 1, Romans 8). That's a pretty depressing status update to put on your social media feed, right?

Wrong. Paul was actually the happiest, most joyful, peaceful, content, satisfied soul you could ever meet. He was the guy who wrote, **"Rejoice in the Lord always"** (Philippians 4:4). He's the Christian we quote when we feel weak: **"I can do all this through him who gives me strength"** (Philippians 4:13). He's the guy we want to be like, because he said, **"I have learned the secret of being content"** (Philippians 4:12). How could a guy who believed he was so bad by nature end up feeling so good? Answer—Jesus. Paul knew that without Jesus he was a mess but with Jesus he was a miracle of grace.

You are too. As a Christian, you are in Christ. You're included in all the love, affection, and attention that the Father gives his Son. God sent his Son and then his Spirit to transform your identity—to make the spiritually dead you live, to make the spiritually blind you see, to make the spiritually hostile you joyfully submit to Jesus' authority.

No, without Jesus we are not good people. But with Jesus we are not just good. We are the best—children of God!

february 6

A reliable, no-strings-attached network
Pastor Clark Schultz

One of the most annoying sounds in the world has to be the busy signal you get when you call and someone is on the other line. Take a moment to hear that sound in your head. You're welcome to scream now.

What about when you call out to God? Do you get that same annoyance? God is never too busy for you to call on him. **"Call on me in the day of trouble; I will deliver you, and you will honor me"** (Psalm 50:15). He promises to deliver us.

When we start with a phone provider, we often get locked into a contract and there are hidden fees, etc. With God there are no hidden fees and our contract is signed in the blood of his Son. No strings attached.

So today when you're reaching for your phone, call on God. Call on him and thank him for today's blessings. Thank him for the troubles too, as crazy as that sounds. God has a plan for those too, and they will work out for your good.

A popular cell phone ad campaign had a guy showing up in places all over the world saying, "Can you hear me now?" The claim was that you could go anywhere and this network was reliable.

With God, when you ask, "Can you hear me now?" the answer is always yes.

Requiem for the middle

Jason Nelson

I noticed it when I was still teaching. The middle seemed to be disappearing. There were exceptional students and special needs students. Few kids were just average. I see it in our society. People either have good incomes and live in big houses or are struggling to make ends meet and find something affordable to live in. Political moderates get voted out. Even the middle child is an endangered species as many couples opt to have just two children. I don't think it's anyone's aspiration in life. Who's hoping to be successful enough just to make it to the middle? I miss the big modest middle. We seem to be engineering it out of existence.

Congratulations if you're highly successful. I really hope you can stay that way. Making the adjustments required to go down is very difficult. May God lift you up if you're not feeling so successful. Please keep striving and never give up. Working your way up is also very difficult, and it can take a long time. And don't feel embarrassed if you're stuck in the middle. You lack nothing. **"A godly life brings huge profits to people who are content with what they have. We didn't bring anything into the world, and we can't take anything out of it. As long as we have food and clothes, we should be satisfied"** (1 Timothy 6:6-8 GW). It's the middle that holds everything together.

february 8

Why believe in Jesus?

Pastor Mike Novotny

Has anyone ever called you crazy for believing in Jesus Christ? "Wait, you actually believe that God was born from a virgin, died on a cross, and then came back from the dead? Seriously?"

If so, check out how the apostle Paul defended his faith in front of two skeptical politicians during his trial in Caesarea: **"Festus interrupted Paul's defense. 'You are out of your mind, Paul!' he shouted. 'Your great learning is driving you insane.' 'I am not insane, most excellent Festus,' Paul replied. 'What I am saying is true and reasonable. The king is familiar with these things, and I can speak freely to him. I am convinced that none of this has escaped his notice, because it was not done in a corner'"** (Acts 26:24-26).

I love that logic. Paul pointed out that Christianity didn't happen in a corner. There were real witnesses of the real things that happened in a real place on our real planet. The early Christians didn't rely on how they felt or what they believed in their hearts. Rather, they put their faith in what they had seen, heard, and witnessed—the words and works of the Savior, who was seen alive publicly after his death by hundreds of witnesses (1 Corinthians 15, Acts 2, Acts 13)!

Their faith, just like ours today, is true and reasonable. You are not a fool to trust in Jesus.

Diversity in the church
Pastor Mike Novotny

There are few things that I love more than seeing diversity in the church. When Puerto Ricans, Pakistanis, Brazilians, African Americans, Caucasians, Hmong, Mexicans, and Germans sing and pray and praise God together, I thank the Spirit for his saving work among every people, tribe, and nation.

Which is why I'm so ashamed to think back to my childhood. I shudder to remember what I found funny back in those days. I'm too ashamed to repeat the jokes I once repeated at recess. And, unfathomably, I was a Christian. I believed in the God who made the world, loved the world, and forgave the world. But somehow that didn't translate into my love for all the world. There's so much I've had to learn, to repent of, and to change.

Are any of you like me? Has God had to open your eyes to his love of diversity? If so, join me in a united confession of sin. And, just as urgently, join me in a grateful sigh of relief. Because Jesus didn't let his Jewishness stop him from justifying Gentiles like me and most of you. He refused to let racial uniqueness stop him from saving sinners, no matter what their skin color or native language. **"For God so loved the world that he gave his one and only Son"** (John 3:16). Those words refuse to let racism into the church. And they offer hope to those who are changing their ways and loving the people whom our Father created and saved.

Feeling overwhelmed
Pastor Matt Ewart

Life can be overwhelming sometimes.

Several years ago, one of my lovely kids accidentally spilled a stinky, dead snail down the back seat of our minivan. It went right down the cracks of the seat. And it was horribly disgusting. When I arrived on the scene and assessed the situation, I came up with the perfect solution: "Let's just sell the van and buy a new one." If only that were an option.

Part of life is that you have to deal with situations where you feel overwhelmed. It's normal. Feeling overwhelmed is your cue that there's something you can't do.

Jesus felt overwhelmed too. It was the evening before his death when he was with his disciples in the Garden of Gethsemane. Crucifixion was on his mind when he shared this with his disciples: **"My soul is overwhelmed with sorrow to the point of death"** (Matthew 26:38).

There was something that not even Jesus could handle, and that was the weight of your sin. That weight would literally overwhelm him to death. The sentence of death was carried out on him so that it would not hang over you. He was overwhelmed much more than you will ever be.

I share this not to minimize the things that make you feel overwhelmed. I share it because Jesus understands what it feels like.

Something might leave you feeling overwhelmed today. When it does, share it with your Savior. The burden of being overwhelmed is not something you have to carry alone.

God and the preacher
Jason Nelson

"Hey, Preacher, why so glum?"

"Nothing I'm doing seems to be working. People aren't coming to church. Money is tight. There's conflict at meetings. And people expect me to do something about it."

"Well, why don't you take a different approach?"

"Are you serious? Don't you know we have a system? I was trained in the system. I need to look like I'm loyal to the system. Besides, the old guard that keeps my church afloat is content with the system. They would grumble if we changed things. I can't afford to lose them."

"But everything is permissible."

"I thought about trying something new, but do you know what they do to you at preacher meetings if you try something new? I mean, we spend most of our time discussing the system and how important we preachers are to preserving the system. It's not safe to question the system. That just puts a target on your back. I don't want to eat lunch by myself. If I ever want another job in the system, I need to fit in."

"Listen, Preacher. It's my church. I married myself to her long before you had a system. I'll still be married to her after your system is gone. It's my Word that matters. It was my Spirit who called you to serve. I want my world saved by my gospel. I put a good head on your broad shoulders. Feel free to use it. I've got your back."

Sleep well. Live free.

Andrea Delwiche

"In peace I will lie down and sleep, for you alone, Lord, make me dwell in safety" (Psalm 4:8).

Do these words of David give you peace or seem naïve?

How about Jesus' words? **"Do not worry about your life, what you will eat or drink; or about your body, what you will wear. Is not life more than food, and the body more than clothes? Look at the birds of the air; they do not sow or reap or store away in barns, and yet your heavenly Father feeds them. Are you not much more valuable than they? Can any one of you by worrying add a single hour to your life?"** (Matthew 6:25-27).

How can David or Jesus throw around phrases like, "I will sleep in peace" and "don't worry"? Maybe they had a better grip on reality. Both Jesus and David knew they lived in a bigger reality than the earthly realities that confronted them.

Both David and Jesus looked at things from the perspective of the kingdom of God. In the kingdom, where we live as believers, our earthly possessions, reputations, and safety can be *loosely* held; this earth is only the beginning, not the end for us.

What we begin *here* continues for us in eternity. While on earth, we can live without our hands clenched in fear and anxiety. We trust the One who holds the world (and us) in the palm of his hand. He will guide us through this life and the next—with peace. Sleep well. Live free.

Scientific or spiritual?

Pastor Mike Novotny

I got an email from a Christian chemistry major: "How can I believe in creation and yet learn the science that directly contradicts such a belief?" She felt stuck between two communities—the scientific and the spiritual. In her life, some people prayed, went to church, and believed in God while other people spent time in labs, recorded data, and tested theories. Did she have to choose between the two?

How do God and science fit together? Maybe you've felt that tension too. Maybe it happened in high school science class. Or when visiting a museum that explains a world without God. Or during a Netflix special on our universe. Countless Christians have wondered if they have to choose between a Jesus-believing heart and a science-loving head.

While I can't dig into every issue here, I can tell you this: **"The heavens declare the glory of God; the skies proclaim the work of his hands"** (Psalm 19:1). The Bible doesn't tell us to shut our eyes to the evidence and "just believe." Rather, it encourages us to open our eyes and see the intricate evidence of a glorious God.

No wonder so many scientists like God! In his study of Nobel prizes awarded during the 20th century, Baruch Shalev found that 73 percent of chemistry winners, 65 percent of physics winners, and 62 percent of medicine winners were Christian!

Do you have to choose to be either scientific or spiritual? No. Just ask the psalmist . . . or that group of Jesus-worshiping, Nobel Prize-receiving scientists!

When I see a puppy

Jason Nelson

I'm not sure what's happening to me. As I've gotten older, I've become more sentimental. There are hymns I can't get through without choking up. My lower lip starts to quiver if family members give me special gifts. My eyes fill with tears when I read what my grandchildren write to me: *"I luv yoo grambpa."* When I see a puppy, I begin to weep. It's become a contest among my offspring. Whose gift or card will get the waterworks going in Dad? My son-in-law is a pharmacist. He knows stuff. He's witnessed this spectacle and has a theory. He told me he thought I had low testosterone. WHAT? Who looks another man in the eye and says he may have low testosterone?

I choose to see it differently. As each of us moves through life toward our own Day of the Lord, the manifestations of the Spirit of God in our lives are age appropriate. God said, **"I will pour out my Spirit on every kind of people: Your sons will prophesy, also your daughters. Your old men will dream, your young men will see visions"** (Joel 2:28 MSG). Little children will give you their love without holding back. Young men and women make big plans and are quick to tell what they think they know. And old men dream about the way they used to be and the things they used to do. And they shed tears.

The flip side of worry

Ann Jahns

I'm a world-class worrier. If it were an Olympic sport, I'd have a house full of gold medals. Nothing is off limits from my worrying scenarios.

But if anyone should've been a worrier, it would've been the apostle Paul. Because he boldly and unabashedly proclaimed his faith in Christ, he endured prison . . . shipwrecks . . . torture . . . stoning . . . starvation. Yet in Philippians 4:6, he declares, **"Do not be anxious about anything, but in every situation, by prayer and petition, with thanksgiving, present your requests to God."**

Years ago, I attended a women's Bible study with an older lady who had unexpectedly lost her beloved husband of 45 years. She expressed that she was grappling with the aching hole in her life. She admitted that she was fearful and worried about the future. But I will never forget something she said: "My worrying has never changed the outcome of anything."

So what's the flip side of worry? What can we do when worry floods our minds, steals our sleep at night, and threatens to rob us of our peace and joy? Paul reminds us that the other side of the worry coin is prayer. When worry looms, take all those worries to the throne of heaven in prayer and lay them at the feet of Jesus. Big or small, present or future—give all your worries to God. Paul promises, **"And the peace of God, which transcends all understanding, will guard your hearts and your minds in Christ Jesus"** (Philippians 4:7).

Jesus' water works
Pastor Mike Novotny

There are two things I love about the "water" that Jesus offers us in the gospel of John. **"Jesus answered, 'Everyone who drinks this water will be thirsty again, but whoever drinks the water I give them will never thirst. Indeed, the water I give them will become in them a spring of water welling up to eternal life'"** (John 4:13,14).

The first thing I love is that Jesus' water isn't work. Notice the words, "the water I *give*." Jesus' isn't charging absurd prices like the fancy bottled water taken from fresh mountain springs. What Jesus is offering you—his unconditional love to quench your thirsty soul—is free. It's a gift. It's grace. If you feel too unworthy or too spiritually poor to afford it, Jesus has good news—his love is free for the taking and enjoying.

The second thing I love is that Jesus' water works. Unlike a bottle of water that can only satisfy us for so long, Jesus' cross is a spring of water that never runs dry. It wells up and offers us life with God every second of every day. That means you can, even in this very moment, look to Jesus and find grace, mercy, hope, and help, without fear that you will use up his precious love.

There are so many things to adore about Jesus, but here are two near the top: Jesus' water (his soul-satisfying promise) is not work, and it works!

His love is for the world
Pastor Mike Novotny

I'm so glad that Jesus wasn't racist. The Novotny family tree reaches its branches back to modern Germany and the Czech Republic. Lots of hardworking, farm-loving, light-skinned folks make up "my people." How about your people? Have you ever studied your family tree? If so, maybe you feel like I do, grateful that Jesus wasn't racist.

After studying Jesus' genealogy in Matthew's opening chapter, I couldn't find any connections to my people. I found Iraqi Abraham and Jordanian Ruth, but no Germans made the cut. Thankfully, Matthew's final chapter makes sure that people like me and you are included in the story of grace: **"Go and make disciples of all nations,"** Jesus commanded (28:19).

Don't you love the "all" in Jesus' parting words too? Jesus wants your nation, your tribe, your people to know that his love is for you. Jesus died and rose and told his friends to go so that people with skin like yours, hair like yours, eyes like yours might be part of the body of Christ. Jesus reached out his hands through their words so that your people would never be less than, never inferior, never segregated to the back rows of eternity. Jesus gave his life so there would be no shame in being black, no guilt in being white.

Jesus told his friends to go into the world because his love is for the world. His love is for you!

Fiercely dependent
Pastor Matt Ewart

One way I would describe myself is that I'm fiercely independent. Fiercely. Independent.

I know it doesn't make sense to all the women out there, but it's to the point where I'll search a store for a good 30 minutes to find what I'm looking for before I'll ask for help. And don't even ask me if I use the directions provided for things that "require some assembly."

Maybe you aren't as fiercely independent as I am, but what I do know is that most people only ask for help when they need it.

So as I was reading through Psalm 119, one of the verses jumped out at me. See if it jumps out at you too. Read it a few times if needed: **"I rise before dawn and cry for help; I have put my hope in your word"** (verse 147).

What stood out to me were two words: *Before dawn.* Before the day even started, this psalmist was crying out to God for help. Well before the help was needed, the cry for help went out. How amazing is that?

What do you need God's help for today? Be fiercely dependent on him. The crazy thing with God is that he loves it when you ask for help before you need it. Ask for his blessing on your day. Pray for his presence before you need it. You already have his word that he will work out all things for your good.

The path of progress
Jason Nelson

I favor progress because I believe in God. He said, **"See, I am doing a new thing! Now it springs up; do you not perceive it? I am making a way in the wilderness and streams in the wasteland"** (Isaiah 43:19). God has been advancing his agenda from the time we messed up the first thing. His forgiveness and other redemptions are new things flowing from his love. I like progress because I see how we benefit from it.

But the path of progress can be pretty choppy. Change can have unintended consequences. There's often a backlash right before we take big steps forward in our society, the church, and our personal lives. The possibilities energize some people to get on board earlier than others. The uncertainty embedded with progress causes some people to fight it to the bitter end. Stalwarts would like to keep things as they are. Reactionaries would like to take things back to the way they used to be. They see new things as passing fads or threats to beloved traditions. Progress could undermine one group's status if it makes things fairer for others. Making progress gives a culture indigestion right in the gut. There's going to be noisy belching as a society expels fear and resentment until the blessings of progress are fully digested.

If you're not a fan of progress, let's have a conversation. What new thing would you like God to take back? And then what?

Start with the Lord
Andrea Delwiche

"Listen to my words, Lord, consider my lament. Hear my cry for help, my King and my God, for to you I pray. In the morning, Lord, you hear my voice; in the morning I lay my requests before you and wait expectantly" (Psalm 5:1-3).

Are you struck by David's confidence in God when you read this psalm? He starts out asking God to hear him and to consider what he's asking of God. He then reminds God about what he, David, does each morning: "I lay my requests before you and wait expectantly." Past experience and knowledge of God have taught David that when he lays requests before God, he will get an answer.

At the end of this psalm, David uses a beautiful word picture: "Surely, Lord, you bless the righteous; you surround them with your favor as with a shield" (verse 12).

How about you and me? Do we start our mornings with the Lord, asking for his help to confront everything we will face in a peaceful way? Do we feel confident that we're covered by the shield of God's favor? Do we sense God's blessings piling up at our feet?

Even if you didn't start out feeling blessed today, take time to see all the ways that God's favor and blessing are evident in your life. Consider starting your day the way David did. Ask the Lord to help. Then David's confident words will be your words too.

Science and spirituality
Pastor Mike Novotny

Recently, Americans celebrated the 50th anniversary of humankind's first ever steps on the moon. The year 1969 marked one of science's greatest achievements. Maybe you remember the details—a 6.2 million pound rocket blasted American astronauts into space at over 25,000 mph. Four days later, they landed on the moon.

But before Neil Armstrong and Buzz Aldrin took those epic first steps, something else happened. Buzz took out bread and wine and celebrated the Lord's Supper, confessing his connection to Jesus. He also read the ancient words of his Savior: **"I am the vine; you are the branches"** (John 15:5). Buzz imitated the astronauts from Apollo 8, the men who read Genesis 1 as they gazed upon Earth from space.

I love those stories. They remind me that the scientific and the spiritual aren't mutually exclusive. You can be a devoted scientist, even the best in your field, while holding on to God, to his Son, and to Christian faith.

Maybe some of the "fruit" that Christians produce is a deep desire to know God more, not just through quiet times and church services but through the vast universe that our Father created. Maybe "Amen!" and "Hallelujah!" can be heard not just in sanctuaries but also in outer space.

Maybe the most scientific among us can also be the more spiritually focused on Jesus. Just ask Buzz!

february 22

What makes someone happy?
Pastor Jared Oldenburg

Webmd.com has changed the landscape of the medical world. Right at our fingertips is enough information to do some rudimentary diagnostics on ourselves: Why do I have a headache? What does blurred vision mean? But when it comes to our spiritual lives, I don't think physical ailments are the only things stealing our joy.

King David is probably the most famous of all the biblical kings. The Bible even describes him as a man after the Lord's own heart. What made him unique among all the kings was not his power or strength but instead his willingness, when confronted by sin, to confess and seek God's forgiveness.

In Psalm 32 we get to see both sides of David. One weighed down by guilt and one raised up by forgiveness. He describes his condition: **"When I kept silent, my bones wasted away through my groaning all day long. For day and night your hand was heavy on me"** (verses 3,4). Have you ever felt that weight of shame and guilt? I think we all have.

Yet see the joy David experiences once the burden has been lifted: **"'I will confess my transgressions to the Lord.' And you forgave the guilt of my sin. Rejoice in the Lord and be glad, you righteous; sing, all you who are upright in heart!"** (verses 5,11).

There's a reason why believers have confessed their sins to the Lord for thousands of years. Joy comes in the Lord's forgiveness. And that forgiveness overcomes our worst ailments.

Follow Jesus with all your heart
Pastor Jeremy Mattek

John Hart is one of the 56 men who signed the US Declaration of Independence. There were many who tried to stop him from signing. At one point, John had to make a choice between supporting his patriotic beliefs and being by the side of his dying wife and their 13 children. He forsook his family and put his signature on the document. It's doubtful that everyone would forsake their family the way he did.

Yet, if you ever have to make a choice between following your family or following Jesus, Jesus expects that you will follow him. **"Still another said, 'I will follow you, Lord; but first let me go back and say goodbye to my family.' Jesus replied, 'No one who puts a hand to the plow and looks back is fit for service in the kingdom of God'"** (Luke 9:61,62).

In Jesus' eyes, not even saying goodbye to a father is sufficient cause to delay in following Jesus. The reason Jesus feels this way is simple. He knows that our families can't save us from hell or pay our debt to God.

But Jesus did. In fact, he keeps our families together even beyond death. His sacrificial death assures us that we will be reunited with our fellow believers in heaven.

Use your time with family and friends to celebrate this gift. Gather around God's Word and encourage one another with his promises so that heartfelt devotion to the Jesus who saves might be the one thing your entire family has in common.

february 24

Are you for real?

Pastor Clark Schultz

"When John, who was in prison, heard about the deeds of the Messiah, he sent his disciples to ask him, 'Are you the one who is to come?'" (Matthew 11:2,3). Undoubtedly as John the Baptist stared at the prison walls, he wondered, "Okay, Jesus, are you for real?"

Don't we do the same thing? We know Jesus, we point to Jesus, we pray to Jesus. But when our prison moment comes—like a health scare, relationship trouble, self-worth issues—we begin to question, "Okay, God, are you really in control? Do you really love me?"

Jesus didn't give John a yes-or-no answer but pointed to his body of work. He pointed to his preaching, teaching, and miracles.

When doubts arise for us, Jesus gives us a similar answer when we say, "Okay, God, where are you?" He says, "I am always with you." He says that he has plans for us. He says, "It is finished," and all our sins are forgiven. God's body of work, his Word, speaks volumes to how much we are treasured. Despite how things look on the outside, God is in control.

So while the world will tempt us to turn away from God or to turn to the idols of drugs, sex, or alcohol to numb our pain, Jesus invites us to turn to him for forgiveness and for love. We can know that he is the Savior, he is our friend, he is our helper, and he will *never* leave us.

Choose the water that works!

Pastor Mike Novotny

In 2010, rapper Lil Wayne expressed a dilemma we all face in life. He assumed "the game" (a career in rap music) would satisfy his soul, but it didn't. All of the money, fame, and pleasure weren't enough to fill the God-shaped hole that his Creator put in his heart.

You don't have to be a rapper to feel the same way. We too often assume that _____ will be enough to satisfy us. Making it into college. Finding a good job. Getting married. Having kids. Making more money. Going on another trip. Remodeling the kitchen. Retiring. Even we Christians assume that if God would just bless us with _____, we would be content. However, those good things break their vows and leave us just as restless as before.

Thankfully, God is still inviting you to a life of deep spiritual satisfaction. Listen to one of the last things he says in the Bible: **"Let the one who is thirsty come; and let the one who wishes take the free gift of the water of life"** (Revelation 22:17). If you're thirsty for love, forgiveness, hope, peace, rest, friendship, acceptance, pleasure, joy, or any spiritual gift, then come to Jesus! Jesus is offering the "water" that will quench the thirst of your very soul. Best of all, he says it's a "free gift," all yours through faith. What an offer!

For many
Jason Nelson

Imagine this scene: **"This is my blood of the covenant, which is poured out *for many* for the forgiveness of sins"** (Matthew 26:28). There's a small group, 11 survivors and Jesus. The faces are familiar to each other, and the conversation is intimate because everyone is comfortable being in the group. But Jesus' words imply that this meal doesn't end there. It doesn't stay there. This may be Jesus' Last Supper, but this little group will not be the last to celebrate it. There is momentum coming out of the upper room. The Spirit of Christ coming out of the upper room expands his kingdom. The Lord's Supper is served at a very big table. His blood is poured out for many. The forgiveness of sins is for many.

How many? *Imagine this last scene:* **"After this I looked, and there before me was a great multitude that no one could count, from every nation, tribe, people and language, standing before the throne and before the Lamb. . . . 'These in white robes—who are they, and where did they come from?' . . . 'These are they who have come out of the great tribulation; they have washed their robes and made them white in the blood of the Lamb'"** (Revelation 7:9,13,14). The body and blood of the Lamb that was given and shed for you was also given and shed for many for the forgiveness of their sins.

Mind your own dirt
Pastor Matt Ewart

The good news of Jesus that changes a person's eternity also transforms a person's earthly life. It's impressive to see what God can do when a person's life is founded on what Jesus has done.

But there are some things that work against God's work. In the parable of the sower, Jesus illustrated how it's like a farmer who sowed seed across various types of soil.

Some seed fell along a path and was eaten by birds. When you don't address your spiritual doubts and misunderstandings, it leaves you vulnerable to the enemy.

Some seed fell on rocky soil and didn't last very long in the sun. When you expect God to work only through good things, your faith will shrivel up at the first sign of trouble.

Some seed fell among thorns and was choked out. When the worries of life and the lies of wealth have your full attention, there's no space for God to create new fruit in you.

The point of Jesus' parable is that when your life isn't transformed the way it could be, that's your cue to mind your own dirt humbly. Look for the things in your own heart that have been robbing you of the fruit that God wants to produce in you. And know that with him it's not only repentance for the past. There's still a miracle crop he wants to produce in you: **"This is the one who produces a crop, yielding a hundred, sixty or thirty times what was sown"** (Matthew 13:23).

God likes science

Pastor Mike Novotny

Don't believe the rumors floating around out there about faith and science. The fact is that God likes science. If God got a bumper sticker, it might say, "I (heart emoji) science." If teenage Jesus had a bedroom poster, it might have been the periodic table. The word *science* comes from the Latin *scientia*, which means "knowledge." Since God likes knowledge, he absolutely likes science.

The apostle Paul explains why: **"What may be *known* about God is plain to them, because God has made it plain to them. For since the creation of the world God's invisible qualities—his eternal power and divine nature—have been clearly seen"** (Romans 1:19,20). God wanted to be scienced, to be known. So what did he do? He created stuff you could touch and taste and test.

God likes it when we study science because praise is data driven. When we know how babies grow from peanut to grapefruit to watermelon in the womb, we end up impressed with our awesome God. When we grasp how sleep and screenings and stress affect our holistic health, we gasp at the connections God wired through our bodies and brains. When we figure out how sunlight and exercise and meditation can combat depression, we are discovering how God put the puzzle pieces of joy together.

God likes it when we get it, because he likes it when we get him. God likes science. You can too.

March

The Lord is not slow in keeping his promise,
as some understand slowness.
Instead he is patient with you,
not wanting anyone to perish,
but everyone to come to repentance.

2 Peter 3:9

All we need
Pastor Jared Oldenburg

"So then, just as you received Christ Jesus as Lord, continue to live your lives in him, rooted and built up in him, strengthened in the faith as you were taught, and overflowing with thankfulness" (Colossians 2:6,7).

If there was ever a sentence that I would tape to my bathroom mirror, I think it would be this one. In just one sentence, the apostle Paul offers all the encouragement we could ever need to live out our lives as believers—and sometimes we can use that encouragement. Life happens. We get busy. We get distracted, and sometimes we lose focus on what matters. The believers in the city of Colossae, whom Paul was writing to, were forgetting what mattered most. They were getting distracted, and some were even being convinced that Christ alone was not enough for their salvation. Pretty scary. To combat this idea, Paul wrote an entire letter seeking to convince them that Christ is truly all they needed in life.

These verses are in the middle of that letter. For the next five days, I want you to walk with me as we look at all the encouragement that the apostle Paul packs into this one sentence.

It starts with this simple phrase that grounds us in our faith when the world seeks to distract us: **"You received Christ Jesus as Lord."** A simple fact: We have Jesus, and he is all we need.

Live in Christ
Pastor Jared Oldenburg

"So then, just as you received Christ Jesus as Lord, *continue to live your lives in him,* **rooted and built up in him, strengthened in the faith as you were taught, and overflowing with thankfulness"** (Colossians 2:6,7).

I don't know about you, but I have an endless list of things I know are good for me—get up early, eat well, get plenty of sleep, live in the moment, never own a cat, etc. The hard part for me is not the *knowing* part; it's the *doing* part. If you're human, I think you can relate. Things come up, the kids get sick, deadlines loom, and life continues. It doesn't take too long for the knowing and the doing to look pretty different.

I think this is a perfect time to pause and take stock of what we know and what we're trying to do in life. Here is what we know—We have Jesus and the forgiveness that comes in his name. And here is what we do—**"Continue to live your lives in him."** When we have Jesus, we have a mission. We have a chance to wake up (maybe even early) and find a purpose. I'm sure the kids will still get sick and deadlines will still loom, but today is a brand-new day to live our lives in him—in his love, in his forgiveness, in his acceptance, and in his strength.

march 3

Build your life on Christ
Pastor Jared Oldenburg

"So then, just as you received Christ Jesus as Lord, continue to live your lives in him, *rooted and built up in him*, strengthened in the faith as you were taught, and overflowing with thankfulness" (Colossians 2:6,7).

OK, I admit it. Yesterday's devotion was just a tad vague. Paul encouraged us to continue to live our lives in Christ. That's pretty encouraging, but also a little bit confusing. What exactly does it mean to live a life in Christ? Thankfully, he explains it more fully: **"Continue to live your lives in him, rooted and built up in him."** Now we're getting somewhere.

With two quick metaphors, we can almost visualize what Paul's talking about. As a tree finds fertile ground and drives its roots ever deeper to find water and security, so we can connect to Christ, the very source of our identity. We're his, we're forgiven, and we're loved. Once we've found this firm foundation in our Savior, it only makes sense to start building our lives on him.

What does that look like? Imagine the confidence you can have in life knowing that even the worst of your sins are wiped away. Imagine the joy you possess, even in the worst of circumstances, when you know that you're living for a greater mission. Imagine the hope you know when things seem bleak, because you're certain that God is working for your eternal good.

That's not vague; that's living life in Christ.

Rest and grow in God's Word
Pastor Jared Oldenburg

"So then, just as you received Christ Jesus as Lord, continue to live your lives in him, rooted and built up in him, *strengthened in the faith as you were taught,* and overflowing with thankfulness" (Colossians 2:6,7).

Even if you're not a weight lifter, you probably know that muscles grow and get stronger only after a workout, when they're resting and recovering. I didn't really understand this as a kid. When you lift heavy things, the force of the effort causes micro tears in the muscles. Once you stop lifting, your body repairs those micro tears with stronger tissue. Thus, you get stronger when you're at rest, not really when you're lifting weights.

This is a pretty accurate parallel as Paul encourages us to be **"strengthened in the faith as you were taught."** I'm not sure what you're going through now—job loss, sickness, mourning a death, stress, anxiety, or just feeling overwhelmed with life. What I do know is that these burdens don't make faith stronger. Trials in life are the things that tear us apart. Your faith, on the other hand, grows stronger when you find rest and rejuvenation in God's Word. It's here that the Holy Spirit mends us together, builds us up with his promises, and prepares our hearts and minds to face whatever challenges the world may throw at us.

Overflow with thankfulness
Pastor Jared Oldenburg

"So then, just as you received Christ Jesus as Lord, continue to live your lives in him, rooted and built up in him, strengthened in the faith as you were taught, and *overflowing with thankfulness*" (Colossians 2:6,7).

There aren't too many positive examples in life that utilize the word *overflow*. The sink . . . the coffee urn . . . the cooking pot . . . or (ahem) the toilet. Most of the time it means the very thing we wanted contained is now where it shouldn't be. It's a mess. It has to be cleaned up. It has to be put back where it came from.

But sometimes what we want to contain isn't just the physical. Have you ever overflowed with anger or frustration? Have you ever lost it and poured out gossip or even hate? As we live lives in Christ, Paul is calling for us to overflow with something else. When we're strengthened in faith. When we understand what God has done for us in Jesus. When we understand the cross or the fact that he drank the overflowing cup of God's wrath. When we grasp Jesus' substitutionary death for a world overflowing with brokenness, God is calling for our hearts to overflow—not with anger or jealousy—but instead with thanks. **"Continue to live your lives in him . . . overflowing with thankfulness."**

Wrong directions
Pastor Clark Schultz

This past May a woman in Ontario was driving at night. She claimed she didn't have good visibility, but she listened to whatever direction her GPS told her. When she should have turned left, she turned right . . . right into a lake. She was able to grab her purse and swim out of her car to safety.

Sometimes we listen to voices that don't always send us in the right direction. Like the unmarried person who throws the words "I love you" in the air to get you to make a wrong turn when it comes to boundaries. We let the problems of this world pull a "recalculating" on our brains to think, "God really must have it in for me to allow this turn to happen in my life."

You can get a beeper to find your keys. If you lose your smartphone, you can use an app to find it. When you start down a road you shouldn't, understand you have the alert of friends, teachers, and parents to guide you. Listen to their counsel.

When we make wrong turns, God invites us to grab our Bibles and swim to him for safety. Listen to his voice. Listen to the voice of the Shepherd, who encourages you to come to him when you're weary and burdened.

"In the same way, I tell you, there is rejoicing in the presence of the angels of God over one sinner who repents" (Luke 15:10).

And with Jesus we know we will never be lost.

Jesus has to

Pastor Mike Novotny

Every kid has asked the timeless question: "But do I *have* to?" My dictionary defines the verb *have* as something you are bound to do or compelled to carry out. Kids want to know if they have the option of getting out of the work they really don't want to do.

Jesus had a different attitude about his "have to." Notice this stunning example—**"Now [Jesus] had to go through Samaria"** (John 4:4). Ancient Israel's map was like a three-scoop ice cream cone with Judea as the southernmost scoop, Galilee on the top, and Samaria squished in the middle. Because first-century Jews didn't associate with Samaritans (John 4:9), they didn't "have to" go through their land. Nor did they want to. Some Jews added extra miles to their trips in order to avoid Samaria altogether because they didn't want to be near such sinful people. But Jesus "had to" go through that land. Why? Because he was on a mission to meet, love, and save a Samaritan woman and her neighbors (John 4:39-42).

I love that about Jesus. Don't you? He has to go to unexpected places, like the place you are right now. He has to do unexpected things, like take time to listen to your smallest prayers and forgive your biggest sins. He has to bless unexpected people, people like you (even if your life is as messy as a Samaritan's). Why does he have to? Because he is the Savior who is bound to his Father's will and compelled by his unconditional love. Even better, his gracious heart wants to. He wants to bless you.

Better than fear
Pastor Matt Ewart

Fear is a powerful thing, and every parent knows it. A little bit of fear will conform the behavior of my children. All I have to do is threaten to take away something they love, and it's crazy to see how fast they go from demonic to angelic. It's tempting to use fear as a permanent parenting tool.

But God's way is different. Perfect love doesn't use fear. It drives out fear.

God is interested in our outward behavior only insomuch as it's a reflection of what's in our inner hearts. If good behavior was what he was after, the angels would have sufficed. If outward behavior was his goal, the threat of hell would be all it takes.

But the loving Father in heaven is after something much more important: your heart. **"For the grace of God has appeared that offers salvation to all people. It teaches us to say 'No' to ungodliness and worldly passions"** (Titus 2:11,12).

Fear conforms your behavior, but grace transforms your decisions.

Today you may have to interact with someone whose behavior isn't okay. Maybe it's a toddler. Maybe it's an employee. *Maybe it's an employee who acts like a toddler.*

I guarantee you that fear will instantly conform the behavior. That's the easy way to go about it.

But what would it look like to treat that person with grace? Find someone today whose life could use some change. But instead of conforming with fear, transform him or her with the same grace that God shows you.

Instant gratification
Pastor Clark Schultz

What's the longest you've had to wait for something? The year was 1980. My fifth-grade teacher had taken our whole class to see the movie *Empire Strikes Back*. The rolling credits, the big reveal of who Luke's father really was, Han Solo getting frozen, and then the ending credits. The movie ended with a cliff-hanger. I turned to my teacher and said, "So, when does the next movie come out?" He said, "Three years." My reaction: "Three years? Holy cow, that's a long time to wait! That's like forever!"

What's the longest you've had to wait for something at the DMV, at the checkout line, or even for a text response? If you're at a drive-through or a stop sign and don't move fast enough, you're often prodded with a honk or something worse.

We've become an instant gratification nation. We're accustomed to getting what we want—right now!

Do you sometimes apply that "right now" principle to God in prayer? "God, it's my prayer; give it to me right now!"

Patience, friends, the Lord's on a different timetable. And his timetable is perfect and for our good.

"Do not forget this one thing, dear friends: With the Lord a day is like a thousand years, and a thousand years are like a day" (2 Peter 3:8).

Make friends with money
Jason Nelson

Please don't misunderstand the title. I'm not encouraging you to use money to buy friendships. Nor am I suggesting you should only be nice to rich people, even though that could pay off when you're down and out. Jesus teases us with that idea in Luke 16:9, but he is really talking about being shrewd managers of our money. The point I'm making is to treat money very well because the two of you are in a long-term relationship.

That's also the point of Erin Lowry's book *Broke Millennial* and why she established brokemillennial. com. She tells the members of her generation that now is the time to get your financial life together (#GYFLT). She knows her audience and realizes from personal experience that no one teaches young people about money.

That's nothing new. No one ever talked to me about money either. A family friend suggested I marry a rich girl because I could learn to love her. But no one said anything about credit scores or diversified portfolios. No one mentioned dollar cost averaging and dividend reinvestment as ways to have more money later in life. No one told me that when you pay off debts it's like giving yourself a raise. What most people know about money is that you earn it and spend it and try to earn more so you can spend more until you can't do either one anymore. So where do broke baby boomers go for advice?

"Suppose one of you wants to build a tower. Won't you first sit down and estimate the cost to see if you have enough money to complete it?" (Luke 14:28).

Faith and facts

Pastor Mike Novotny

Some people claim that Christians are people of faith while atheists are people of facts. A more accurate description would be that both Christians and atheists claim to have facts that back up their faith.

Take the universe for example. As a Christian, I have faith that God created all of it. **"By faith we understand that the universe was formed at God's command"** (Hebrews 11:3). I wasn't there when creation happened. I can't find a YouTube clip to check it out. By faith I believe in God the Father, the Maker of heaven and earth, but I didn't see God the Father make heaven and earth.

Yet my faith is backed up by some stunning facts. The design of the universe is powerful evidence for a Designer. The odds that life exists on the earth—that we are just so far from the sun and the gravitational force is just so—are nearly impossible unless an all-powerful God fine-tuned it. The last time I investigated the evidence, the odds of life just happening on earth would be like winning the Powerball jackpot not once but 342,000,000 times in a row! It turns out that our faith is not blind but supported by powerful facts.

The next time you find yourself in a healthy discussion about doctrine and data, remember that Christians are people of faith . . . and people of facts.

Be careful, Pharisee
Pastor Clark Schultz

If Jesus was here today, where would he be? I asked that question a few years back to a group of church ladies I taught, and they all gave me answers like this: church, in a pulpit, or here at the ladies meeting.

The ladies looked shocked when I said, "Yes, those answers are nice and all, but more than likely Jesus would be hanging out at bars, drug houses, or even the local street corners where the ladies for hire normally gather."

Does this picture put a look of horror on your face or these words to your lips: "My Jesus would never visit such places"? Then I'll say to you what I said to that ladies group: "Be careful, Pharisees. Listen to these verses."

"Now the tax collectors and sinners were all gathering around to hear Jesus. But the Pharisees and the teachers of the law muttered, 'This man welcomes sinners and eats with them'" (Luke 15:1,2).

Jesus met people where they were. He didn't act as if he was better. He loved all people from all walks of life. This servant attitude made up Jesus' ministry and even had many turn against him because they thought he shouldn't be associating with "sinners." Rather than looking at outward appearance, he looked at the heart, reached out to those who needed help, invited them to dine with him, and took the riffraff of society to be his followers. To whom do we need to apply this same love to today?

Follow Jesus in weakness

Pastor Jeremy Mattek

"Pastor," the woman on the phone said, "I need you to stop by the house as soon as possible. It's very urgent."

"What's wrong?" the pastor asked.

"I need to give you my church offering for this coming weekend," the woman replied.

"Why don't you bring your offering with you to worship on Sunday?" the pastor asked.

"Because if I don't give it to you now," she said, "I'm going to spend it on alcohol tonight."

This woman had struggled with alcoholism for many years. The temptation exposed her spiritual weakness over and over. Yet that day she found strength to keep fighting against it, a strength that came from knowing that Jesus didn't die to save the people who prove they're strong enough to follow him. He died to save a world full of sinners who regularly prove that they're not.

Maybe you feel weak against this same temptation. Or maybe the temptation is entirely different. But no matter what, Jesus already died to forgive that weakness. God loves you. He's still here for you. He has already prepared a place in heaven for you.

That's a special gift that will always provide the strength you need to keep fighting against your weakness.

This is why the apostle Paul wrote, **"I will boast of the things that show my weakness"** (2 Corinthians 11:30). His weaknesses, and the truth that they were forgiven in Jesus, provided powerful encouragement and strength to Paul and to anyone who has ever felt weak against temptation.

My favorite reason to believe
Pastor Mike Novotny

My favorite reason to believe in the Bible is, admittedly, not all that logical. It's much more personal and intensely emotional. It might not be persuasive enough to change an unbeliever's mind, but I still hope it tugs at an unbeliever's heart. That reason is Jesus' uniqueness.

There's no one like Jesus. There's no god, no philosophy, and no religion that offers what Jesus offers. Listen to how the prophet Isaiah described him: **"He was pierced for our transgressions, he was crushed for our iniquities; the punishment that brought us peace was on him, and by his wounds we are healed"** (Isaiah 53:5). Who else offers to take our place and our punishment and give us peace? Only Jesus!

A young skeptic approached me after church and asked what I thought of other religions that, like the Bible, teach us to love one another. I replied, "I agree with that, but what do they offer me when I fall short of love? What can they promise me when I sin?" Many spiritual people and religious paths can tell us how to love, but only the Bible proclaims a Savior who loves the unloving. Only one Scripture gives us grace, full and free, to you and me.

Yes, the Old Testament prophecies are persuasive. Yes, the New Testament apostles give compelling testimony. But, in the end, it's the uniqueness of Jesus Christ that wins over Christian hearts and compels us to trust the Bible that Jesus trusted. That's why we believe.

You can't bring your slippers with you

Ann Jahns

Would you agree that our society is crazy about stuff? Clothes, cars, the latest digital gadget—every savvy marketer's goals are to get us to buy more stuff and to convince us that we can't live without it. Channels like HSN and QVC give us 24/7 access to items we simply *must* have. He who dies with the most toys wins, right?

When my father suffered a debilitating stroke at the age of 81, medical professionals gently advised our family to move him to a hospice facility where he could comfortably live out his final days.

Do you know what my dad brought with him to his hospice room? The clothes on his back—and a pair of slippers. Guess what? He didn't even use those slippers.

The world tries to convince us that our worth is determined by our worldly possessions. Don't buy that lie. Even over two thousand years ago, Jesus knew that possessions vie for first place in our hearts. In Matthew 6:19-21, he said, **"Do not store up for yourselves treasures on earth . . . but store up for yourselves treasures in heaven. . . . For where your treasure is, there your heart will be also."**

At the end of your life, the only thing that matters is the treasure of your faith—your relationship with Jesus. You can't even take a pair of lowly slippers with you. If you believe that Jesus is your Savior, your treasure in heaven is already waiting for you.

Why?

Pastor Mike Novotny

Did you hear about that jury trial for the evil cat who murdered the innocent mouse? Snuck up on her while she was trying to get some cheese for her babies, poor little thing. Did you catch that on Court TV?

No, you didn't. We don't have court cases for cats or lawyers for lions. We don't call it murder when a dog drags home a backyard catch. But we do for humans. Why the difference? If the atheist is right and we're just evolved animals, why doesn't survival of the fittest fit into our consciences? Why do we march for justice and equality? Why do we care about the innocent and defenseless? Why don't we just let the strongest survive?

Answer—Because we're not animals. We're people, created in the image of God. The apostle Paul wrote, **"When Gentiles** (non Jews)**, who do not have the law** (the Bible)**, do by nature things required by the law . . . they show that the requirements of the law are written on their hearts"** (Romans 2:14,15). Where did this idea of good and evil come from? From God. For morality to make sense, you need the law of God.

The next time an unbelieving friend calls something good/bad, uses the moral word *should* in a sentence, or reveals a concern for justice, ask a thought-provoking question—Why? Why would anything be just, unjust, bad, or good . . . unless there was a God who declared it to be so?

Water is work

Pastor Mike Novotny

Back in 1697, an English pastor named Henry Maundrell found a well of water in the middle of ancient Israel. He measured it to a depth of 105 feet. Can you imagine how much work getting that water must have been? According to Google, a gallon of water weighs 8.34 pounds. Picture yourself standing on top of an eight-story building, 100+ feet above the ground, hauling up your 8.34 pounds (plus bucket weight) as a tattered rope rubs against your raw hands. Ouch.

Maundrell's well is believed by many to be the very spot where Jesus made a stunning promise to a woman who was tired of working for water. Jesus smiled, **"The water I give them will become in them a spring of water welling up to eternal life"** (John 4:14). Jesus' "water" isn't like well water that you have to get to. It's something that springs up to get to you. It's not work, but a gift from God.

That was Jesus' picturesque way of describing eternal life. The love of God, acceptance of God, peace of God, grace of God, family of God, inheritance of God, and every other spiritual blessing aren't hauled up by your own spiritual strength. Instead, they are like a spring that gushes up to get to you and constantly satisfies your soul. Eternal life is not by works but simply by the grace of God. That is why Jesus' water quenches the thirst of our tired souls. And that is why we love him so much.

Reveal yourself
Andrea Delwiche

"Lord, **do not rebuke me in your anger or discipline me in your wrath. Have mercy on me, Lord, for I am faint; heal me, Lord, for my bones are in agony. My soul is in deep anguish. How long, Lord, how long? Turn, Lord, and deliver me; save me because of your unfailing love**" (Psalm 6:1-4).

Sometimes, as Christians, we're afraid to be honest, even in our own church. We're afraid to ask questions of each other, our pastors, or God. We're afraid to say how we really feel: "I'm depressed." "I'm feeling faithless." "I'm just plain tired."

King David wasn't afraid to be honest—honest with God and with anyone else who reads his words. Over the course of the ten verses of Psalm 6, he begs. He questions. He cries. He experiences relief and an answer to his prayer.

We get to see right into David's deepest fears and grief. His transparency leaves nothing hidden. We're refreshed and blessed by his honesty thousands of years later.

Do we reveal ourselves with this sort of honesty to God? Do we trust the Holy Spirit to work with us to speak our needs? Do others see this godly honesty in us so that they have a space where they can speak with transparency in return?

In the peace of Christ, we can offer our hearts honestly to God and each other. As we live transparently, we will experience relief from the Lord and be God's channels of relief to those we meet.

The God of hope
Pastor Matt Ewart

To some degree, you willingly arrange your life around every single hope that you have.

One of the times I arranged my life around a hope was a few years into marriage. My wife and I began to pay a lot of attention to how many bedrooms our future house would have, what kind of cars we were driving, and what kind of career paths we were on. You know why we did all of that? Because we hoped to have kids. They rearranged our lives before we ever had them.

You do this in your life too. High school students take the long route to class with the hope that they run into that special someone. Athletes put in extra workout time with the hope of winning. Employees add extra effort with the hope of being promoted.

What hopes will you arrange your life around today? There's a big hope that permeates through all the others. Jesus settled your sin at the cross and rose again three days later. You have the hope of eternal life. You have the certain hope that someday you and everyone who falls asleep in Christ will be raised to life again.

What would today look like if you arranged your life around that kind of hope?

"May the God of hope fill you with all joy and peace as you trust in him, so that you may overflow with hope by the power of the Holy Spirit" (Romans 15:13).

Man, that's deep!
Pastor Clark Schultz

The Challenger Deep in the Mariana Trench is the deepest known point in the earth's oceans. In 2010 the United States Center for Coastal and Ocean Mapping measured the depth of the Challenger Deep at 10,994 meters (36,070 feet) below sea level with an estimated vertical accuracy of ±40 meters. If Mount Everest, the highest mountain on the earth, were placed at this location, it would be covered by over one mile of water. Man, that's deep!

You know what else is deep? God's wisdom! **"Oh, the depth of the riches of the wisdom and knowledge of God! How unsearchable his judgments, and his paths beyond tracing out!"** (Romans 11:33).

How about you? Where do you find your wisdom? Do you go with the latest fad? Do you buy into the "party it up now" idea? Do you feel you are in control of your life and your destiny?

God's wisdom was to send his Son to die for you! This wisdom also includes whatever situation you're dealing with right now—it will work out. If you doubt, go back to just how deep God's love is for you. It's deeper than the Challenger Deep; and that, my friends, is deep! God's Son scaled more than the Mariana Trench; he towered over the trenches of sin and has forgiven you.

So as the waves of life come crashing in on you, hold on to the only true life preserver there is, the wisdom and knowledge that only God gives.

A desire for meaning

Pastor Mike Novotny

Did you hear about that Hollywood dog who was depressed because she didn't have a meaningful life? She got carried down red carpets in a Gucci purse, but she was miserable that she didn't make a difference in the world. Did you catch that story in *People* magazine?

No, you didn't. Because the desire for meaning is reserved for humankind. Mosquitoes don't change college majors. Puppies don't read *The Purpose Driven Life*. Cats don't cry out, "But what does it all mean?!" No, most animals are happy with supper, sex, and safety. So why doesn't that work for us? Why do we long for love, friendship, purpose, and meaningful work? Why do we talk about legacy and impact?

Because of God. Old King Solomon said it like this: "[God] **has made everything beautiful in its time. He has also set eternity in the human heart**" (Ecclesiastes 3:11). God set eternity in your heart. God placed a desire in you to find him, the eternal God and the eternal blessings that endure forever. Your desire to be connected to the supernatural and eternal is proof that you're not an animal. You're more than what science's lab can examine and explain. You have a soul that will never be satisfied until it sees God.

As one famous saint used to say it—Your heart will always be restless until it rests in him. So, seek him today. Study the world around you to know God more. Then, through Jesus, know God better than ever before.

For you
Jason Nelson

"And he took bread, gave thanks and broke it, and gave it to them, saying, 'This is my body given *for you.'* . . . He took the cup, saying, 'This cup is the new covenant in my blood, which is poured out *for you'*" (Luke 22:19,20).

This somber occasion was made more somber by Jesus' demeanor and his talk of suffering and betrayal. He said this would be his last Passover until his kingdom comes. Judas was already gone. The table talk after the meal revealed one more time that his closest followers still didn't understand Jesus. They argued about who would be greatest. Peter overplayed his hand, insisting he was ready to die with Jesus. What did Jesus mean when he said this is a new covenant? Is this a new kind of Passover? Is this a new way of relating to God?

When I look around the upper room, my eyes get wide and my jaw drops a little. It's still hard to understand what it all means. But there's something to remember always. With the bread, Jesus gave us his body; with the wine, he gave us his blood. The forgiveness of our sins is intensely personal for him and for us. He said, "Peter, this forgiveness is for you. James, this is for you. Luke, this is for you. Jason, this is for you too."

Why does racism exist?

Pastor Mike Novotny

A few years ago, I tried to explain racism to my kids. I defined racism as the belief that races are not distinct equals but that one race is better than another. I walked through the ugly American history of slavery. When I finished, my daughters looked at me and asked, "Daddy, why?"

I asked myself a similar question the other day. Why does racism still exist? Why, after all of our prayers and progress, do so many people harbor prejudice in their hearts? Why would any Christian come to the conclusion that some races are better than others?

After studying Paul's words in Romans chapters 1-3, I think I found an explanation. Because "they" don't sin like "us." In Paul's day, the Gentiles didn't sin statistically like the Jews. They tended toward pagan idolatry and sexual immorality. The difference, however, led many Jews to a feeling of superiority. It led to racism. Paul, in turn, had to spill major ink to prove that all people, regardless of race, are sinful and need the gospel of Jesus' unconditional love (confer Romans 1:18–3:20).

Allow me to warn you gently about the same temptation today. Statistically, some groups commit certain sins more than other groups and vice versa. That reality makes a feeling of superiority so very, very tempting. So, when you feel that temptation, go back to Paul's words and remember this: **"All have sinned and fall short of the glory of God, and all are justified freely by his grace"** (Romans 3:23,24).

Then I am strong
Pastor Matt Ewart

I struggle to figure out why everyone doesn't at least want the message of the Bible to be true. It seems pretty awesome to me that God would become human, have a wrestling match with death, and come out victorious on our behalf.

This good news tells the clear message that there's an almighty God who thinks the universe of us. We're a big deal to him.

But that can make it difficult when it doesn't feel like we're a big deal to him.

Unforeseen circumstances can completely change the trajectory of your life in an instant. Sometimes the good things that God promises you seem to fade amidst all the bad things happening. Does he still love you? Does he still care?

God's perspective is eternally greater than ours. Our default is that we want God to bless us for this short period of life. But his goal is to use this short life to shape us for eternity.

So while God blesses you with things that are good, he ultimately shapes you with things that are not.

When money is tight, our prayer for daily bread becomes sincere. When doctors don't know what to do, our hope falls back on what God has already done. When the inevitability of death hits home, the resurrection comfort becomes alive.

"That is why, for Christ's sake, I delight in weaknesses, in insults, in hardships, in persecutions, in difficulties. For when I am weak, then I am strong" (2 Corinthians 12:10).

Struggles with Genesis?

Pastor Mike Novotny

For many, the struggle with science and religion starts in Genesis. "You're saying God created the universe with just a few words? And Adam and Eve were real people? And Noah built a boat and marched animals on board? Why would anyone call this nonfiction?" My short answer is—We believe in Genesis because Jesus did.

But why follow Jesus' lead? Logic and love. Logically, it's reasonable to trust the guy who predicted his own resurrection and then pulled it off. Study the works of Gary Habermas and realize how reasonable it is to believe Jesus came back from the dead. Or read 1 Corinthians chapter 15 and the book of Acts and follow the apostles' line of thought—"Jesus is alive! We are witnesses! If the resurrection is true, that Jesus had the divine power to conquer death, he must be God. And, if he's God, then we can trust what he trusts, Genesis included."

Or consider trusting Jesus because of love. Jesus loves us illogically. God dying on a cross doesn't compute, but that's what God did. God not counting our sins doesn't agree with the accountant in us, but that's what God says. God remembering no more what we can't forget doesn't make sense to us, but that's God's bottom line. No human loves like that. Only God does. Which points to a Jesus who can be trusted.

There are many hard parts about holding on to Genesis. But know this—Jesus loves every page of the book that begins the Bible. That's why we can too.

Peace at all costs
Pastor Matt Ewart

Right now you may be feeling some tension with someone in your life. Maybe you did something to create the tension. Maybe the other person did. Either way, here you are with some unresolved tension between the two of you, and you don't like how that makes you feel.

One reason we tend to put off these tensions rather than address them is because it always costs something to establish peace with someone.

It may cost you a piece of your pride.

It may cost you an evening of your time.

It may cost you discomfort as you open an old wound.

Wherever there's tension, it'll cost something to be resolved. And sometimes that cost can be high.

Today I want you to dwell on the peace that God initiated with you and all humankind. Think about the peace on earth that the angels sang about at Jesus' birth. Think about the unthinkable cost that Jesus paid gladly to establish peace between you and his Father.

Now since the tension between you and heaven is erased, take to heart what that means for you:

"If it is possible, as far as it depends on you, live at peace with everyone" (Romans 12:18).

Part with your pride. Spend your time. Put up with the pain. Pay whatever is necessary on your end to resolve the tensions you feel. There's no guarantee that things will be resolved right away. Maybe today is just about that first step.

Thirsty?

Pastor Mike Novotny

Have you ever wondered why it's so hard to be satisfied? If you're like me, living in a prosperous country, you have/own/enjoy more blessings than 99 percent of human beings in history. Yet it is so easy to feel bored, empty, and aching for more. Why is that?

God knows the answer. **"My people have committed two sins: They have forsaken me, the spring of living water, and have dug their own cisterns, broken cisterns that cannot hold water"** (Jeremiah 2:13). Why do our souls feel so thirsty for more? Because we've forgotten God, the spring of living water, and turned to someone or something else to satisfy. But no matter how many dollars you make, how many trips you take, or how many rounds of golf you play, it's not enough to fill that desire in your heart. Those are "broken cisterns."

Thankfully, God is still giving away living water. We can come to Jesus today and find eternal life in his name. We can find a gushing source of love that never runs dry, a mercy that bubbles up new every morning, and a grace that endures forever.

Recently, the man who sold Minecraft, the popular video game, for $2.5 billion dollars admitted that his mansion, champagne, and celebrity friends didn't cure his loneliness. His story reminds us that even the biggest "cisterns" on earth are broken. Praise God that we have something better in Jesus, a spring of living water that never runs dry and can always satisfy our souls.

The King deserves our praise

Pastor David Scharf

Around the world, it's not uncommon for the people of a country to hold a parade for the soldiers who are going into battle on their behalf. They cheer their troops on to encourage them and to show their thanks to those who may give up their lives for their fellow man.

Five hundred years before Jesus' birth, the prophet Zechariah pictured a similar parade. We know it as Palm Sunday: **"Rejoice greatly. . . . See, your king comes to you, righteous and victorious, lowly and riding on a donkey"** (Zechariah 9:9). Jesus rode into Jerusalem to the praise of the people. Jesus rode in to do battle and win. The only difference between this parade and all others like it is that Jesus rode into Jerusalem *knowing* that he was going to die . . . and yet he still marched into battle! He did it for you. What a King!

Now what? Zechariah tells us: "Rejoice greatly!" You usually rejoice in proportion to the news you receive. If you win free cable for a month, you'll rejoice with a "Yes!" If you win free groceries for a year, you'll rejoice even more with a "This is amazing!" every time you check out of the grocery store for free that year. Even better, Jesus brings you the righteousness you need and the victory you crave. How can you not rejoice GREATLY with a lifetime of praise?

So rejoice. No, even better, rejoice GREATLY today!

Wrapped in the identity of God
Andrea Delwiche

"But you, Lord, are a shield around me, my glory, the One who lifts my head high" (Psalm 3:3).

What does it mean to say that the Lord is my glory? *Glory* can also mean, "honor." What does it mean to say, "My honor as a person is found in God?"

Sit with that for a while. King David probably did something similar when he wrote this psalm. It wasn't a glorious time in David's life. He had fled from his son Absalom. Terror, anguish, and uncertainty hung around his kingship like a cloud of smoke.

Yet the cloud became the fragrance of incense. David's personal splendor had collapsed, but he wore the Lord's mantle of glory. It covered him in peace and security to the point that he was able to write, **"I lie down and sleep; I wake again, because the Lord sustains me"** (verse 5).

As David assessed his life situation, he saw the Lord. His reputation, his well-being, rested in the character of God. He knew he belonged to God; therefore, he knew he was secure.

How much of my sleeplessness is because I'm looking to save myself? How much of my restlessness is rooted in my perception of my importance, honor, and prestige? Can I picture myself stripped bare of artifice and wrapped instead in the identity of the triune God? Can I picture the Lord saying to me, "Take off that dusty, tattered cloak of identity; it's too heavy. Wear mine instead. Let me be your glory. Rest in me."

A multiracial Messiah
Pastor Mike Novotny

The other day, I tried to track down all the Jesuses in my office. I gathered every painting, picture, icon, and action figure. Then I studied the look of Jesus. It made me realize that every artist has to make important choices—Which paint color do you use for his skin? What size and shape do you make his nose and eyes? How much melanin is in the God-man?

We don't have to guess entirely about the answers to those questions. Just read the words that open the New Testament: **"Abraham was the father of Isaac, Isaac the father of Jacob, Jacob the father of Judah and his brothers. . . . Boaz the father of Obed, whose mother was Ruth, Obed the father of Jesse, and Jesse the father of King David"** (Matthew 1:2,5,6).

Do you know these people and the places they came from? Abraham was from modern Iraq, Jacob's mom from modern Syria, righteous Ruth from modern Jordan, and famous David from Bethlehem in the Palestinian West Bank. Jesus' genetic story starts with Iraqi, Israeli, Jordanian, and a mixture of Middle Eastern countries and culture.

What might change if we remembered that we have a Middle Eastern Messiah? How might we react to the news stories involving "those nations" and "those people" if we recalled that they were Jesus' people? What attitudes might evolve if we read the first page of the New Testament and discovered a divine Son with darker skin, a multiracial Messiah?

Stay tuned

Pastor Clark Schultz

Agree or disagree: Streaming TV services have saved or ruined TV watching as we know it?

I disagree. If you're patient, you get to watch an entire season all in one sitting!

God asks us to be patient with him. Good things come to those who wait. And I mean patiently wait! It's not like drivers who take off fast from a stoplight only to be stopped at the next light and the next light. Hurry up, stop, hurry up, stop.

But our lives are "hurry up and wait" at times. God wants us to be patient and wait for him. Does God love you? Yes! Does it always seem like that? Not always. Does God always keep his promises? Yes!

"The Lord is not slow in keeping his promise, as some understand slowness. Instead he is patient with you, not wanting anyone to perish, but everyone to come to repentance" (2 Peter 3:9).

A life of following God may mean denying some of the things that others are doing around you. There might be some commercial breaks that you wish you could fast-forward through. But understand that God has not left you! God doesn't want you to fail! But when you mess up, he wants you to run to him, not away from him! So stay tuned to him and be patient!

April

[Jesus] then began to teach them that
the Son of Man must suffer many things and
be rejected by the elders, the chief priests and
the teachers of the law, and that he must be
killed and after three days rise again.

Mark 8:31

The Lamb on the throne

Pastor Mike Novotny

There are two wonderful words that don't often appear together outside of Christianity—*lamb* and *throne*. **"And they cried out in a loud voice: 'Salvation belongs to our God, who sits on the throne, and to the Lamb'"** (Revelation 7:10).

A throne is a place for a king, a position of power and honor and authority. If you sit on a throne, you get what you want. You have the last word. You live in a palace filled with servants, far from the pain of the streets. A lamb, on the contrary, is a symbol of humility, sacrifice, and substitution. In the Bible, lambs died on altars so that kings could sit on thrones.

But in heaven we find something unique—the One on/near the throne is a lamb! As the Lord of lords, King Jesus could have stayed in the comfort of the palace. Instead he chose the pain of the altar we call the cross. As the Son of God, Jesus could have used his authority for his own security. Instead he chose humility, adversity, and tragedy. Jesus was our King but, in love, chose to become our Lamb.

That thought is enough to send the saints and angels into endless praise. Will you join them today? Salvation belongs to our God! Hallelujah and Amen!

Temptation
Christine Wentzel

During the time before Easter, our thoughts dwell particularly on the enormous price paid to restore our relationship with God. The variety of temptations that confront us can be as pesky as a fly or as alluring as a desert mirage. When wrestling with a particularly strong temptation, we may conclude our ugly weakness stands apart from the exposure Jesus experienced. Ha! If we truly understood!

"We have a chief priest who is able to sympathize with our weaknesses. He was tempted in every way that we are, but he didn't sin" (Hebrews 4:15 GW).

Think about being bombarded with every temptation known to mankind; the devil had a field day. We don't need an itemized list. It's enough to know that Jesus was "tempted in every way." We can well imagine the rest.

Consider how easy the devil convinced angels living in heaven to follow him to hell and for Eve and Adam to doubt God while living in Paradise. Beware! The devil was beyond smug. Our grace giver allowed the tempter a shot at Jesus and then had him fleeing in failure. Hallelujah!

Jesus, the mediator between God and us, proved his qualifications to understand our weaknesses. There is nothing he can't empathize with. There is nothing he will allow to overtake us. Amen.

What love is
Sarah Habben

I know my husband loves me. He doesn't surprise me with candlelit dinners or flowers. But he cleans the house on his day off. Chooses not to sigh when I'm the last one ready. Plans amazing family trips. I'd be a fool to wait for flowers as proof of his love when the clean floor is proof already. I'd be wrong to complain about his missing "romance gene" when my husband cheerfully does the dishes after a long day at work. His love serves me every day.

I know my God loves me. At least I claim I do. But when I beg him for more resources or less pain or a snappy resolution to my conflicts and God seems silent . . . well, then my confidence wobbles. I want God to prove his love with a yes to all my prayers. Preferably with one-day delivery. But if I limit God to my personal terms of love, I'm a fool. **"This is how we know what love is: Jesus Christ laid down his life for us"** (1 John 3:16).

My heavenly Bridegroom scrubbed the filthy floor of my heart with his holy blood. He cheerfully provides me with food and clothes and energy for each day, even when I don't thank him. He doesn't sigh when I come to the Lord's Supper—"That wrongdoer and those sins *again*?" He strengthens my faith, encourages me with his Word, and has an amazing plan for my eternal life.

Lord, I know you love me. Thank you for all the ways you prove it. Amen.

Easter is about/for real people
Pastor Mike Novotny

Easter is more than a story. It's history. Because history is about real people, places, and things, which are exactly what we find in John's gospel. Just look at the real people from real places that we meet on the day Jesus rose from the dead—**"Early on the first day of the week, while it was still dark, Mary Magdalene went to the tomb and saw that the stone had been removed from the entrance. So she came running to Simon Peter and the other disciple, the one Jesus loved"** (John 20:1,2).

First, there's Mary from the town of Magdala (that's what *Magdalene* means). Then there's Peter, a fisherman from Bethsaida, six miles northeast of Capernaum, who was courageous (and impulsive) enough to sprint straight into the tomb, even though grave robbers were rumored to have snatched Jesus' body. And then there's John—the "other disciple." John must have been one of those quiet, competitive types, because he later mentions how he whooped Peter in the first Easter 5k and made it to the tomb first. Mary, Peter, and John were real people.

Which is really good news. It means that Easter was about real people back then and is for real people even now. Real people like you and me who find joy in talking today to the living Jesus and who will one day run through our own tombs into eternal life. Thank God that Easter is history, a real event that really blesses real people!

Easter is about/for real places

Pastor Mike Novotny

The Church of the Holy Sepulchre in Jerusalem is believed by most scholars to mark the actual tomb of Jesus. This church was built in the 12th century A.D. on top of the ruins of the original church, built around A.D. 326 by Roman Emperor Constantine. Why did Constantine pick this particular spot in Jerusalem? Because that's where Emperor Hadrian built a pagan temple to his gods around A.D. 135. And why did Hadrian build his temple in that spot? Because he wanted to cover up the very location where Christians claimed that their God, Jesus, defeated death.

I love that history. It points to the real place back then where Easter happened and the real places today where Easter is still happening. As Jesus later put it, **"And surely I am with you always, to the very end of the age"** (Matthew 28:20). Just like Jesus appeared in a real place to Mary, Peter, and John, he also is really present where we spend the minutes and seconds of our days. We are never alone in our homes, offices, or morning commutes. The Jesus who defeated death is present to offer us eternal life.

Today, take some time to acknowledge the presence of Jesus in your personal space. And thank God that Easter is more than another story. Easter is history!

Easter is about/for real events

Pastor Mike Novotny

The most frequently used words in John's account of Easter morning are . . . "saw" or "looked" (John 20:1-20). Mary *saw* the stone rolled away. John *looked* into the tomb. Peter *saw* the strips laying there. Unlike many modern "testimonies," Mary didn't say, "I just felt God saying to me . . ." Peter didn't preach, "I just believe that Jesus was reaching out to me." No, these people gave their eye witness accounts of the events they *saw*. Because they didn't want another subjective story. They wanted objective history!

I love that detail from the first Easter morning. In a world of varied beliefs and religions, I crave something concrete, something rooted in the real events of real history. Don't you? Because a Jesus who is historically risen and literally alive is present for the real events that you will go through this week. The sleepless nights. The staff meetings. The visits to the ER. Everything. Christians never face anything alone, because Mary, John, and Peter reported the real event, which would alter every real event that followed.

Are you worried about an upcoming event in your life? Don't be. Jesus is no longer in some tomb. He is alive, well, and with you always, working out everything for the good of his church. Just ask Mary, John, and Peter.

A place for lost sheep

Jason Nelson

Is there a place in your heart for lost sheep? They'll return if we don't give up on them, if reclaiming them is our priority. Think about what Jesus is saying here: **"I was sent only to the lost sheep"** (Matthew 15:24). He cares so much about lost sheep because we all start out that way.

The nice thing about lost sheep is that they hide in plain sight. You can spot them a mile away and very close to home. Lost sheep make the other sheep nervous because, for a while, lost sheep will look and act lost. But all the sheep benefit from being in a place that's safe for lost sheep.

Lost sheep don't like jumping through hoops. They get discouraged easily. They would rather stay lost than risk getting sheared one more time. But they'll eventually wander in through wide open doors. Do you invite them in? Does your church have special ministry to help them recover from being lost? Are they welcome at the Lord's Supper when they desire the five things present there: bread, wine, body, blood, and forgiveness? Are they welcome so they won't be lost anymore?

When lost sheep return, there's some kind of buzz in heaven over it. So, until they come back, leave an empty chair at the dinner table, a reserved seat in the back of church, an open chamber in your heart just for them.

The Holy Spirit is predictive text
Linda Buxa

It's a little creepy, but my work email knows what I want to type before I even type it. With predictive typing, I start typing a few words and—all of a sudden—a complete sentence magically appears.

There's a moment in the Bible when Jesus told his disciples that their words would be supplied for them, just like predictive text. As they were about to go out to share their faith—and would get in trouble for doing so—he said, **"Do not worry about how you will defend yourselves or what you will say, for the Holy Spirit will teach you at that time what you should say"** (Luke 12:11,12).

So far I haven't been called to testify about my faith in front of people who could throw me in jail (and not many of you have either I bet), but we've all been in situations where we had no idea what to say. Yet somehow, we spoke God's words of witness, comfort, hope, kindness, gentle correction, wisdom, and encouragement. That's the Holy Spirit giving us the words we need when we need them.

The apostle Paul once asked people to pray for him **"that whenever I speak, words may be given me so that I will fearlessly make known the mystery of the gospel"** (Ephesians 6:19). Pray that prayer for yourself, your friends and family, and your fellow believers too. Pray for the right words. Then thank the Holy Spirit as he fills them in for you.

april 9

A new mindset on money
Pastor Mike Novotny

Ti is a tiny word in the Greek language, one of the smallest that you'll find on any given page of a Greek New Testament. But it has a big meaning in Acts chapter 4: **"All the believers were one in heart and mind. No one claimed that any of their possessions was their own, but they shared everything they had"** (verse 32). Our English versions translate the Greek word *ti* with our word *any*. None of the early Christians claimed that anything, not even the tiniest trinket, was his or her own.

That passage is a powerful example of what some Christians call stewardship. It's the idea that nothing we have, own, wear, drive, possess, etc. belongs to us. It all belongs to God. He owns it. We just manage it. God, in his generous love, gives us so many blessings to use to his glory and others' good, but we must remember that everything, even the tiniest *ti*, belongs to him.

That truth can confront us if we hold on to money too tightly. Yet it can also comfort us. The God who owns everything has chosen to put so much into our hands. Through generous parents, job opportunities, birthday gifts, and annual raises, he has chosen to entrust his stuff into our lives. He gave us the privilege of being his channel for giving to those in need so we can experience the joy of his generous heart.

What a powerful mindset! Look around for a moment and consider all the things, down to the smallest possession, that our Father has put into your hands.

Jesus makes you a winner
Pastor Clark Schultz

Ad executive and inventor Reyn Guyer was hired to work on a promotional display for a shoe polish company. He was working with the idea of colored polka dots on a mat when it struck him that it might be better as a board game—using people as pieces. He hired some designers to help, and eventually Milton Bradley produced the game that we now know as Twister.

Have you ever played that game in real life? You and I do it all the time. Instead of twisting our bodies, we take a spin at a sin because everyone else is doing it. Then we twist what Scripture says to make up for that sin. For example, "Hey, I can get drunk this weekend. I know God will forgive me." Or, "God says I should love my neighbor. But *that* person isn't really my neighbor, right?"

Take heart and focus on the yellow dot that reminds us of the sun—more specifically, the Son of God. Jesus allowed his hands and his feet to be on display for the amusement of those who mocked him. He shed his blood and allowed himself to be twisted on a cross so that you and I can look forward to heaven after this game of life.

Christ made it possible for all of us to be winners: **"But he was pierced for our transgressions, he was crushed for our iniquities; the punishment that brought us peace was on him, and by his wounds we are healed"** (Isaiah 53:5).

A new joy and understanding

Andrea Delwiche

"When he was at the table with them, he took bread, gave thanks, broke it and began to give it to them. Then their eyes were opened and they recognized him, and he disappeared from their sight. They asked each other, 'Were not our hearts burning within us while he talked with us on the road and opened the Scriptures to us?'" (Luke 24:30-32).

Do you recognize the voice of your risen and ascended Lord? Do you know the heartburn that comes when the Lord is opening Scripture to you? The two followers of Jesus who have come to be known as the Emmaus disciples were unable to recognize their risen Savior when, on that first Easter, he appeared to them and began to untangle the momentousness of his suffering, death, and resurrection.

After Jesus had handed out the dinner bread, they recognized him and identified what it was that confirmed for them that their visitor was their Lord: "Were not our hearts *burning within us* while he talked with us?" In hindsight, they were able to recognize the burning in their souls that they normally felt as they learned from their Teacher and Master and Savior.

As you celebrate Christ's resurrection, ask the Holy Spirit to give you new joy and understanding. Ask the Spirit to untangle for you the deep significance of the newness of life connected with Christ's resurrection. What are some of the ways that Christ's resurrection changes your life now and forever? Praise God for his indescribable gift!

Follow a leader worth following
Pastor Jeremy Mattek

Would you want a surgeon to operate on you if he only made a half-hearted effort? Would you want an attorney to represent you if she practiced law half-heartedly? Would you want teachers in your children's classrooms if they only had half-hearted feelings about children?

It wouldn't be worth following a Savior who was only half-hearted about saving you either.

Thankfully, Jesus wasn't.

"As the time approached for him to be taken up to heaven, Jesus resolutely set out for Jerusalem" (Luke 9:51).

When this verse says that "Jesus resolutely set out for Jerusalem," it could literally be translated, "He fixed his face for Jerusalem." In other words, he was absolutely determined to get there. Why? What was going to happen in Jerusalem?

He was going to die, and you were going to be forgiven.

He was going to suffer, and you were going to be given a place in heaven.

He was going to be punished for your sins, and you were going to be given the right to walk through life knowing each day that your Father in heaven is smiling in your direction.

Jesus wasn't half-hearted about being our Savior. He was all in. He poured his whole heart and his whole life into his mission to forgive the whole world.

That's a leader worth following.

Study skills
Jason Nelson

Ezra was a professional copyist. He transcribed Moses' scrolls so God's Word could be passed around to more people. What Ezra worked on worked on him. He **"committed himself to studying the Revelation of God, to living it, and to teaching Israel to live its truths and ways"** (Ezra 7:10 MSG). After some captivity, **"he arrived from Babylon, a scholar well-practiced in the Revelation of Moses that the God of Israel had given"** (verse 6). Ezra had good study skills. He educated himself in God's Word. That paid dividends in his life and in the lives of others. We can do the same thing. We can copy the copier.

Read: Written words don't have meaning unless we read them. God's words on a screen or in a book are there to read. When we do, we begin to understand God's big plan and notice our special little place in it.

Write: Forming words with our hands somehow unlocks their power. We can underline, rewrite, or script a *prayer-a-phrase* of favorite psalms, proverbs, and sayings of Jesus and post them to our thoughts. The important things we write down tend to stick with us.

Speak: Conviction is the author of our spoken words. Verbalizing passages that we've tucked away reveals our commitment to them. Quoting the Bible to other people expands the Holy Spirit's universe and God's kingdom.

Remember: When we read, highlight, and take to heart the Holy Scriptures, we get faith that will never fade away.

Grace teaches us

Pastor Mike Novotny

Grace has supernatural power to change people. Just ask that wee little man. If you grew up in church, you might have learned a song about a wee little (and wicked) man named Zacchaeus. He was a money-loving hustler from Jesus' day whom all his neighbors loathed, a man who loved to get and hated to give. Until one day when he stood up and said, "I want to give half of everything I have to the poor. And if I ever cheated anyone out of anything, I want to give it all back. No, I want to give back four times what I took."

That's change! So, how did that happen? Grace. Jesus saw Zacchaeus, morally small, greedy and unworthy, and he said, "I have to hang out with you today." The neighbors muttered, "With him?" Jesus smiled, "Yes, with him." Jesus' shocking love and gracious presence moved Zacchaeus in a way that the shame of his neighbors could not.

The apostle Paul wrote about that same life-changing power of grace: **"For the grace of God has appeared that offers salvation to all people. It teaches us to say 'No' to ungodliness and worldly passions, and to live self-controlled, upright and godly lives in this present age"** (Titus 2:11,12).

Grace has the power to change all people. Even people like Zacchaeus. Even a person like you. I'm not sure what change you want to make in your spiritual life, but I do know that grace is always the best place to start.

Don't be afraid; just believe

Pastor David Scharf

Jairus was a man in the Bible who was told his beloved daughter was dead. He turned to Jesus for comfort and heard, **"Don't be afraid; just believe"** (Mark 5:36). Believe what? What could Jesus possibly do to make this better?

We've all been there. We know Jesus loves us, we know he promises to care for us, we know he promises all will work out for our good according to his will . . . we know, but what could he possibly do to make *this* (you fill in your "this") better? The answer comes at the end of the account. Jesus raised Jairus' daughter from the dead. And that's not the only astounding thing he did. He healed the sick, turned loaves of bread into food for thousands, and raised himself from the dead. This all-powerful One also happens to love you. Just look at the cross and empty tomb for the evidence.

As marvelous as raising Jairus' daughter is, do you know what my favorite part of this account is? It's the last line after he raises Jairus' daughter from the dead: **"[Jesus] told them to give her something to eat"** (Mark 5:43). Her parents knew to feed her, but Jesus made certain to say it anyway. Do you see what that means? Jesus cares for you down to the last detail. It may seem that nobody notices you, but Jesus notices. Whether your "this" is big or small, don't be afraid. Just believe.

Peace and forgiveness in Jesus' hands

Pastor David Scharf

What makes you nervous? What brings fear and anxiety to your heart? On Easter Sunday evening, Jesus' followers had reason for anxiety and fear. First, they thought their lives might be in danger. The Jewish religious leaders had put Jesus to death. How hard would it be for them to get the disciples? Additionally, they were struggling with guilt. For whatever reason, they had not gotten it when Jesus told them he would rise from the dead. They should have believed him. How would the risen Jesus deal with them? In anger and judgment? Here's how:

"On the evening of that first day of the week, when the disciples were together, with the doors locked for fear of the Jewish leaders, Jesus came and stood among them and said, 'Peace be with you!' After he said this, he showed them his hands and side" (John 20:19,20).

In the place of fear, there was forgiveness. Why? Because Jesus had really died and risen. The sight of Jesus' nail-scarred—but risen!—hands drove fear out of their hearts!

Picture Jesus. He's standing in front of you, smiling, hands outstretched. You can see the nail scars on his hands. He says to you, "Peace be with you." There in his words of peace, in his nail-scarred yet risen hands, is the antidote to fear, all fear. For there, in the hands and words of Jesus, is forgiveness.

At the empty tomb with Mary—Part 1

Christine Wentzel

"When Jesus rose early on the first day of the week, he appeared first to Mary Magdalene, out of whom he had driven seven demons" (Mark 16:9).

It's hard to imagine what life was like for Mary Magdalene before Jesus healed her. Perhaps anyone on intimate terms with mental illness can glimpse into the chaos of her mind and soul. Filled with divine compassion, Jesus drove out the demons. In a blink of an eye, Jesus restored her. He made her whole—physically, emotionally, socially, and above all spiritually.

In this new life, she committed to the needs of the traveling teacher/healer with a radical message. She witnessed the wonders he performed. Yet she saw him through the eyes of her expectations: a heaven-sent earthly king.

Her view from the foot of the cross contradicted everything she learned from her Messiah. Fear and doubt attempted to crowd out her faith and mess with her reason. Everything she thought she came to believe was about to die.

The holy Lamb of God looked down on the people below him while braced against the splintery wood of the cross as every sin of mankind was nailed into him. He knew the worth of his perfect work for friend and foe alike. His joy was made complete when he breathed out, **"It is finished"** (John 19:30).

At the empty tomb with Mary—Part 2
Christine Wentzel

"At this, she turned around and saw Jesus standing there, but she did not realize that it was Jesus. He asked her, 'Woman, why are you crying? Who is it you are looking for?'" (John 20:14,15).

Mary Magdalene was grieving for three days. She was spent. When the Sabbath was over, she was determined to help give her healer and teacher a proper burial. When she looked in the tomb, she saw heavenly beings instead of a dead body. Perhaps she lost her mind as well as her Master after all.

Mary, muddied by grief, drew conclusions based on circumstantial evidence and not on Jesus' promises. The last thing on her mind was seeing him alive, let alone standing near her in love—once again ready to heal her pain and give her the greatest news.

Assuming Jesus Christ was a gardener, she asked for an explanation. He patiently encouraged her to remember who called out the demons, healed bodies, calmed storms, walked on water, and raised the dead all the while he spoke of his prophetic identity and mission.

But she saw her Savior die! Nothing about this made any sense! Her grief and confusion clouded over the memories of miracles and messages of messianic fulfillment.

How many times do we struggle with our own expectations and wisdom over God's? It's wasted energy. As C.S. Lewis once put it, "I gave in and admitted that God is God."

At the empty tomb with Mary—Part 3

Christine Wentzel

"Jesus said to her, 'Mary'" (John 20:16).

The Word made flesh holds the power to create from nothing, but with a gentle breath, he drove out Mary's unbelief and grief by speaking her name.

She remembered. She might have wanted to collapse on him in relief and repentance for her blindness. We do the same every time he reminds us of his presence no matter how bad things appear.

With Jesus' salvation mission at an end, his relationship with Mary and the rest of his people changed. He would no longer live on earth among them, but he would promise not to leave them alone to their own devices. He sent her on her way to spread the good news to his disciples.

Mary did as she was told—with an eagerness we do well to emulate. She didn't need a degree from a Bible college or a seminary school. She simply spoke what the Lord had told her. She didn't need to worry about anything beyond that. We have those same abilities, the same urgent mission. Go and tell!

Thank you, Lord. The account of Mary Magdalene is especially meaningful for your daughters. You honored a woman to be the first witness of your resurrection. You know our need to be reassured of your love and that we are of worth in your eyes. Open ours to see the encouragement, purpose, and promise forever preserved in the account of Mary at the empty tomb. Amen.

Communicate or fight
Jason Nelson

Communication is the art of avoiding a fight. Playwright George Bernard Shaw said, "The single biggest problem in communication is the illusion that it has taken place." People think they've communicated when they haven't. That's why **"you will hear of wars and rumors of wars, but see to it that you are not alarmed. Such things must happen, but the end is still to come"** (Matthew 24:6). We will hear of conflicts among nations, in the church, at work, and between the lady of the house and the man of the house. But don't panic. It doesn't mean everything will blow up. People need to de-escalate the situation with better communication.

Repeating the same thing a little louder is not communicating. Communication is being honest about problems and transparent about attempts to solve them. Communication is being willing to involve as many people as possible in the process. Everyone affected by decisions needs an opportunity to pick through the same dump of information so he or she can weigh in. Then there's a chance to build consensus. Otherwise people will fill in the blanks with uncharitable assumptions about other people's motives.

You can't overcommunicate. Share more information with more people. Take more time to ask if everyone understands. Show more willingness to listen to another's take on circumstances. Be more patient when someone just doesn't get it. Be willing to engage in one-on-one repentance and forgiveness. Enjoy a little more peace on earth.

Remember what God said

Pastor Jeremy Mattek

Sports fans nervously pace the room when their favorite team is losing. But when the team pulls out a last-second win, they get pumped. Their feelings go from anxiety to excitement.

On Easter morning, the women were sad and scared as they approached Jesus' tomb. But then they saw an angel who said, **"Remember** [what] **he told you, while he was still with you in Galilee"** (Luke 24:6). What Jesus had told them was that they were going to see him delivered into the hands of sinful men. He would be crucified, and then on the third day he would rise again.

The women remembered and believed, and their hearts that were so heavy one minute became light and joyful.

They ran to the disciples and told them that Jesus was alive. The angel helped them remember the promise he made, and that promise made the difference.

What promise would the angel remind you of if he spoke to you today? "Didn't God say that there is nothing in all creation that can separate you from him?" "Didn't God say that you don't need to worry about anything?" "Didn't God say that all things work out for the good of those who love him?" "Didn't Jesus say to his disciples that they would see him again?"

He did. And they did. Just like we will. One day we will see. But each day until then, the very best thing you can do is open his Word and listen.

Hard words, happy hearts
Pastor Mike Novotny

I recently heard about a girl who was raised in a religion that added conditions to the gospel. "Believe in Jesus and you are God's child," her church said, "*and* when you speak in tongues, you'll know you truly believe." She did believe in her Savior, but no matter how hard she tried (and she tried hard), that mysterious gift never arrived. So she assumed she wasn't saved.

Thankfully, she met some Christians who believed in the no-strings-attached gospel. "Jesus alone saves," they said. "Jesus alone makes us good enough for God," they smiled. "Jesus is all you need," they insisted. They encouraged her to put her hope in Christ alone. They told her that through faith she was already a child of God. As peace filled her heart and the Spirit lifted her burden, that young woman wept for joy.

Confronting false teaching can be hard, but its goal is joy through Jesus. Paul once wrote, **"Rebuke** [false teachers] **sharply, so that they will be sound in the faith"** (Titus 1:13).

Is there someone in your life who has helped protect your faith through such a rebuke? If so, thank them for their courage today. Is there someone in your life who needs to be protected from false teaching? If so, take Paul's words to heart and act. Their future faith will thank you.

#beautiful

Sarah Habben

When I look in the mirror, I see what lots of 40-somethings presumably see: sags and wrinkles and thinning hair. You older folks are likely muttering, "Just you wait." You younger folks might find your pointy nose or scrawny pecs to be cruel and unusual punishment in a society that worships sexual allure.

But here's a thought: When I feel ugly and unworthy, maybe it's not because I'm a victim of the big, bad world and its unhealthy obsessions. Maybe the problem is that *I* worship beauty too. I offer this idol my time as I obsess over my selfies and profile pictures, as I follow the lives and diets of gorgeous celebrities. I offer this idol my income as I load my cart with products to halt or hide the aging process.

So . . . should I be *relieved* when God says, **"People look at the outward appearance, but the LORD looks at the heart"** (1 Samuel 16:7)? Ha! Maybe if I could borrow someone else's heart—one not filled with vanity, jealousy, and idolatry! The truth is that my inside is worse than my skin-side.

Thankfully, I don't have to borrow a better heart. I've been given one. It's Jesus' heart. Jesus, who had no beauty or majesty in his outward appearance but who is nevertheless perfect in every way. Jesus, who died to remove my ugly sins and make me lovely in God's eyes.

When I look in the mirror, I can see what God sees: Jesus, my beautiful Savior.

God doesn't show favoritism
Pastor Mike Novotny

God's kind of like Blake Shelton, one of the celebrity judges from the *Voice*. It's a reality show where singers try to impress a panel of judges. Except there's a catch. When the singers first perform, the judges' chairs are turned backward. Why? Because they don't want the judges to be biased toward beautiful people. They want Blake and his friends to hear the voice and not just see the face.

Sounds a lot like God. The apostle Peter confessed: **"God has shown me that I should not call anyone impure or unclean. . . . I now realize how true it is that God does not show favoritism but accepts from every nation the one who fears him and does what is right"** (Acts 10:28,34,35). God doesn't show favoritism. His favor isn't just for people with that color skin, with that kind of hair, with those shaped eyes, or from that part of our planet. No, God accepts from every nation the one who fears him and does what is right.

That's a good word for a world with so much racial division. What matters most to God and, hopefully, to his people is the soul and not the skin. A heart that trembles in God's glorious presence and longs to do what is right is worth choosing, applauding, and imitating.

It's so easy to judge a book by its cover and people by their appearance. Ask God today for the ability to hear "the voice" of someone's soul.

3 reasons to be religious

Pastor Daron Lindemann

Fewer and fewer of today's people practice organized religion.

So permit the Bible a few minutes to make its claim why religion is important. All of this comes from a religious man named James.

First, the main culprit that gets in between people and God is pride. We think we know more than God. Not true. **"He chose to give us birth through the word of truth, that we might be a kind of firstfruits of all he created"** (James 1:18).

God made people. People don't make God. God made you. God planned you, created you, and chose you to be his child by faith. Not just any child, but his favorite child. You are the firstfruits of all he created.

God saves you by sowing the seed of his Word, his message of forgiving grace, in your heart. **"Humbly accept the word planted in you, which can save you"** (James 1:21). We're all just a bunch of dirt until God makes us his beautiful garden.

Finally, **"every good and perfect gift is from above, coming down from the Father of the heavenly lights, who does not change like shifting shadows"** (James 1:17). God doesn't stand forgetfully at the fridge wondering why he opened it, and he doesn't forget about you.

God forgives you, and he doesn't change his mind.

You won't find a religion better than that. Including no religion at all.

The diversity of eternity
Pastor Mike Novotny

This past month, I immersed myself in trying to understand issues of race in contemporary culture, including inner city poverty, unconscious prejudice, and mass incarceration. What did I learn? That it will take superhuman amounts of humility, honesty, and selflessness to remedy the struggles so many face today. To be candid, I'm not certain if our finger-pointing society has the virtue required to do it.

Which is why I needed to dream with Jesus' friend John—**"After this I looked, and there before me was a great multitude that no one could count, from every nation, tribe, people and language, standing before the throne and before the Lamb"** (Revelation 7:9). Look at the uncountable crowd in John's dream! From every nation. From every tribe. From every people. From every language. The saved are Africans, Americans, Asians, Canadians. They speak English, Arabic, and all the accents you can choose for Alexa. Your people, my people, all people are there. If unrepentant racists were allowed into heaven, they would hate the VIP section. Because in heaven there is fellowship without discrimination, praise without hesitation, and worship without segregation. If you love diversity, you will adore eternity.

That glimpse gives me the motivation I need to keep fighting so that God's will might be done here on earth as it is there in heaven. I pray that it fuels up your heart to fight for truth and justice too.

Serenity
Jason Nelson

Reinhold Niebuhr was pastor of Bethel Church in Detroit during the time between two devastating World Wars. He had the habit of writing eloquent prayers to accompany his sermons. One has endured as part of our spiritual consciousness: "God, give us grace to accept with serenity the things that cannot be changed, courage to change the things that should be changed, and the wisdom to distinguish one from the other." This prayer can be found on coffee mugs, wall art, and is recited at addiction recovery meetings. It gained traction because it wasn't just a prayer for struggling people; it was the prayer of a person struggling to do what the psalmist said: **"Surrender yourself to the LORD, and wait patiently for him. Do not be preoccupied with an evildoer who succeeds in his way when he carries out his schemes"** (Psalm 37:7 GW).

I wish we could get the juice for serenity loaded into our annual flu shot. I wish we could be immunized against despair and strengthened for our duty to be Christian activists in a scary world. It's not easy to overcome evildoers. We don't want to enable them by sitting on our hands. A broken world demands more from us than a perfect one would. Where is the peace that surpasses understanding? Do we work hard to make the world a better place, or do we just accept it as it is? Following Jesus gives us wisdom to distinguish one from the other.

Jesus is the password

Linda Buxa

Website passwords are challenging. You know, between the capital letters, the special characters, and the lowercase letters, it's hard to keep them all straight. Because we're told to use different passwords on different sites, how in the world can we remember them all and get access to our online accounts?

Personally, I can't. This is why I love the auto-fill feature on my computer. It does all the work for me, putting in the password so I can have access to my shopping, my banking, my work.

You know what? Membership in God's family requires a password too. Not one with capital letters or numerals or special characters, but one that requires perfection.

How in the world will we ever get access with that kind of requirement? We won't. At least not on our own.

This is why I love Jesus.

By dying on a cross for us, he met God's requirement for punishment. By rising from the dead, he defeated Satan for us. And now he did all the work for us so we can have access to what we need—a relationship with the Father here on earth and the promise of eternal life in heaven.

Jesus said, **"I am the way and the truth and the life and the password. No one comes to the Father except through me"** (John 14:6).

Okay, technically he didn't say he was the password. But he was—and he still is.

Hey, you kids!

Pastor Daron Lindemann

My ten-year-old buddies and I were messing around in a home under construction in our neighborhood. It was nighttime. We weren't damaging anything, but we shouldn't have been there.

"Hey, you kids!" we heard from a truck pulling over in front of the house. Man, did we scram!

Getting called out isn't always a bad thing, though.

"Hey, you kids!" the server at the restaurant says to a few tables of high schoolers having a good time, and he hands out free ice cream sundaes.

The apostle Paul called out kids when he wrote the letter to the church in Ephesus. He expected that the children would be listening to someone reading this letter or perhaps reading it themselves. And he called them out!

"Children, obey your parents in the Lord, for this is right" (Ephesians 6:1). See that? He called out the kids. Talked directly to them.

God's Word is for everybody. And no matter what your intellect, attention span, or maturity level, God has something he wants to tell you.

By the way, Jesus suggested that adults should be more like children when it comes to believing him and following him. So let's keep kids close to us and close to God's Word.

Add an "and"

Pastor Mike Novotny

A few years ago, I learned the power of the word *and*. I was preparing for a series called *Gay & God*, and I knew people would have so many reactions and emotions to the intersection of sexuality and Scripture. So we came up with this little tagline—Loving everyone God made *and* everything God wrote. I suspected the only way the series would work would be to include the *and*, to think deeply about real people *and* real passages, to care about grace *and* truth. As it turns out, that series became one of the most powerful in all my years of ministry.

And. That three-letter word is so powerful when you remember it. Think of the applications—Prayer is effective . . . and sometimes God says no to your most passionate pleas. Life is hard because of your past sins . . . and God still loves and forgives you. God is love . . . and God is holy. Faith is a personal connection with God . . . and it takes a community for that connection to be strong. A wife must respect her husband . . . and husbands love your wives. Do you see how much depends on *and*? *And* prevents sentences from ending too soon. *And* puts commas where the father of lies would love to put periods.

Meditate on one of the Bible's best *and*s with me— **"All have sinned and fall short of the glory of God, *and* all are justified freely by his grace"** (Romans 3:23,24). What does each part of that sentence add to your faith? What other *and*s might our Father want to add to your thinking today?

May

Only be careful, and watch yourselves closely
so that you do not forget the things
your eyes have seen or let them fade
from your heart as long as you live.
Teach them to your children
and to their children after them.

Deuteronomy 4:9

My Father's world
Jason Nelson

This is my Father's world: The birds their carols raise, the morning light, the lily white, declare their Maker's praise.

God put people in a unique position. We are like everything else he made. We have the same basic needs other living things have. We are also like him. When God made us rational beings, he delegated some of his power to us. We can act in ways no other creature can. We can alter, even destroy, the planet we live on. It's not as durable as we think it is. The universe is infinite. Our planet isn't.

"The earth is the Lord's, and everything in it, the world, and all who live in it" (Psalm 24:1). This is our Father's world, and we need to take better care of it. Christians haven't said much about the environment. Other than St. Francis, few big names reflected on nature. Maybe it's because we think it's out of our hands. We don't need to worry about having a livable planet. That's God's problem. But we need to be responsible stewards. I don't hug trees, but I've seen maps plotting where cancers occur more frequently and I wonder why. We exploit things we don't need to exploit because we can make money. We leave open wounds on the landscape and ignore toxins seeping into our drinking water. Let's take a deep breath of fresh air while we still can and remember:

This is my Father's world: He shines in all that's fair; In the rustling grass I hear him pass, he speaks to me everywhere.—Maltbie D. Babcock

Pastors should be more preachy

Pastor Mike Novotny

Don't you love it (I mean, double-heart-eyed emoji love it) when people preach at you? No? *Preaching* isn't the most popular word these days, is it? "Don't preach at me." "I like that the pastor isn't too preachy." In our lingo, "to preach" has the idea of being arrogant and condescending.

But that's not what the word originally meant. A preacher, in Bible lingo, is a messenger who comes with authority. Instead of sharing some personal feeling or subjective opinion, a preacher comes from the throne of the king to let the people in the streets know what the king has decreed.

In the New Testament, preaching is often connected to the stunning promises of King Jesus. Paul declared, "[God] **has brought** [eternal life] **to light through the preaching entrusted to me by the command of God our Savior**" (Titus 1:3). God commanded Paul to run through the streets of the world and preach eternal life through faith in Jesus Christ.

So every time you go to church or open another Grace Moments email, you should be saying, "Pastor, preach at me! Pastor, I don't need your opinion (no disrespect). No, I need a word from God. Preacher, you've been listening to the King and studying his Word. So, what does he say? Tell me. Please!"

That's preaching. It's the way you find rock-solid peace amidst the white noise of human opinions in our world.

When you've been hacked
Linda Buxa

On Facebook it's easy to tell when your friend's account has been hacked. You go from seeing family photos and funny stories to being tagged in an offensive video that tells you, "You won't believe this! It will blow your mind!" That's when you reach out to let your friend know it's time to change her password.

Isn't it interesting that the person who was hacked always says thanks and then sends a post apologizing and letting people know she's taken steps to secure her account?

In our personal lives, it's easy to tell when our friends' lives have been hacked by temptation and brokenness. People who used to walk closely with God are falling away and are making choices inconsistent with God's good plans. Just like we reach out after a social media hacking, the Bible tells us to reach out to the people we care about. **"Brothers and sisters, if someone is caught in a sin, you who live by the Spirit should restore that person gently"** (Galatians 6:1).

You know what, though? People will react far more defensively about this kind of intervention than they will about a social media account. But that doesn't let you off the hook. God says it is an act of love to say, "Hey, the messages you're sending are different than who you really are. Don't give the devil, the world, and your bad nature freedom to wreak havoc. Change your password."

"Remember this: Whoever turns a sinner from the error of their way will save them from death and cover over a multitude of sins" (James 5:20).

Progress & perfection
Pastor Mike Novotny

Do you think God's happy when you're making progress but not yet perfect? Consider that question as you listen to Paul: **"Brothers and sisters, we instructed you how to live in order to please God, as in fact you are living"** (1 Thessalonians 4:1). That verse is fascinating. These Christians weren't yet perfect (as the next verse implies), but Paul applauded them nonetheless. They were facing intense persecution and daily temptation, yet they were still following Jesus, and Paul couldn't help but smile.

Paul is like the coach of a little kids' football team. He calls them together, claps his hands, smacks them on the helmets, and shouts, "Yes! You did it! You ran the play just like I called it! Now, let's try again and do it even faster!"

What a fresh way to approach spiritual growth! We shouldn't take sin lightly. We dare not minimize the pain that our imperfections cause. Yet there is a time and place to thank God for growth, for every small step in his direction. As some Christians have said, "I'm not what I will be, but I'm not what I was!"

Today I'd like you to think about how you've grown as a Christian. What parts of your faith have gotten stronger in the past year or the past month? Take a moment and celebrate like an apostle. Thank God for progress even as you pursue perfection!

Pay attention to God's "wonderful deeds"

Andrea Delwiche

"I will give thanks to you, Lᴏʀᴅ, with all my heart; I will tell of all your wonderful deeds. I will be glad and rejoice in you; I will sing the praises of your name, O Most High" (Psalm 9:1,2).

These are King David's words. How do they apply to me? How would things change if I spent more time praising God *and* telling of his wonderful deeds as David did? How do *I* go about giving thanks to the Lord with all my heart?

In order to praise something sincerely, I need to know it. I can't write a glowing review of a movie that I haven't seen. I can't tell of God's love and mercy if I haven't paid deep attention to Scripture to see how he worked wonders in the past or noticed and reflected upon how he has acted in my *own* life. I need to be aware.

Then, as the Spirit works in my heart, I will honestly testify to the Lord's greatness because I will remember.

How will things change as I pay attention to God's "wonderful deeds"? In addition to speaking from experience to *others* about the goodness of God, I will be changed myself. Reflecting on the works of the Lord will transform my heart and mind. It will bring me into deeper adoration of my Savior-God. It will increase my trust in him—what he can accomplish *for* me and *through* me in all areas of my life.

Christ's autopsy
Pastor Jon Enter

How do you know for sure Jesus died? Some say Jesus passed out from the pain and later recovered in the tomb. It's eternally crucial that Jesus did in fact die on the cross. If he didn't, we suffer forever.

Whenever you have a question about the Bible, look at the immediate context. When Pilate heard Jesus had died, he was surprised that it had happened so quickly. So Pilate sent a soldier to test if Jesus truly was dead. **"One of the soldiers pierced Jesus' side with a spear, bringing a sudden flow of blood and water"** (John 19:34).

This proves medically and scripturally that Jesus died. It all has to do with how God created our bodies to react to being injured. When a body is cut or punctured, the wound instantly contracts, closing up the hole, and then blood clots the wound to heal it. This only happens if the body is alive. If the body is dead, there's no instantaneous, automatic reaction. The hole stays open. Whatever is inside comes out.

This is how autopsy results show if a victim was stabbed while alive or after death. If the body died, even a split second earlier, the wound stays open. The soldier was watching to see how Jesus' body reacted to being pierced. Jesus' wound stayed open; what was inside—blood and water—came out. Jesus died. Without a doubt, Christ died and paid the price for your soul's salvation. You are forgiven by his death and saved by his life!

Ask God to give you himself

Pastor Daron Lindemann

"Enough about me; tell me more about you."

The desire to get to know someone more deeply signifies that a relationship is there. It's growing and enjoyable.

God, who knows everything about you, still can't get enough of your prayers. It's like a parent asking his one-year-old, "What does the lion say?" Even though the kiddo knows the answer and the parent knows the answer, the parent loves hearing it. Relationship. Growth. Joy!

And so the apostle Paul prayed for believers to love getting closer to God: **"I keep asking that the God of our Lord Jesus Christ, the glorious Father, may give you the Spirit of wisdom and revelation, so that you may know him better"** (Ephesians 1:17).

One of the blessings of prayer is getting to know God better. Picture yourself jumping up on your heavenly Father's lap because he wants to hold you for a while and tell you a story. Without you squirming away.

I can still remember my grandpa scooping me up on his lap. I can smell his cheap cologne. Feel his strong hands. See his smile up close. All of it created pleasant memories. Intimacy. Closeness.

Prayer is more than a duty or a transaction. Make your prayers more than just asking God to give you things. Ask him to give you himself.

Thank him for being him. Praise him for his true words. Enjoy him because of his character. Spend time with him, rejoicing in his promises.

How is your "walk" with God?

Pastor Mike Novotny

Have you ever heard Christians talk about their "walk" with God? The idea comes from passages like this: **"We instructed you how to live in order to please God, as in fact you are living"** (1 Thessalonians 4:1). The original Greek of the verb that we translate "to live" is "to walk."

But why would Paul choose the idea of walking to describe the Christian life? Here are two reasons— First, walking involves direction. Unless you're walking in place (which looks weird!), you're walking in some direction. It's the same with Jesus. Your life can move toward him or away from him, but every day your soul is moving in some direction. Second, walking involves pace. You can walk quickly or slowly. You can slowly seek God, taking a step here or there when you have the time; or you can seek him with all your heart, running the race to win the prize.

So, how's your walk? The comfort of Christianity is that Jesus makes us worthy even while we're "walking." As we try to fix our eyes on Jesus and pick up our spiritual pace, we know that we're already loved, pleasing, and perfect in the eyes of our Father. Therefore, Christian, take a deep breath. Your soul is safe with Jesus.

Knowing that, let's walk even straighter and even faster for our Lord and Savior!

You should be proud

Pastor David Scharf

What are you proud of? Maybe you've made it through rigorous schooling or run a marathon or lost a bunch of weight or you have a great family or home or job . . . the list could go on and on. It's wonderful to thank God for the gifts and abilities he's given us. We can be "proud" of those things. But when those things make us think we're better than someone else or even that somehow those things make us look better in God's eyes, then that becomes the sin of pride. It's a mindset that we've all fallen prey to.

So what can you be proud of? You can be proud of being humble. Huh? That may seem like a contradiction, but humility leads me to see myself for the selfish person I am, and it leads me to see even more clearly the Savior whom I have in Jesus. C.S. Lewis said, "Humility is not thinking less of yourself; it's thinking of yourself less." A truly humble person will boast in only one thing because there is only one person to think of: Jesus. First Corinthians 1:31 says, **"Let the one who boasts boast in the Lord."** Jesus is my heart's true boast! Take the world, but give me Jesus!

Today, thank God for your gifts and abilities and then ask him to help you use them to show your pride in Jesus to everyone you see.

Even for me?

Pastor David Scharf

One of Satan's biggest lies is to try to convince people that Jesus is not for people like them. They know what Jesus did, but it has no impact on their lives. They slip further and further from church and from hope, comfort, and joy as well. Maybe you've been there.

Remember Rahab? She's not the most glamorous character in the Bible. She was a prostitute who helped some Israelite spies. She wanted to be saved by the God who would destroy her people. The spies told her to tie a scarlet cord in the window and she would be spared. Think this through. How could God be for her? She was a prostitute. She was a pagan foreigner. And she knew full well what this God did with the unbelieving nations. How could God be for her? Because our God is for everyone . . . and she knew it. **"And she tied the scarlet cord in the window"** (Joshua 2:21). What a beautiful act of faith!

What will be your scarlet cord today? What will you do that shows you know Jesus is for you? Can I encourage you to do something specific this week? Tell someone what Jesus means to you. If you're holding a grudge, forgive as God has forgiven you in Jesus' cross. When you look out at the people God has placed into your life, remember that Jesus is for them . . . even for you. Then hang your scarlet cord in their lives.

He was raised to life for you

Pastor Jeremy Mattek

In 1994 Nevest Coleman was working his dream job as a groundskeeper for the Chicago White Sox. That's when he was convicted of murdering a 20-year-old woman. He received life in prison for a crime that, in November 2017, he was proven innocent of committing. Coleman was released from prison. A few weeks later, for the first time in over two decades, Coleman showed up for his dream job again. The Chicago White Sox gave him his job back.

I'm sure during those 23 years Coleman never dreamed of this happening. Kind of like times we may be convinced that our hearts will never smile again, that our brokenness will never go away, or that we'll never heal. That's how the disciples felt as they woke up on Easter morning because they thought Jesus was dead.

But at various times over the following weeks, Jesus, who had also been wrongly convicted and who really did die, was standing right there in front of them. He was fully alive even after he had died, showing them very clearly that, in the end, death doesn't get the final say in a person's existence. Jesus does. In the end, death doesn't win. Jesus did. But it wasn't his own victory he was most eager to show the world. It was yours. **"By this gospel, *you* are saved,"** Scripture says (1 Corinthians 15:2).

You. No matter how weak, exhausted, guilty, or broken you feel from day to day. You. Are. Saved.

Dear Mom

Jason Nelson

Dear Mom,

I miss you every day. Your motto rings in my ears: **"Put on the full armor of God"** (Ephesians 6:11). I appreciate everything you taught me about faith and life. You seemed so certain about it. You must have had doubts, but it never showed because you were wearing the armor. There were things in your life to be sad about, but you drove away despair by keeping yourself busy. Did God tell you? One of your projects is still going strong. It's a blessing to many and even generating money for God's work. You'd be proud of it, but you wouldn't take the credit.

I tried living up to your example. But I did some things I never told you about because I knew you would be disappointed with me. I'm still trying to live up to your example. As you know, sometimes the armor of God is very heavy and doesn't fit very well. But we put it on anyway.

You'd be delighted with your grandchildren and great grandchildren. They are special, and we speak of you often. There is lots of you in them. They are wearing the armor too. They loved playing with your can full of buttons more than toys. They give people monster cookies in empty oatmeal boxes because they saw you do it. They learned how to love from you.

Mom, I miss you every day, and your motto rings in my ears.

—Jason

Why obey God?

Pastor Mike Novotny

Anyone who's studied God's instructions on Christian living knows they're not easy. To love God more than anything? To love everyone as much as I love myself? Even you-know-who from work? Nothing is harder than obeying those two commands.

So why would you? Here's Paul's answer: **"For you know what instructions we gave you by the authority of the Lord Jesus"** (1 Thessalonians 4:2). Paul's reason for obeying God's instructions comes down to a single title—"the Lord Jesus."

It's easy to miss the implications of that name. The title *Lord* means that Jesus gets the last word. He's the master, the general, the coach, and the king. We're the servants, the soldiers, the players, and the citizens. That's the blunt reality behind Christian obedience. Jesus is God, and you are not. So do what he says!

But there's more to that title. Do you know what the name *Jesus* means? It means, "He saves." Jesus' very name implies that he rescues you from danger. In other words, Jesus is not just bossing you around. He wants to bless you. He gifted you his life, his perfection, so that even while you're working hard to obey God's commands, you're already covered in God's compassion.

There's nothing more motivating than pure, undeserved love. That's exactly what we find behind and before all the commands of Christianity. We obey because our Lord's name is Jesus. He saves!

The faces of Mom and Dad

Christine Wentzel

Picture your parents in your mind's eye. In all that you see, do you also envision the face of God superimposed over theirs? In every case, they're your parents because your Lord God put them there as his authority over you. As such, he commands you to honor their parenting as you would his.

"Children, obey your parents in the Lord, for this is right. 'Honor your father and mother'—which is the first commandment with a promise—'so that it may go well with you and that you may enjoy long life on the earth'" (Ephesians 6:1-3).

Incredibly, your heavenly Father adds an incentive to following his already perfect order. It will "go well with you" to respect your parents as his representatives "that you may enjoy long life" while here on earth. Imagine the benefits for all of you as you live together under the same authority of a just and loving God!

If your parents don't know their privileged position comes from God, then you have the opportunity to show them the face of his Son, Jesus, so you might win them over to Jesus and their purpose as his children. Your days will be more difficult, but you will not go at it alone. The Holy Spirit is living in you, helping you every step of the way.

Honor your mom and dad. Acknowledge their noble stations—they come with a heavy responsibility. You will increase the confidence and joy in their roles of a lifetime!

Take refuge in him

Andrea Delwiche

There are times when we want a safe place to go and let someone protect us. We wish someone would shoo people away when we're sick or feeling besieged. Perhaps we're preoccupied with bad news, and we'd like someone to take our problems and hang them on a hook so we could be free from the burden for a little while.

For David, the Lord himself was the ultimate place of refuge. David needed rest and protection. He asked the Lord to fulfill that role for him:

"Lord my God, I take refuge in you; save and deliver me from all who pursue me, or they will tear me apart like a lion and rip me to pieces with no one to rescue me" (Psalm 7:1,2).

What does this mean for us? Can we enter this refuge? Yes! We're part of God's family, already under his protection. Sometimes, though, we struggle to live as if this is the ultimate reality of our lives.

David wrote down his conversation with the Lord. He took time to articulate what it meant that the Lord was his refuge. We see that conversation worked out in many of the psalms. David asks that the Lord would rise up and protect him; vindicate him; and provide refreshment for his soul, rest for his body, and delight for his heart.

If you were to write a request to the Lord asking for refuge, what would you say?

Be assured that God's arms are already around you. He's eager to be your sanctuary.

may 16

God became a victim again
Pastor Daron Lindemann

Guys break up with their girlfriends because they aren't ready for a committed relationship. Gals break up with their boyfriends because they're interested in someone else.

Both were true of Adam and Eve when they broke up with God. They ate the forbidden fruit, choosing someone else (the devil and his lies) and not being ready to commit to God (but committed to their own desires and ideas).

Adam and Eve left God as a lonely lover. For the first time in eternity, God became a victim. Hurt. Broken.

Not ready to give up on his relationship with humanity, God reached out to Adam and Eve in the Garden of Eden. They made excuses. They blamed each other and him.

God's curious questioning of Adam and Eve turned to cursed condemnation—not directed at them but at the devil.

"I will put enmity between you and the woman, and between your offspring and hers; he will crush your head, and you will strike his heel" (Genesis 3:15).

One offspring of Eve—Jesus Christ—would be born and become Satan's conqueror, crushing his head. God would defeat Satan and sin by becoming a victim a second time! He would suffer and be crucified.

God became a victim first by the sinful choice of humanity in Adam and Eve. He was willing to become a victim again by his own choice, suffering for our sins and saving us forever.

Sin is short-term pleasure

Pastor Mike Novotny

Back in 2011, Miami rapper Pitbull released a song that would flood the airwaves and dominate the charts. In its chorus, he sang about drinking more than he should that night and taking someone home and making sure she felt good that night because there might not be a tomorrow. Tonight might be the last.

Did you catch the fatal flaw in Pitbull's logic? He wants to get drunk tonight and have sex tonight because tonight might be all he's got. Sin always says that. It focuses on how tonight could feel, on how here-and-now could go, on the short-term pleasure of crossing one of God's moral boundaries.

But Paul knows a better way. He writes, **"[Grace] teaches us to say 'No' to ungodliness and worldly passions, and to live self-controlled, upright and godly lives in this present age, while we wait for the blessed hope—the appearing of the glory of our great God and Savior, Jesus Christ"** (Titus 2:12,13). You can say no to today's passions (getting drunk, getting him back, getting your way, etc.) because you are waiting for tomorrow's pleasure. Because of the grace of your Savior Jesus, you have a blessed hope—you are going to see the glory of God, a sight that will make all of life's joys seem small.

So when that old pet sin comes knocking on your door and, like Pitbull, promises to make you feel good tonight, tell it that you are too busy waiting for your eternal and happy tomorrows.

Loving the unlovable

Sarah Habben

Dealing with a difficult person is, well, really *difficult*. Maybe it's a spouse who nags and snipes. An aggressive coworker. An in-law who makes you feel like you never quite measure up. A defiant child. When you're near that person, your stomach hurts; your blood pressure rises. You can't imagine how Jesus expects you to love that person when there is no love in return.

But honestly? We've *all* been that difficult person. We excuse our own venom, saying someone bit us first. We avoid the messy effort of fixing a broken relationship and call it "tolerance." We withhold the seeds of love because they will only fall on hard ground.

How . . . *why* . . . does Jesus expect us to love the unlovable? Because he did it first—he loved us to death! He covered our sins. He connects us to God's power and glorious might. He gives us *great* endurance and patience, not a half-hearted measure that says, "This far I will go, but no farther."

Today, before you encounter that difficult person, ask God to **"fill you with the knowledge of his will through all the wisdom and understanding that the Spirit gives, so that you may live a life worthy of the Lord and please him in every way: bearing fruit in every good work, growing in the knowledge of God, being strengthened with all power according to his glorious might so that you may have great endurance and patience"** (Colossians 1:9-11).

Then, in that strength, go sow God's love.

The urgency of evangelism
Pastor Mike Novotny

One afternoon I was staring at the screen of my laptop, trying to come up with a sermon theme for an upcoming message on evangelism. What would capture the urgency of Jesus' mission for Christians to spread the good news and not let the fear of people's reactions get in the way? Then I heard it—ticktock. My office clock was counting loudly the passing seconds—ticktock. That sound, that one little word, grabbed my heart.

Because every person you know and love is like that clock. Their lives are ticking down to their last second, their final breath. Even before that moment, your relationship with them is ticking down to the final conversation. Picture an hourglass over every head you see today, as the sands of life fall closer to their final hour. While everyone has an eternity ahead of them, there is a limited time to hear the good news about Jesus so that eternity is filled with happiness.

I'm not suggesting you sprint through the streets and scream at everyone: "Do you believe in Jesus?!" But please remember the window of opportunity God has given you to bring Jesus to them. Paul writes, **"Be wise in the way you act toward outsiders; make the most of every opportunity"** (Colossians 4:5).

There's a fancy phrase I learned growing up to summarize that idea. I've heard that limited time to trust in Christ is called our "time of grace."

Sounds important enough to name a ministry after it, doesn't it?

may 20

Comfort and confront
Pastor Mike Novotny

I'm so glad the doctor told me the bad news. Back in the year 2000, I suffered a traumatic injury during a soccer game. Suspecting broken ribs, the medical staff X-rayed my chest but were surprised to discover that all of my ribs were intact. So they handed me a bag of ice and wished me the best . . . until the doctor came rushing into the room. "Son, you need to call your parents," he insisted, pointing to the X-ray that showed a small dark blot—my collapsed lung.

I'm grateful he broke the bad news. After surgery and a painful recovery were over, I got back on my feet. These days, the only things left to remind me of that injury are a few scars.

Good churches act a lot like that doctor. "[The pastor] **must hold firmly to the trustworthy message as it has been taught, so that he can encourage others by sound doctrine and refute those who oppose it"** (Titus 1:9). The best pastors (and churches and Christians) hold so tightly to their Bibles that they can tell you when your faith is healthy and when you need spiritual surgery.

We all would prefer the former, but sometimes we need the latter. So when someone wants to talk seriously about your behavior, your beliefs, or your attitude, please don't run away. They might just be God's hands in doing some surgical work on your soul.

When it's all over and you heal from the sting of the hard conversation, you will thank God for that person's courage.

Healed

Sarah Habben

Dumb mosquito. It bit me, and a week later I was flat on my back. My temperature shot up to 104 degrees. An ice pick stabbed my skull. My bones hurt; my skin hurt. Sweat poured off me as I shivered with cold. For eight days I lay in bed—dehydrated, feverish, pain competing with nausea. That dumb mosquito had given me dengue fever.

All that long week I thought about the hemorrhaging woman in the Bible. She had bled for 12 years. Her lifesavings had bled away in search of a cure. **"When she heard about Jesus, she came up behind him in the crowd and touched his cloak, because she thought, 'If I just touch his clothes, I will be healed'"** (Mark 5:27,28). If I'd been anywhere near Jesus' cloak, I likely would have ripped the hem right off in desperation.

Can you relate? Maybe your health or your marriage is bleeding away. Maybe you feel like a social leper. Maybe you feel ugly on the inside and out. Satan's sting has convinced you that you are unloved, untouchable, unwelcome. You are desperate for healing. Where can you turn?

Like that woman, seek out Jesus. Find him in the Bible. Like that woman, don't just touch his cloak—grab on to his reputation. Jesus the Promise Maker is also a Promise *Keeper*. He has taken a world of untouchables and healed us: by loving us, dying for us, forgiving us, and—at just the right time—welcoming us to his heavenly home.

America needs a conscience
Jason Nelson

America needs a conscience. We're in a moment that's begging for a leader with integrity who can help us form a national conscience out of our very disparate pieces of faith, knowledge, and philosophy. America doesn't need petty voices railing against one another. We don't need the peep, peep of little voices pulling us in different directions. We need one of those rare big voices that can impress us and draw us closer to the kind of community Jesus ultimately wants us to live in. **"How often I have longed to gather your children together, as a hen gathers her chicks under her wings, and you were not willing"** (Matthew 23:37).

A conscience does more than get us to comply with a checklist of dos and don'ts. It's a righteous inner voice that works behind the scenes to elevate our character. A good conscience knows when to speak out. "There comes a time when one must take a position that is neither safe, nor politic, nor popular, but he must take it because conscience tells him it is right" (Martin Luther King Jr.).

God made history by raising up leaders who in good conscience ignited reformations, great awakenings, and left us committed to justice for all. Their gift to future generations is a good conscience they can call their own. A social conscience cannot be formed behind closed doors or in inner sanctums. A social conscience comes from what we see leaders do in broad daylight.

Why the Father lets you suffer
Pastor Mike Novotny

Have you ever wondered why our loving Father lets his children suffer? At any time, God could push the big red button in his office and end the world. Jesus would come flying down to earth with millions of angels, and all of your pain and suffering would immediately end. Yet he doesn't. He waits. Why?

The other day I talked to a new Christian about this very thing. Why wouldn't Jesus just end her pain? So I asked her, "If five years ago another Christian just like you was hurting just like this would have prayed this same prayer, what would have happened to you? If God ended his people's suffering back then, would you have been ready for eternity?" She then realized why Jesus waits. It's not that he doesn't love us. It's just that he also loves them. He wants all people to be restored to a right relationship with God.

I'm sure your heart asks Jesus the same question his first followers asked: **"Lord, are you at this time going to restore the kingdom to Israel?"** (Acts 1:6). Jesus' answer for you is the same he gave back then: **"It is not for you to know the times or dates the Father has set by his own authority. But you will receive power when the Holy Spirit comes on you; and you will be my witnesses in Jerusalem, and in all Judea and Samaria, and to the ends of the earth'"** (verses 7,8).

The Father lets us suffer for the sake of their salvation. So pray today for strength, and spread the only message that saves.

God is not Dropbox

Linda Buxa

I love Dropbox. It's a place in "the cloud" where I keep files so I can access them whether I'm working from a phone, a work computer, or my home computer. Except . . . the other day it turned out that I had deleted a file I needed.

Thankfully, Dropbox has a "restore deleted files" feature. The smart tech people knew that you might throw away something you later need. So I clicked on the "restore" button, and what was gone got brought back.

I'm a lot like Dropbox. I know that when Jesus died on a cross and rose from the dead, God deleted my sins and guilt. Yet I often click on the "restore deleted sins" button, bringing guilt and remorse back as I ponder why I was so dumb when I was young (and not so young).

This is why I'm extra grateful that God isn't like Dropbox at all. When he deletes my wrongs, they're gone forever. He promises: **"For I will forgive their wickedness and will remember their sins no more"** (Hebrews 8:12). Now, when we try to bring them back, God looks at us questioningly and says, "Sins? Guilt? What are you talking about?"

There *is* a "restore" button that God is interested in, though. It's the one King David talked about after he asked for—and received—forgiveness for adultery and murder. He pleaded with God: **"Restore to me the joy of your salvation"** (Psalm 51:12).

God happily clicks on that button. Over and over and over.

The Lord observes and acts
Andrea Delwiche

Do you believe God looks on the everyday situations in your nation, in your city, in your home and knows what's going on? Do you believe in God's power to act based on what he sees? Do you believe as a child of God that you're given authority and have a responsibility to act in the face of evil, or do you shake your head and say, **"When the foundations are being destroyed, what can the righteous do?"** (Psalm 11:3). Beyond resignation to our own hopelessness, does that question also indicate a lack of trust in God?

David reminds us, **"In the Lord I take refuge. How then can you say to me: 'Flee'?"** He continues, **"The Lord is in his holy temple; the Lord is on his heavenly throne. He observes everyone on earth; his eyes examine them. . . . He loves justice; the upright will see his face"** (Psalm 11:1,4,7).

The Lord knows what's going on in every situation here on earth, and he acts on behalf of his people. Life isn't hopeless.

We can trust God and speak with hope rather than discouragement when evil threatens. We can trust the Lord to provide in every situation. We can stand with the Lord's help in the face of adversity and ask, "What can I do to live out your love here on this earth?"

Having been comforted and protected by the Lord, we in turn can give comfort and protection to others.

Humanity + Divinity x Eternity
Pastor Mike Novotny

Whenever the headlines of racism and injustice get me down, I turn to one of the Bible's most inspiring parts, Revelation chapter 7: **"Therefore, 'they are before the throne of God and serve him day and night in his temple; and he who sits on the throne will shelter them with his presence. "Never again will they hunger; never again will they thirst. The sun will not beat down on them," nor any scorching heat. For the Lamb at the center of the throne will be their shepherd; "he will lead them to springs of living water." "And God will wipe away every tear from their eyes""""** (verses 15-17).

Does it get any better than that? One day the nations will stand before the throne of God. One day people from all races will enter his temple. One day we will feel the cool shadow of his presence. One day Jesus will bring us to the springs that satisfy the soul. One day God will bless us with everything we've ever wanted—love, freedom, acceptance, attention, justice, joy—everything will be ours. Because we will be with God.

What a dream the apostle John had! A dream with no majority or minority. No unfamiliarity or insensitivity. No negativity or disparity due to diversity. No monstrosity of slavery. No brutality of inequality. Only a glorious community of every ethnicity. Only diversity gathered in flawless unity. Only the beauty and fraternity of final victory. Only humanity and divinity for all eternity. Oh, come quickly, Jesus! We can't wait for this day!

God intervenes himself and through us

Andrea Delwiche

Psalm 10 opens with two questions that people still ask today: **"Why, Lord, do you stand far off? Why do you hide yourself in times of trouble?"** (verse 1). The middle verses detail the cause of the trouble. The psalm concludes with a confident expression of faith: **"You, Lord, hear the desire of the afflicted; you encourage them, and you listen to their cry, defending the fatherless and the oppressed, so that mere earthly mortals will never again strike terror"** (verses 17,18).

Take some time to read Psalm 10. What changes from the beginning to the end of it? Did the psalmist write the first 13 verses, hear an update, and become satisfied that the Lord *had* heard his prayer and *had* called to account the evil person? Did the Spirit simply remind him about the times he had seen the Lord's helping hand come to the defense of the helpless? Did he go out as a servant of God and bring relief to a terrorized person?

Somehow, the psalmist's question is stilled, and he sees God overseeing the movements of the world for the good of the afflicted.

Do you ask these questions? Are the psalmist's words an answer for you?

God is capable of intervening by miraculous means to bring relief and protection. He also uses us to defend the fatherless and the oppressed. Have you experienced this deliverance? Are there ways you can work to deliver someone else who needs protection or justice?

Lord, prepare me to serve you!

Jesus bridged the gap

Pastor Mike Novotny

Have you ever heard of the Mackinac Bridge? It's an architectural marvel that connects the upper and lower peninsulas of Michigan. Opened in 1957, the bridge spans five miles. The over 11,000 workers used over 1,000,000 bolts, nearly 1,000,000 tons of concrete, and 42,000 miles of cable wire to build the massive structure. It makes you wonder—Why would people give so much time, energy, and money just to build a bridge? Answer—Because sometimes connecting here to there is worth it.

Just ask Jesus. Jesus knew that sin pushed us apart from God. An eternal chasm separated his holy presence from our not-so-holy lives. That's why Jesus became our bridge. Paul wrote, **"The Lord Jesus Christ . . . gave himself for our sins to rescue us"** (Galatians 1:3,4). Jesus didn't give a few years of time or a few million bolts to bridge that gap. He gave himself. His very blood. His sacred life.

The result? You are rescued! Rescued from the land of darkness, from the land of shame, from the land of not being good enough for God. You no longer have to live in the land of worry or anxiety or fear that something will keep your Father far away, because Jesus gets you to God—to peace, to rest, to mercy, to love.

Building a bridge is no small task. But Jesus was willing to do the work so that your connection to God could start now and last forever.

Does God always give good gifts?
Pastor David Scharf

Jimmy asks his dad for some eggs for breakfast. Dad gets out of bed, lumbers over to the refrigerator, pulls out a live scorpion, and drops it on Jimmy's plate. That afternoon as they are fishing, Jimmy, still skeptical of what happened when he asked for eggs, asks his dad for a fish fry for dinner. His dad opens up the live well in the boat and hands Jimmy a live rattlesnake.

True story? No! No father, even the worst of criminals, would do that to his children when they ask for food! That is precisely Jesus' point. He says, **"If you, then, though you are evil, know how to give good gifts to your children, how much more will your Father in heaven give good gifts to those who ask him!"** (Matthew 7:11). Even imperfect fathers know how to give good gifts. What about a perfect Father in heaven? He gives perfect gifts. In fact, God loves it when you ask! Jesus says, **"Ask and it will be given to you; seek and you will find; knock and the door will be opened to you"** (Matthew 7:7). Followers of Christ can pray boldly! And when we pray, we know that God will give us perfect gifts. God has already given you the greatest perfect gift in Jesus, who has given you a relationship with his Father by dying on a cross.

Use it! Pray boldly as a child asks his father!

Before Bethlehem
Pastor Jon Enter

Was Jesus "Jesus" before he was born in Bethlehem? The second person of the Trinity, God's holy Son, first received the name Jesus at his Bethlehem birth. But Jesus is eternal and always existed as God even before the creation of the world. Jesus was Jesus before Bethlehem; he just went by a different name.

Jesus appeared to believers in the Old Testament as the "angel of the LORD." When God spoke to Moses from the burning bush, it was the "angel of the LORD" speaking. It was Jesus talking. When the Israelites were unfaithful, Jesus confronted them: **"The angel of the LORD went up from Gilgal to Bokim and said, 'I brought you up out of Egypt and led you into the land I swore to give to your ancestors'"** (Judges 2:1). The "angel of the LORD" is recorded 51 times in the Bible referring to Jesus before he took on human flesh; Jesus has always been here among us.

Before the world was created, Jesus was and is God. Before Bethlehem, Jesus was and is the promised Savior. After Bethlehem, Jesus was and is the Savior who delivered on God's promise to rescue the world. Jesus has many names. Which is your favorite? Jesus. Savior. Angel of the Lord. Good Shepherd. Messiah. You don't have to pick! They're all him; they all reveal who Jesus is. He's the One who confronted the devil, rescued you from his clutches, and holds your hand through this life into paradise!

Scapegoating
Jason Nelson

It started as a beautiful thing. On the Day of Atonement, the high priest made sacrifices for himself, the people, and everything contaminated by sin. But there was this one goat that was kept alive **"to be used for making atonement by sending it into the wilderness as a scapegoat"** (Leviticus 16:10). Aaron laid the sins of the community on the head of a homely little goat, and some poor guy was elected to take the goat way into the wilderness and leave it there. Then he hurried back before the goat could follow and bring guilt and shame back where it belonged.

We put the scapegoat on steroids. Politicians display him in an absurd sideshow. Everything bad is the other party's fault. What do they teach their children about taking personal responsibility? The rest of us join right in. We look for someone to blame so we can avoid that hot, sweaty feeling of admitting our own mistakes. I think we should send all the people who never uttered the words "I was wrong" to a distant planet and leave them there.

There's only one way to be forgiven for scapegoating, including the way I did it in the preceding paragraph. Our blame has been placed on Jesus. **"We all, like sheep, have gone astray, each of us has turned to our own way."** Let's change those ways because **"the Lord has laid on him the iniquity of us all"** (Isaiah 53:6).

June

As a father has compassion on his children,
so the Lord has compassion on those who fear him.

Psalm 103:13

For men 50 and older
(and those who love them)—Part 1
Pastor Mike Novotny

Of all the official members of my church, about 7 percent of them are what the apostle Paul called "older men," a Greek word that points to ages 50 and up. If that's you, or someone you know, listen up: **"Teach the older men to be temperate, worthy of respect, self-controlled, and sound in faith, in love and in endurance"** (Titus 2:2).

Those are wise words. Men tend to thrive when they feel respected in life. As they get older, however, their muscles droop, their minds lose their edge, and the next generation passes them by in company value and technological skill. That reality causes many men to become bitter, the "grumpy old men" who gripe about everything under the sun.

Paul wants better for our older brothers in Christ. He wants them to be different, and, through Jesus, they can be. When they fill up their hearts with the promises of God, they don't need the world's respect. Instead, grace's guarantees allow them to age gracefully, to grow in spiritual strength even as their bodies grow weaker.

Guys, if you take Paul's words to heart, you will be a great blessing to the next generation. Your experiences in war, business, and family will help guide them through the treacherous years of young adulthood and lead them to the one thing that truly matters—God. So ask the Holy Spirit today to make you an older man who is worthy of respect.

For men 50 and older
(and those who love them)—Part 2

Pastor Mike Novotny

If you've ever witnessed a baptism, you might have seen a small crowd of people gathered in front of church. When a child is baptized, the parents will often choose a sibling, cousin, or close friend as a godparent. This human tradition is a way to (1) honor someone's faith and (2) increase the "village" that will help keep this kid close to Christ.

A few years ago, however, a young couple from our church chose a unique godfather for their son, a man named Tom. Tom (and his wife, Pam) are grandparents of two teenagers, yet they were asked to help little Henry grow up to be a strong man of God. Why? Because of the way Tom and Pam live their faith.

Their story makes me think of Paul's words to Pastor Titus: **"Teach the older men to be temperate, worthy of respect, self-controlled, and sound in faith, in love and in endurance"** (Titus 2:2). That's Tom. People respect him. He is sound and healthy in his faith. He loves the love of Jesus, which causes him to seek God in his life. He is not perfect, but he adores the cross and is eager to honor God in all he does.

There are many families that are dying to find good examples to help them raise the next generation to love Jesus. Join me today in asking the Holy Spirit to raise up more believers like Tom and Pam, Christians whose faith is noticed and respected, regardless of their age.

For women 50 and older (and those who love them)

Pastor Mike Novotny

Paul wrote some curious words about older women: **"Teach the older women to be reverent in the way they live, not to be slanderers or addicted to much wine, but to teach what is good"** (Titus 2:3). *Hmm* . . . why would Paul say those specific words to this specific group in the church? Here's my theory—words and wine are very tempting to older women.

Younger women are often so busy with school and work and raising exhausting children that they don't have a lot of personal time to unwind. But as women grow older, when work slows down and the kids are out of the house, they get to spend more time with friends. Wine is poured. Words fill the room. And reverence for God can be quickly forgotten.

Paul warns older women about this because he knows the power of a godly woman (read Titus 2:4,5). A sober, self-controlled woman can mentor young Christian women. She can teach them how to do good in God's name, how to avoid the most common pitfalls of female life at home and in the world. Most important, she can urge the next generation of women to seek God, to find her identity and wholeness in the rock-solid promises of God through Christ.

If she slurs her words or is known as a gossip, the message might not get through. But if she can speak clearly and confidently about Christ, her impact can't be measured. Let's pray that God fills our churches and the nations with women like that!

For men 18-49
(and those who love them)
Pastor Mike Novotny

Godliness for younger guys is simple. In Titus chapter 2, Paul gives older guys a long list (be temperate, self-controlled, loving, etc). Older women get many boxes to check (don't slander, get drunk, etc.). Younger women receive seven separate to-dos. But younger guys? Just one.

"Encourage the young men to be self-controlled" (Titus 2:6). That's it! Apparently, Paul knew enough young Christian men to summarize his advice in a single word—*Don't*! Guys, I know you're thinking about it, but don't! I know your buddies are doing it, but don't! I know part of you really wants to, but don't! Don't be the next guy who cares more about video gaming than about God, who has ingested more Hot Cheetos and Monster Energy drinks than Communion's bread and wine, who wastes his 20s seeking the temporary things of life and forgets the eternal blessings of God.

Man, I wish I would have heard those words when I was 15. There are years that I can't get back and sins I can't un-commit. Thankfully, there is mercy for the younger me and grace that motivates me to leverage my remaining years as a "younger man" (Psalm 25:7).

If you're a young Christian guy, pray over Paul's words today. If you're not, ask our Father to strengthen his wrinkle-free sons. Lord, raise up a new generation of men who love God with all of their hearts and use their strength to serve others.

For women 18-49
(and those who love them)

Pastor Mike Novotny

If you're a female under 50, who's the best person at church to teach you how to live a God-pleasing life? (Hint: It's not the pastor.)

While the apostle Paul told Pastor Titus to teach older men and women as well as younger guys, he seemed to miss one major demographic in the church—younger women. Actually, he didn't forget but rather entrusted their discipleship to those who might be best equipped. "[The older women] **can urge the younger women to love their husbands and children, to be self-controlled and pure, to be busy at home, to be kind, and to be subject to their husbands, so that no one will malign the word of God**" (Titus 2:4,5).

While Paul's assumption that younger women would mostly be married mothers isn't as true in modern America, his wisdom still stands. There are some things about the female experience that a man like me will never fully grasp. That's where experienced sisters in Christ are so valuable. They can sympathize and relate to unique struggles that younger women face. They can urge the next generation to honor Jesus in all they do at home and in the world for the health of their families and the reputation of God's Word.

Younger ladies, is there an older woman in your church who might mentor you? Seasoned sisters, is there a younger woman in the faith who could use your wisdom? Make a connection today, for your own growth and for God's glory.

Sober eyes

Jason Nelson

The addiction recovery group at my church has dubbed itself "Sober Eyes." It was started by a recovering addict. He knew other addicts who wanted to recover and gathered them together. The moderator is a church member who is an AODA counselor. Our pastor sits in, not to force religion on anyone but to respond to spiritual questions that may come up. Spiritual questions always come up because addicts need a power greater than their own in order to recover. Every Sunday night, a handful of young adults shows up at group, where they are honest with each other and help each other see the world through sober eyes. Some of them have come to Bible classes and worship services. The rest of us welcome them and love on them.

The rest of us are also recovering people. We all need support to see the world with sober eyes. **"We don't yet see things clearly. We're squinting in a fog, peering through a mist."** Very little in life is crystal clear. It's 50 shades of blurry because we suffer misery of body, mind, and spirit. We can lose perspective and lose hope. We need to be with other recovering people who trust steadily, hope unswervingly, and love extravagantly. They keep us going until **"the weather clears and the sun shines bright! We'll see it all then, see it all as clearly as God sees us, knowing him directly just as he knows us!"** (1 Corinthians 13:12 MSG).

Jesus isn't afraid of your fears

Pastor Daron Lindemann

Researchers say that at least 645 known fears exist. Like the fear of heights, fear of spiders, fear of change, fear of failure, fear of lists . . .

Fear is a feeling that can tell us something about ourselves, our hopes and priorities—if we're willing to listen. That doesn't mean fear is the boss. More like a tour guide.

Jesus' own disciples experienced fear after he was crucified. Fear that they'd be next! Fear about the future. How did the risen and alive Jesus help them calm their fears?

Jesus' wounds rescued them and us from our fears.

Like battle scars, when Jesus rose from the dead, he showed these saving wounds from his crucifixion to his disciples. **"See my hands. . . . Stop doubting and believe"** (John 20:27). These are the receipt of payment for sin accepted.

Jesus' words reframe our fears.

Have you seen Jesus? touched the nail marks in his hands? felt the scar from the spear plunged into his side? No. "Good," Jesus says, reading your thoughts as you wish you could touch him and then you'd really believe. **"Blessed are those who have not seen and yet have believed"** (John 20:29). That's you. Blessed by Jesus' promises, as much or even more than the disciples who touched Jesus.

No circumstances can create fear in you bigger than the faith in you that the wounds and words of Jesus create. Your fears aren't afraid of you. They will continue to assault you. But they are afraid of Jesus.

Jesus is our autosave

Linda Buxa

I love Microsoft Word. It's the program I use for my devotions and blogs and freelance work. There's only one problem. It doesn't have an autosave feature. It stresses me out to know that if I don't remember to hit save every so often, all my work will be lost if the application freezes or my computer crashes.

While I don't love Google Docs, I've come to appreciate its autosave feature. It's so much more relaxing to know I can keep plugging away because all the saving is automatically done for me.

That's how life is for Christians too. If we constantly think we have to earn our way into heaven by doing good deeds—which is really just thinking that we have to do the saving ourselves—we'll be constantly stressed out. What if our self-control crashes, our day goes wrong, we lose our tempers, or we relapse into addiction? Even if we think we've done good things, will they really be enough? How do we know?

That's why we're grateful for Jesus, who's done all the saving for us. He **"has saved us and called us to a holy life—not because of anything we have done but because of his own purpose and grace"** (2 Timothy 1:9).

Now we get to relax because Jesus is our autosave. Thanks to his grace, he's got our salvation all taken care of. We can keep plugging away as we tell others about his salvation.

Hold firmly to the Word

Pastor Jeremy Mattek

Would you dig through 8 tons of garbage? One husband and wife did. The wife had taken off her 12.5-carat wedding ring to do the dishes on a Sunday afternoon. She didn't remember the ring until the next morning. When she went to look for it, it was gone. She soon figured out that it must have fallen into the garbage, which had already been taken out and picked up by the garbage truck. The couple found the truck just minutes before it dumped its load in a landfill. The truck driver dumped out the dirty, stinky, who-knows-what-that-was trash onto the street instead. The couple jumped in and found the ring.

You don't need to go to that much trouble to find something far more valuable. In the risen Christ, you have the God-given right to look at death and expect to find life. You have the right to know that even your greatest pain will not separate you from the greatest joy God can give any of his children. Easter is the priceless treasure of knowing that you're going to be okay.

You only need to dig through the Word of God and look on any one of its pages to find the promises that will breathe life into your heart and soul, which are so often broken. That's why we are told to **"hold firmly to the Word"** (1 Corinthians 15:2). In that Word, you'll always find life, strength, forgiveness, and heaven. Because in that Word, you'll always find Jesus.

How can it be?

Pastor Mike Novotny

A few years ago, three songwriters handed Lauren Daigle, a Christian artist, some lyrics they wanted her to consider for a new song. The lyrics talked about how Jesus pleads our case before God. He wipes out everything we've done wrong. He gave his life so we can be free. How can that be? The message moved her. If you Google Lauren's performance of "How Can It Be," I bet it will move you too.

The more you're aware of your own spiritual brokenness, the more you'll ask the same question. How can it be that God would choose someone like me? How can it be that the eternal Father, who was perfectly content without me, would nevertheless want to spend the rest of eternity with me? How can that be?

I don't know, but elected/chosen/wanted is exactly what Paul says you are as a Christian: **"Paul, a servant of God and an apostle of Jesus Christ to further the faith of *God's elect* . . ."** (Titus 1:1). The teaching of election (that God chooses us to spend forever with him) baffles the mind while it also uplifts the heart. Logic can't quite make sense of it all, but we love to remember the truth that pops up on so many pages of the Bible. God elected us! God chose us! God wants to be with us!

How can that be? I have no clue, but I love it anyway. Don't you?

As sweet as honey
Andrea Delwiche

Psalm 12 speaks about untrustworthiness in human relationships, but the psalmist starkly contrasts the words and communication we receive from God. It's a very specific description: **"The words of the Lord are flawless, like silver purified in a crucible, like gold refined seven times"** (verse 6). The words of the Lord are "flawless." Other translations of the Bible say, "pure." Either way, it's a pretty big deal. *Flawless* means "without any blemishes or imperfections; perfect. Without any mistakes or shortcomings." The words of the Lord are without blemishes or imperfections. Free from lies and doublespeak. Able to be trusted.

Elsewhere in the Bible, the Lord says to his prophet Ezekiel, **"Son of man, eat this scroll I am giving you and fill your stomach with it."** Yes, digest the Word of the Lord. And how does Ezekiel describe the flawless words of the Lord? He says, **"So I ate it, and it tasted as sweet as honey in my mouth"** (Ezekiel 3:3).

How many times in a day do you doubt the words of others? How many times during the day do you doubt your own words, whether the words you speak out loud or the words that populate the thoughts in your head? Do you long for words that are backed up by action and truth?

In the midst of chaos and uncertainty, spend time each day digesting the words of God. They are always applicable, and they will always nurture and sustain— flawless and as sweet as honey.

The punishment in Paradise

Pastor Jon Enter

Why did God put a tree in the Garden of Eden that Adam and Eve couldn't eat from? Did he set them up for failure?

God created that tree as a unique opportunity for worship. The word *worship* comes from the Old English word *WORTHship*. In worship we show God what he's worth to us. When Adam and Eve refused to eat the forbidden fruit, they showed God what he was worth to them. They, however, selfishly ate the fruit, wanting something more than God. One sin, one bite of the forbidden fruit and BOOM, they were banished from Eden.

God placed an angel and flaming sword to guard Eden's entrance. Why? Next to the forbidden tree was the tree of life. Its fruit confirms the spiritual state a person is in. If they ate from it, they'd be eternally sinful. So God, in love, kept them from hurting themselves further by eating from the tree of life.

Revelation 2:7 reveals its new location: **"To the one who is victorious, I will give the right to eat from the tree of life, which is in the paradise of God."** The tree of life is in heaven. When we eat of it, we're confirmed in the perfection given to us by Jesus.

Adam and Eve destroyed their relationship with God by a tree. God amazingly, lovingly, graciously restored that broken relationship by a tree, by the cross. God loves you. He never, absolutely never, sets you up for failure. He leads you into forgiveness.

Sow more Jesus seeds

Pastor Daron Lindemann

Your influence grows in others like a seed growing into a strong tree. People hear your faith in Jesus; even more so, they see your faith in Jesus.

Your friends on social media. Your neighbors waving and watching. Your children developing character based on your patterns of behavior. Your church family aware of your life decisions or how you act when your church is making decisions.

"For as the soil makes the sprout come up and a garden causes seeds to grow, so the Sovereign LORD will make righteousness and praise spring up before all nations" (Isaiah 61:11).

You are sowing Jesus seeds all the time: by the way you drive in heavy traffic and by how you treat checkout clerks at the store. By showing kindness to those who hurt you. By the way you remain calm when others panic. By the way you obey your parents, study for exams, post on Instagram, or party.

You are constantly sowing seeds.

The "righteousness and praise" of the Lord starts small in your heart by his grace and then grows to become a towering way of thinking and living. Like acorns falling from an oak, you drop seeds of the Lord's righteousness and praise all around you.

You never know who's watching. But you do know this—your Lord God is watching. He smiles when the oak drops its acorns, doing what it's supposed to do, praising him. And he smiles when you do the same.

Hidden but revealed

Pastor Jon Enter

Someone at work or school stops you: "Hey, you're a Christian. I heard God being three persons yet one God is just a New Testament thing made up by Christians. Where is God as three yet one in the Old Testament?"

What do you do? Run away. Stare blankly forward until the person walks away. Those are options. This explanation is better!

In Deuteronomy 6:4, God defines himself as ONE: **"Here, O Israel: The Lord our God, the Lord is *one*."** In Genesis 1:26, God refers to himself in the plural, hinting at being three persons: **"Let *us* make mankind in *our* image, in *our* likeness."** Then in Numbers 6:24-26, God narrows down his plural nature into three: **"The Lord bless you and keep you; the Lord make his face shine on you and be gracious to you; the Lord turn his face toward you and give you peace."** There are THREE "the Lords." Father. Son. Holy Spirit. Here God gives the job description of each person of the Trinity. The Father blesses and keeps you as an earthly father should and as your heavenly Father does. The second "the Lord" is Jesus, who pours grace and forgiveness into your life. The last "the Lord" is the Spirit, who brings you to faith, resulting in peace being in your life.

Father, Son, and Spirit, since before creation, throughout the Old Testament and throughout your life, rule and reign over your life. What comfort to know he always was, is, and will be!

Two tips for church
Pastor Mike Novotny

If you're part of a local gathering of Christians, how could you make your church even better? Paul encourages growth when he writes, **"Brothers and sisters, we instructed you how to live in order to please God, as in fact you are living. Now we ask you and urge you in the Lord Jesus to do this more and more"** (1 Thessalonians 4:1). What would that look like in church?

Let me offer two tips. First, seek God. During every song, every prayer, every minute of the pastor's message, seek God. Our brains love autopilot. Familiar settings allow them to zone out and conserve energy (like driving home from work). So fight for your focus and seek God as soon as you enter the sanctuary. I'm sure you don't want to spend an hour in church just to check some religious box. So I urge you to seek God with every song lyric, bullet point, and prayer request.

Second, serve people. Especially before and after church, find ways to connect with, engage, and love people. Put others first. Sit a few seats in so that you silently invite others to sit next to you. Ignore your church friends and invest in a guest. Make the experience the best it can be for others.

I love church. Hearing about my Savior and gathering with his people is the highlight of my week. But for the good of others and the glory of Jesus' name, I want to do it even better. May God help us do greater things!

Forget about it!

Pastor David Scharf

Looking back can be dangerous. Once unthinkable, Roger Bannister broke the four-minute mile on May 6, 1954. Forty-six days later, John Landy broke Bannister's record. A month later, the two ran against each other in a matchup known as "The Miracle Mile." Landy was favored to win, but he kept thinking as he ran, "Where is Roger?" Unable to help himself, just before the finish, Landy looked back over his left shoulder and Bannister passed him on his right. Landy lost the race. Looking back can be dangerous.

Speaking of his own race, the apostle Paul wrote, **"One thing I do: Forgetting what is behind and straining toward what is ahead, I press on toward the goal to win the prize for which God has called me heavenward in Christ Jesus"** (Philippians 3:13,14).

What past sin plagues you? Paul says, "Forget about it!" That's easier said than done. How can we forget all of those things that hurt others and, worse, offended a loving God? We can forget about them because God has. Never open the filing cabinet of memories unless you're holding the key of mercy. Your wrongdoings and guilt are gone because of Jesus. When it comes to your failures . . . forget about it!

Then strain toward what's ahead like a runner reaching for the tape. By doing that you'll be reminded constantly of God's love, your purpose in life, and the home that awaits you in heaven!

Four false teachings
Pastor Mike Novotny

Faithful pastors (and committed Christians) must have the courage to call out false teaching. **"[The pastor] must hold firmly to the trustworthy message as it has been taught, so that he can encourage others by sound doctrine and refute those who oppose it"** (Titus 1:9).

There are four main false teachings for you, your church, and your pastor to refute. First, refute people who add to God's law, demanding that, for example, you have to wear dress clothes to church or stick to Friday fish during Lent or say the Apostles' Creed every Sunday in order to make God happy. Second, refute people who subtract from God's law, brushing past financial and sexual sins since few people keep those old rules these days. Third, refute people who add to God's gospel, insisting that you have to believe in Jesus *and* be circumcised, speak in tongues, do your penance, etc. to be saved. Finally, refute people who subtract from God's gospel, claiming you don't have to believe in Jesus at all as long as you are somewhat spiritual and a decent human being.

Adding to God's Word feels exclusive, allowing people to think they are not like "those people" in the church or the mediocre types of disciples. Subtracting from God's Word feels like a loving way to reach more people for Jesus. But God knows what is best for his church and for our world.

So stick to the Word. Nothing more, nothing less.

Thankful for the thorn

Christine Wentzel

"I begged the Lord three times to take it away from me. But he told me: 'My kindness is all you need. My power is strongest when you are weak'" (2 Corinthians 12:8,9 GW).

This is a great go-to section if you're feeling down by chronic pain. It reminds you and me that the pain is there for a holy reason. If it serves no sanctified purpose, then God is just an all-powerful bully and our faith in him is false. But that would contradict every promise God spoke through his Word and every blessing so lovingly given to us, his adopted children.

Just like us, the apostle Paul experienced frustration—physically, emotionally, and spiritually. Just like us, he thought the Lord's work would be better served without those frustrations. But God knows us better than we know ourselves. Paul says it was to keep him from being conceited. We don't always receive a clear-cut reason for our pain.

However, there's an incredible testimony to be found in Christians who suffer. Through the pain made by the thorns, the Source of life blazes brightly. So if Christ uses our weakness to demonstrate his strength to the world, praise God!

Fixes aren't quick

Jason Nelson

"Whoever starts to plow and looks back is not fit for God's kingdom" (Luke 9:62 GW).

Do you know how far along we would be if we didn't keep setting ourselves back? I can cite examples of organizations that had a good thing going and then backed away from it. It happens in every enterprise: commerce, religion, government, and even families. We have trouble plowing straight furrows because we second-guess the direction we're headed. And if the leadership regime changes and brings in a different set of priorities, good initiatives go back on the shelf or become footnotes in history. Sears is gone even though Mr. Roebuck pioneered home delivery of just about everything that Amazon is feasting on.

Sustainability isn't just a buzzword thrust upon us by the granola crowd. It's a way of God. Operating so we can keep it going is a way of God. That requires a firm grip on the plow handle and a dedicated focus on what's ahead. It takes wisdom born of experience to fight the siren call of the quick fix. There are fixes for most of our problems. But they are seldom quick. They are the blessings of sustained effort and being able to pass the plow from one generation to the next. The postmortems on lost causes come from early retirees with good memories. They meet for coffee. They talk about someone's newfound success. They say, "We used to do things like that."

june 20

Luminous like the moon
Andrea Delwiche

Picture a clear night sky. It may be a wide view if you live in the country or just a glimpse if you're a city dweller. The moon pulls up over the horizon or over the roof of the house behind you. Maybe it's a full, pearly moon. Maybe it's a pale sliver.

Consider yourself in the same night; small and seemingly insignificant in comparison to the vast, bright moon. Like a speck of starlight. Perhaps that's what David thought when he asked, **"When I consider your heavens, the work of your fingers, the moon and the stars, which you have set in place, what is mankind that you are mindful of them, human beings that you care for them?"** (Psalm 8:3,4).

"Nothing," you might say. "I'm nothing in comparison to God's works of moon and stars."

But David continued, **"You have made them a little lower than the angels and crowned them with glory and honor. You made them rulers over the works of your hands; you put everything under their feet: all flocks and herds, all the animals of the wild"** (verses 5-7).

Can you hear David's nearly incredulous joy? In God's eyes, you're individual and important. You're luminous like the pearly moon. You're full of wonder. Loved. Crowned with glory and honor. Given responsibility for the rest of the created world.

Think of God's creativity and love in making *you.* Then finish with David's cry of joy: **"Lᴏʀᴅ, our Lord, how majestic is your name in all the earth!"** (verse 9).

Our fingerprints are on the cross

Pastor Jeremy Mattek

"As the soldiers led [Jesus] **away, they seized Simon from Cyrene, who was on his way in from the country, and put the cross on him and made him carry it behind Jesus"** (Luke 23:26).

Simon was grabbed from the crowd and commanded to carry the cross when it became too heavy for Jesus. He is one of the few named individuals whose fingerprints are on the cross. But he's not the only one with fingerprints on it.

Our fingerprints are on that cross too. Not because we were there but because its slivers never would have pierced Jesus' skin had you and I not sinned against God. Jesus chose to be there for us. He put his fingerprints on that block of wood because he looks at your heart and can clearly see that it's burdened. And there's no hope that you can ever lift it off.

He gave the world one place to which we all can look to see that his blood was abundant enough, thick enough, and precious enough to completely cover every sin and fingerprint that belongs to you and me.

When Jesus cried, **"It is finished"** (John 19:30), it wasn't a cry of relief that his suffering was finally coming to an end. It was a declaration that your heart no longer needs to feel burdened ever again.

Does God dream about you?

Pastor Daron Lindemann

Olympians dream of gold medals. Busy moms dream of quiet privacy to relax for five minutes without cleaning ketchup off the dog. Oh, and I just took a dream vacation in the beautiful state of California.

Dreaming is our way of connecting with the ideal.

Jacob had a dream, but it was more than Jacob's dream. It was God's dream for Jacob, who had tricked his brother, lied to his father, and was running away from home.

Does God dream about you? If so, what's his ideal for you? What does he want from you more than anything?

Jacob's dream has the answers: **"He had a dream in which he saw a stairway resting on the earth, with its top reaching to heaven, and the angels of God were ascending and descending on it"** (Genesis 28:12). Jacob wasn't thinking about God. Jacob wasn't calling out for help from God. Jacob didn't even say his bedtime prayers.

But God was thinking about Jacob. God was coming to help.

God's ideal for you is not that you accomplish better obedience, not that you ascend the religious ladder and climb to heaven. What God dreams about as he thinks of you is keeping all his promises.

Even when—in weak moments of little faith—you're not asking, not looking, not thinking of him, not praying as much as you should. No conditions. No condemnation. God is your ideal.

Dear Dad

Jason Nelson

Dear Dad,

I miss you every day. Your prayer rings in my ears: **"Out of the depths I cry to you, Lord"** (Psalm 130:1). There were low points in your life, and they started very early on. No little boy should ever be physically and psychologically abused and then suffer throughout life because of it. But you battled back every time. God lifted you out of the depths with love and support from others.

You told me you prayed regularly that God would raise up a new Nelson generation. Did he tell you? He did. We all remember you with great affection. I know you doubted if you were worthy of anyone's love, including God's. Grace was a difficult thing for you to accept. Yet you managed to be incredibly loving every time you came out of the depths. You were a complicated character and could be a bit volatile. But you had an uncommon ability to be honest about yourself and sniff out dishonesty in others. I thank you for that gift.

You had so little to call your own but were very generous. You could be friendly to a fault. There were no strangers in your world. You always made unimportant people feel important because you could relate to them. I guess you understood grace after all. I am trying to pick up where you left off.

Dad, I miss you every day. Your prayer rings in my ears.

—Jason

Jesus is our autocorrect
Linda Buxa

It took me an incredibly long time to be comfortable with texting. After using a normal-sized keyboard for 30 years, I wasn't comfortable with the tiny keyboard on my smartphone. I hunted and pecked with my index finger—and my kiddos laughed because it took me forever to send a single text message. Eventually, I learned how to use both thumbs, but I was constantly hitting the wrong buttons. This was humbling for someone with a reputation for being a stickler for spelling, punctuation, and capitalization in communication. Then technology gave us autocorrect to save me from all my spelling mistakes.

Because I'm full of brokenness from birth, there's no way I can ever get things right. All my own attempts at holiness would be fumbled and misguided. Then God gave us Jesus. He **"made** [Jesus] **who had no sin to be sin for us, so that in him we might become the righteousness of God"** (2 Corinthians 5:21).

Now every wrongdoing we commit, whether intentional or not, is autocorrected by Jesus—replaced with his perfection. Our feeble efforts are glorious, because Jesus gives us credit for our efforts. God takes our destination for hell and replaces it with eternal life in heaven.

One last thought. Sometimes autocorrect gets a bad reputation because it guesses wrong. (There's even a website about that.) That's not how it works with Jesus. He gets it right every single time.

A father who broke the rules

Pastor Daron Lindemann

I'm a rule keeper. A rule giver. That's a confession more than a boast.

I reflect on the many rules I laid down for my sons. Pick up your shoes. Get out of bed for school. Say your prayers. Get good grades. Make 80 percent of your free throws. Flush the toilet. Keep it quiet while I'm napping. Mow the lawn. Keep it quiet while you're mowing the lawn.

The rules themselves weren't always bad or wrong. But what did my sons grow to believe about my expectations? Keep my rules, and I approve and accept you. Don't keep them, and I don't approve and accept you.

Ah, parenting is a difficult thing when it comes to laying down the rules.

Kids need them. Families need them. But rules must not be the master. They must be the servant. Rules must be administered in a spirit of forgiving grace.

So I appreciate Jesus' parable of the lost son (Luke 15:11-32) whose loving father broke the rules. He broke the rules of legalism (rules are master, not servant) that often force themselves into relationships. He refused to scold, "I told you so!"

God my Father forgives me and promises I can be a gracious father too.

What is more powerful than laws? Love. What is more powerful than rules? Relationships where forgiving grace is the best "rule" of all. Then all other rules have their proper place as servants, not masters.

God answers

Andrea Delwiche

"How long, Lord? Will you forget me forever? . . . How long must I wrestle with my thoughts and day after day have sorrow in my heart? How long will my enemy triumph over me?" (Psalm 13:1,2).

Four questions from King David that we ask God when problems line up and cause disaster, heartbreak, and stress: "Why?" "When will it stop?" "Have you forgotten me, Lord?" "Will they get the best of me, God?"

David's questions are followed by a plea: **"Look on me and answer, Lord my God. Give light to my eyes, or I will sleep in death, and my enemy will say, 'I have overcome him,' and my foes will rejoice when I fall"** (verses 3,4).

Then in verses 5 and 6, David considers something new. His questions and pleading turn to praise: **"I trust in your unfailing love; my heart rejoices in your salvation. I will sing the Lord's praise, for he has been good to me."**

What changed? Perhaps David spent some time with the Lord, listening. Perhaps in fear, grief, or even anger he spoke his heart to the Lord and then, as in all good conversation, he waited to hear from the Lord. God answered with a recollection of unfailing love and protection. David's spirit was renewed.

Take the tough questions to the Lord and plead with him. Ask for help from the Spirit to wait in quiet with a searching and open heart. God's unfailing love will uphold you and answer your questions.

The joy of generosity

Pastor Mike Novotny

If I promised I wasn't trying to boast, could I tell you the story of the $600 tip? Years ago, my buddy Jason and I got some late-night appetizers at Applebee's. After learning about the biggest tip our bartender had ever heard of ($300), I whispered to Jason, "Let's give her $300 . . . each!" And we did! We scribbled the absurd amount on our bills, scurried out the doors, and jumped into our cars before she could check the receipts. But before we drove out of the parking lot, the front doors of Applebee's flew open and a shocked, trembling, wide-eyed, hands-extended bartender came rushing out. Jason and I sped away, laughing uncontrollably all the way home.

That night I learned a valuable spiritual lesson—the result of extreme generosity is joy. I remember the joy of that night. I remember how happy it made me to give an absurd amount. I remember being living proof of Jesus' words, **"It is more blessed to give than to receive"** (Acts 20:35). Have you ever experienced that kind of blessed joy?

I'm not sure if you've been there, but your Savior has. Millennia ago, he didn't give $600 but his very life to make you eternally happy. The author to the Hebrews writes, **"For the joy set before him he endured the cross"** (12:2). The cross hurt like hell (literally), but the thought of you being with God forever gave Jesus great joy. What a Savior! What a Giver!

Reflect on Jesus' gift, and you just might feel more blessed than a bartender with $600 in her pocket.

Always surrounded
Pastor Jon Enter

The math doesn't work. 1+1+1=1 What? It doesn't add up. God clearly reveals he's three. Three distinct, individual persons: Father, Son, Holy Spirit. Yet these three are one. Just one God. The triune nature of God is one of the most confusing characteristics of our Lord, but it's also one of the most comforting. Do you know why?

There are multiple analogies to define what's nearly indefinable: how God is three yet one. There's the state of water as gas, liquid, and solid; yet it's still water. There's the three-leaf clover; three individual leaves yet one plant. Those can work, but they lack comfort. They lack the *why*. They lack the purpose of God being three yet one. And when you know, what clarity and comfort it brings!

Each person of the Trinity has focus over different portions of your life. God the Father rules and reigns over the PRESENT so you need not fear what's happening right now. The Father's got it! God the Son rules and reigns over your PAST, protecting you from your sins so you need not fear what you did back then. The Son's forgiven it! God the Holy Spirit rules and reigns over your FUTURE, protecting you into your future so you need not fear what your future holds. The Spirit's guiding it!

Your triune God—Father, Son, and Holy Spirit—protects you in your present, from your past, and into your future. How blessed you are by your loving triune God!

If you build it, they will come

Pastor Mike Novotny

"If you build it, they will come." That was the classic line from the classic baseball movie *Field of Dreams*. A mysterious voice from the cornfields of Iowa told Kevin Costner's character that if he built a baseball field, they would come. Spoiler alert—Kevin did, and they (old baseball legends and new fans) did too.

For many years in America, the same was true for churches. If you built it, a new church, new people came. They were drawn to the newest worship service on the block. But I question if the same is true in America today. As more and more people are post-Christian, that is, past the supposed need for a church family, I'm not sure if a new building and a fancy logo will get them to come. If you build it, they might not come. They might not even care.

But that might change if the "it" in that famous line was not a building but a relationship. If you invested in people, allowed them into your personal life, and let them see how Jesus' love gives you hope and peace despite your sins and challenges, they might come. If they saw, up close, how you didn't fear death because of Jesus' empty grave, they might be curious enough to stop by.

Perhaps the age of assumed religion is fading away. But our mission stays the same. So take Jesus' call to heart. **"You will be my witnesses in Jerusalem, and in all Judea and Samaria, and to the ends of the earth"** (Acts 1:8).

Number one
Sarah Habben

A certain fifth-grade class has had a dodgy reputation since kindergarten. They tattle and talk back and can't form a line without arguing about who's first. But in private, any one of them will calmly discuss how disrespectful and disruptive their *classmates* are. They can't fathom that they're part of the problem.

King David says the wicked are like those fifth graders: **"There is no fear of God before their eyes. In their own eyes they flatter themselves too much to detect or hate their sin"** (Psalm 36:1,2). The "wicked" have no respect for God's majesty. No fear of his judgment. They elbow through life, quick to detect others' sins and blind to their own.

But let *me* hear the warning too. God's child though I am, my sinful nature still makes noise. It blinds me to my awfulness by yammering about my awesomeness. It convinces me that I've earned special attention from God just for being less trouble than the guy in the next cubicle.

Yet what do I deserve from God? Pretty much what a snail deserves from a gardener. The boot. Salt.

Not love.

How I marvel, then, with David: **"Your love, LORD, reaches to the heavens"** (Psalm 36:5). God stooped down in the person of his Son, not to crush me but to lift me from my sin. His priceless, unfailing love changes me. I don't have to look out for "number one." I can, in fact, be last in line . . . because the *Holy* One is looking out for me!

July

You, my brothers and sisters, were called to be free.
But do not use your freedom to indulge the flesh;
rather, serve one another humbly in love.

Galatians 5:13

Gentle rain
Jason Nelson

I was listening to an agronomist talk about the relative infrequency of gentle rains. He had data showing we are getting more and more heavy downpours and fewer quiet soaking rainfalls. One consequence is that topsoil is washing away. So farmers need to use more fertilizers and weed killers to grow crops in poor soil. Then the chemicals wash into streams and rivers in the next downpour. Another consequence is that generations to come may never know the peacefulness of listening to a gentle rain.

The Word of God is a gentle rain. **"As the rain and the snow come down from heaven, and do not return to it without watering the earth . . . so is my word that goes out from my mouth: It will not return to me empty"** (Isaiah 55:10,11). The Ten Commandments, the wisdom of the prophets and poets, and everything there is to know about Jesus need soak time. God promises when we meditate on his Word steadily, good things will spring up in us.

In grade school science, there's something called the hydrological cycle. The mass of water on earth is fairly constant and moves continuously above, on, and below the surface of the earth. Climate changes intensify how moisture moves around. But the Holy Spirit isn't full of bluster. He doesn't want to come down hard on people. He descends like a dove into people's hearts through the gentle rain of the gospel.

Your #1 motivation
Pastor Mike Novotny

If there's a gap between the person you are now and the person you want to be, what gets you to change? If you want to be more self-controlled with your words online or your drinking on the weekends or your attitude about work, how do you do it? If you want to let go of your anger toward your dad or be a better role model for your kid or have a you-first marriage that makes your home blessed, how do you do it?

The Bible's best answer is actually in the Ten Commandments. If you're a longtime Bible reader, you might assume that the Ten Commandments begin with the First Commandment, but that isn't true. **"I am the Lord your God, who brought you out of Egypt, out of the land of slavery. You shall have no other gods before me"** (Exodus 20:2,3). What comes before the First Commandment? The relationship—I am your God. What comes before the life change? Grace—I brought you out. What is the Bible's #1 way to motivate you? God's love.

There are many wonderful ways to get fired up for a change—setting goals, accountability, motivational apps, etc.—but the greatest source of change-producing power is grace. Focus on God's love for you, the love that set you free from the slavery of sin, and you will tap into the greatest motivation of them all.

Value of conviction

Pastor Jon Enter

If you tell someone, "I believe the Bible. I value what God values," you can be mocked, targeted, and called awful names. It's hard. It's growing increasingly difficult on college campuses, in workplace environments, and even at family gatherings to be a proud and positive Christian.

In our culture today, personal truth is actually celebrated as strength. So be strong. Stand firmly yet respectfully on the truths of the Bible.

Being a Christian with conviction doesn't mean you have to know everything about the Bible. You don't have to memorize the 12 tribes of Israel or correctly spell all 12 disciples' names. To be a person of conviction, a person of Christian values, simply be confident that Jesus loves you and is your Savior. Value what God values.

Paul, a pastor who worked with new believers, gave a strong encouragement not to be ashamed of the gospel, to be confident that Jesus loves you and is your Savior despite what the world says about you. Why? **"It is the power of God that brings salvation to everyone who believes"** (Romans 1:16). God's Word has power! Trusting God's Word has power. In fact, the word for *power* here is where we get our English word *dynamite* from. Be a person of conviction. Faithfully trust God's power, which blasts away a lifetime of sin and shame. And be bold in your faith that Jesus truly, truly loves you. Hold firmly to that conviction, and you will see the power of God in your life.

They'll never take our freedom!
Independence Day
Pastor David Scharf

Do you recognize the name William Wallace? Perhaps you're familiar with Mel Gibson's depiction of William Wallace in the movie *Braveheart*. Wallace was a fierce fighter for Scottish independence in the late 13th and early 14th centuries. You may not have seen the movie or know anything about him, but you are probably familiar with his famous, inspirational battle line quote: "They may take our lives, but they'll never take our freedom!"

Today we thank God for the freedoms we enjoy in our country, especially our freedom to exercise our faith. When we look at the history of the Christian church, few places have had the religious freedom we enjoy. This is a special blessing from God. There are many places around the world where Christians are persecuted to the point of death for their faith. Thank you for our freedom, Lord.

Today we also recognize that the freedom we enjoy in our country is temporary and not promised by God. Political freedom is tenuous at best. We can never say the Wallace line with any certainty in our country. Isn't it nice, though, that we can say it to our greatest enemies, sin and death, who threaten our lives? Jesus said, **"So if the Son sets you free, you will be free indeed"** (John 8:36). Because Jesus lived perfectly for you and died in your place, you have been declared free. Period. No one and nothing will ever take your freedom!

God loved you first
Andrea Delwiche

Did you know God has been pursuing you from the first? Don't believe me? Read this: **"Yet you brought me out of the womb; you made me trust in you, even at my mother's breast. From birth I was cast on you; from my mother's womb you have been my God"** (Psalm 22:9,10).

Long before your first remembrance of God, he looked at you, tiny in your mother's womb, and couldn't wait to see the person you would become. He knew you, loved you, and wanted to draw you into a loving relationship. He's been calling you by name from the beginning.

Can you think of your earliest remembrance of God? Was it the first time you heard the story of Jesus and were in awe of his love for you? Or maybe God began making you aware of his presence through the beauty of his created world. **"The heavens declare the glory of God; the skies proclaim the works of his hands"** (Psalm 19:1). Even as you see God's hand in nature, his Spirit is wooing you and calling you to him.

Never underestimate how dearly God wants you for his own. He still works daily to draw you closer and to delight you with his goodness. Where will God show you signs of his love today? In his Word? In a neighbor? In a sunset?

O Lord Jesus, through your Spirit, give us eyes to see and hearts that believe that you have always loved us! Amen.

Going in the ditch
Linda Buxa

On the way to school one snowy morning, my kids hit a slippery patch and slid off the road. Now, the kids were fine and the car was fine, but they were a little shaken up. They couldn't get out of the ditch by themselves, so they called us. Immediately my husband jumped in the car and went to help, because that's what fathers do.

When we run our lives into a ditch, we aren't fine, but it seems our first reaction isn't to call our heavenly Father. After all, we know he's holy and we're not—and we're afraid of his anger or disappointment. May I reassure you? Your Father is waiting—longing—for you to "call," to pray, to reach out.

There's a Bible story about a young man who disowned his family and then ran his life into a ditch. Ultimately he realized he needed help and—ashamed—went back home. **"But while he was still a long way off, his father saw him and was filled with compassion for him; he ran to his son, threw his arms around him and kissed him. The son said to him, 'Father, I have sinned against heaven and against you. I am no longer worthy to be called your son'"** (Luke 15:20,21).

What the son said was true. He had sinned and wasn't worthy, yet the Father still hugged him, welcomed him, and then threw a huge party.

Make the call. Your Father wants to help, because that's what fathers do.

Are you a success?

Pastor Matt Ewart

The biggest thing that determines your personal success is how you personally define *success*.

So how do you define it? Is success a certain amount of money? Is it related to social media? Is it something you park in your garage? How about a number you see on a weight scale?

The good news is that you get to define what success means for you. The bad news is that you and I often pick the wrong definition.

Goals we strive for and numbers we want to reach are fine and all. Everyone needs something to aim at in life. But accomplishing a goal doesn't necessarily make you a success. It just means you have to set another goal, then another one, and so on.

But remember these words from Jesus: **"What good is it for someone to gain the whole world, yet forfeit their soul?"** (Mark 8:36).

God isn't impressed when people set amazing goals and then reach them. He isn't interested in marathon medals or padded portfolios. What he's most interested in is who you are and who you become.

Put another way, God is most interested in the person you would have to become in order to accomplish the goals you set. That means the best definition of *success* is simply to pursue a goal that draws you closer to the identity and purpose that Jesus won for you.

You are not the groom

Pastor Mike Novotny

Can you imagine a best man who wanted more attention than the groom? Picture the bride walking down the aisle with her dad as her husband-to-be wipes away tears at the end of the aisle. But just before the great exchange from father to groom, the best man leaps into the aisle, shakes the dad's hand, and whispers to the bride, "You look beautiful." Imagine him cutting in on the first dance: "Don't mind if I do . . ." That best man would be the worst! Because a wedding is not a competition for attention.

In the Christian life, it's vital to remember that we're not the groom. We are more like the friends who celebrate the attention that Jesus and his church receive. John the Baptist said, **"The friend who attends the bridegroom waits and listens for him, and is full of joy when he hears the bridegroom's voice. That joy is mine, and it is now complete"** (John 3:29,30). John wasn't jealous but joyful, because he saw his job was to help Jesus get more attention.

There will be many times in life when God uses other people, and not you, to draw more attention to Jesus. Their church grows (yours shrinks), their ministry thrives (yours barely survives), their lives make an impact (yours goes unnoticed). Friend, that's okay. God never called you to compete with your brothers and sisters in Christ. Instead, like John, rejoice that people are paying attention to God's Son. It's not about you. It's all about Jesus!

Bless others!

Andrea Delwiche

Did you know that you can bless other people? Look at this extravagant blessing that the writer of Psalm 20 extends to another person.

"May the LORD answer you in the day of trouble! . . . May he send you help from the sanctuary. . . . May he grant you your heart's desire and fulfill all your plans! May we shout for joy over your salvation, and in the name of our God set up our banners! May the LORD fulfill all your petitions!" (verses 2,4,5 ESV).

Have you considered blessing any person in your life in a similar manner?

When we utter a blessing over someone, we're not making a wish. We're extending the power of the name of God as a fragrant and fruitful promise from God. God is all about blessing people. In fact, God gave his people a blessing that we still use today: **"The LORD bless you and keep you; the LORD make his face shine on you and be gracious to you; the LORD turn his face toward you and give you peace"** (Numbers 6:24-26).

Beyond blessing those we love, Jesus told us to love our *enemies*, and the apostle Paul counsels, **"Bless those who persecute you; bless and do not curse"** (Romans 12:14).

Whether a person is a friend or enemy, we should be authentic and deeply present to them in the moment of blessing. These aren't idle words. They carry the weight of God's abundance. Ask the Lord to show you the way forward to blessing others.

Better is good
Jason Nelson

Forget about perfect. It's not going to happen. Only God is perfect. I suggest we focus on something more attainable like being better. We can start tomorrow because Jesus forgives us for not being perfect today. He loves it when we are better. **"The Lord takes delight in his people; he crowns the humble with victory"** (Psalm 149:4). One victory God gives humble people is the ability to get better.

After WWII, an American engineer named W. Edwards Deming helped Japan transform its economy. The Japanese tried rising from the ashes of war by producing low-priced products in inhumane factories with harsh managers. Quality was poor, and "made in Japan" was the punch line for jokes. But Deming made Japan the global leader of reliable products with 14 points of Total Quality Management. Quality was not some inspector's job at the end of the line. It was everyone's job during production because everyone was involved in the process of assessment and improvement. Toyotas got a reputation for being better. And that forced other automakers to get better.

Where in your life would better be really good for you? **"For this very reason, make every effort to add to your faith goodness; and to goodness, knowledge; and to knowledge, self-control; and to self-control, perseverance; and to perseverance, godliness; and to godliness, mutual affection; and to mutual affection, love. For if you possess these qualities in increasing measure, they will keep you from being ineffective and unproductive in your knowledge of our Lord Jesus"** (2 Peter 1:5-8).

Go big

Jason Nelson

The story of Babel is a cautionary tale. The lesson is that being self-aggrandizing never ends well. When our motives are to defy God and make a name for ourselves, God finds ways to bring us back down to earth. Yet, in the face of misguided use of human imagination, God makes a stunning observation about that big tower. When people come together around a common cause and speak the same language, **"nothing they plan to do will be impossible for them"** (Genesis 11:6).

We can put this ability to good use. Across America, withering little churches, even in the same branches of Christianity, are dying on the vine. Many are less than a gallon of gas away from each other. What if they consolidated their efforts around a bigger vision by working together? They could have more impact on their communities with the gospel. Antique shops and funky diners can survive as quaint, out-of-the-way places, but not many churches can.

Old buildings weren't designed to accommodate modern technology and a variety of activities. Limited staff can't provide adequate pastoral care to struggling people from different generations. The calendar of events doesn't appeal to people who don't enjoy eating green bean casserole. If there are visitors, they don't want to sit in conspicuous seats in the very front. Loyal members are very dedicated. Maybe we could also be more efficient with limited resources. We don't want to commit the sin of Babel on a small scale.

God still has work for *you*

Ann Jahns

My friend Donna was recently taken home to be with Jesus. For years she struggled with infections that trapped her in a dizzying pattern of rotating between home, the hospital, and rehab. At times she pleaded with God to take her to heaven, wondering what purpose she still served on this earth while living in a failing body.

But during one of Donna's stays in rehab, she shared her hope in Jesus with a new friend—who later asked to be baptized. Did God still have work left for Donna to do? You bet he did.

Maybe Simeon from the Bible felt the same way. For years he hung out at the temple and waited for Jesus to be born. And waited. And waited some more. God had promised him that he wouldn't die before he saw the Savior. When Mary and Joseph brought baby Jesus to the temple 40 days after he was born, Simeon cradled the child in his arms and marveled, **"Sovereign Lord, as you have promised, you may now dismiss your servant in peace. For my eyes have seen your salvation"** (Luke 2:29,30). But while Simeon was waiting to see his Savior, I'm guessing this **"righteous and devout"** man (verse 25) wasn't sitting idle and merely biding his time. God still had work for him to do.

Like my friend Donna and Simeon, does God still have work for you to do? Even though your body and mind may be failing, be assured that God has a good plan—and his work—for you to do.

Peace in persecution
Pastor Jon Enter

Hours before Jesus' death, facing down the cross, he used some of his final breaths to give Christians a warning and a blessing: **"In this world you will have trouble. But take heart! I have overcome the world"** (John 16:33).

Jesus' words poured peace into millions of Christians before being murdered for their faith. In 2016 every six minutes a Christian died for believing in Jesus (nearly 90,000 deaths). It's impossible to count how many more endured mockery, ridicule, and abuse for the faith you share with them in Jesus.

How have you been mocked at school/work?

What fights happen in your family over religion?

Persecution is going to happen and increase as our world walks steadily away from honoring God's Word. So Jesus warned, **"In this world you will have trouble."** Jesus knows. He knows the pain you've felt; he's experienced it himself. He knows the mockery you've faced. He knows your trouble, so he promises peace and protection. That's why he went to the cross. Christ assures you, **"But take heart! I have overcome the world."**

If you are persecuted for your faith, you're in good company. You stand with Jesus as Jesus stands before you. He is your shield and your deliverer. He is your Good Shepherd who fought back that roaring lion looking to devour you for eternity. He won! He lives! He reigns! In this world you will have trouble; persecution will be here, but take heart because Jesus has overcome the world. You are his . . . forever!

Amazing!

Sarah Habben

My pastor husband once had this conversation with a Grade 3 student:

"How was your day, Taeja?"

"Amazing!"

"Really? What made it amazing?"

"Oh, I dunno. I guess every day is amazing to me!"

When was the last time I was *amazed* by an ordinary Thursday? I'm ashamed to say I can't recall.

Psalm 103 was written by King David, who sounds as jubilant as Taeja: **"Praise the Lord, my soul; all my inmost being, praise his holy name"** (verse 1).

Sometimes my praise is smothered by discontent. I have eyes only for what annoys me and miss God's simple blessings of breakfast or clean sheets. Sometimes my joy is robbed by illness, stress, or exhaustion. My eyes turn inward, and I miss God's invitation to find rest in his Word. Sometimes my joy today is hobbled by yesterday's regrets. I plod forward, dragging a load that Jesus wants me to leave behind.

I'm not sure what Taeja's secret is, but David's joy centers on our amazing God, who does what we don't deserve: **"Praise the Lord, my soul, and forget not all his benefits—*who forgives all your sins*"** (verses 2,3).

In Christ, God forgives our sins of discontent, self-absorption, and doubt. And, oh, the blessings that follow on the heels of forgiveness! Read the rest of the psalm—we are healed, redeemed, loved, satisfied, renewed.

Covered by God's forgiveness, we can give thanks for every ordinary, amazing day.

Our Savior saved us
Pastor Mike Novotny

My firstborn daughter was just a little peanut on the day she almost drowned. Everything was sun and smiles at our friends' backyard pool until she decided to take off her floaties in water that was deeper than she was tall. My mind still possesses a frozen image of her brown hair, shimmering beneath the surface of the pool.

But then my wife leapt into action. She jumped in, still clothed, and lifted our little girl up into the air. Kim rescued her from danger into the oxygen-filled atmosphere. Or, to put it in Bible terms, she "saved" her.

Just like our Father. We too were in danger, in over our heads spiritually. But then Jesus jumped in. Fully clothed in human flesh, he jumped into our world to save us. To rescue us from danger. To bring us to the safest place in the universe—the arms of our heavenly Father.

In some of his best words, Paul wrote, **"But when the kindness and love of God our Savior appeared, he saved us, not because of righteous things we had done, but because of his mercy"** (Titus 3:4,5). Even before we were his beloved children—because of his kindness, love, and mercy—he saved us.

And because he saved you, you are not in danger. You can breathe the air of God's presence today, knowing you are safe at your Father's side. Meditate on what your life would be like if you had no Savior. Then thank God for the fact that, through faith, you do.

Our reality

Andrea Delwiche

The Lord looked down from heaven and saw that his creatures, the ones he had crafted by hand out of the dust of the earth, lived as if he didn't exist. Totally inept, they were willing to will him away in order to justify their choices as they wreaked havoc upon each other. He looked down and saw there was no one who did good. Not even one (see Psalm 14:1-3).

But he didn't just look. He stepped down. And he didn't just step down with cosmic footsteps. He committed to live as they did. He took on the form of his creatures and walked with them.

King David, so many years before Christ's birth, death, and resurrection, cried out, **"Oh, that salvation for Israel would come out of Zion! When the Lord restores his people, let Jacob rejoice and Israel be glad!"** (Psalm 14:7).

David's fervent prayer is our reality. He knew it was coming, but he didn't live to see it. We know that it happened. Do we see it as the new reality in which we live—daily, hourly? Are we glad as David hoped?

Good Father, thank you for your love. Christ, you stepped into our world and made all things new. Holy Spirit, let me see with eyes of faith the reality of the life that Jesus has won for me! Amen.

july 17

It's about Jesus
Pastor Mike Novotny

Amy Carmichael was a Christian missionary who served in India until her death in 1951, bringing the love of Jesus to countless women who suffered in heartbreaking conditions. She spent her entire adult life in that country, pouring out her gifts and trusting in God to do what he wanted and willed, no matter what the earthly results. After her death, a loved one studied all of the photos that Amy had taken in India. In the entire collection, she couldn't find a single picture of Amy herself. Not one selfie!

Amy imitated Jesus' friend John the Baptist. During that crucial time in history when John's followers instead turned their attention to Jesus, the Baptist confessed, **"He must become greater; I must become less"** (John 3:30). John found immense joy whenever people gave their attention to Jesus.

Believers like John and Amy found all the attention they needed in God. When you know that God himself pays attention to you, listens to your prayers, and has the very hairs on your head numbered, it has a way of filling up your need for attention. You can gladly turn the focus toward Jesus' glory, Jesus' name, and Jesus' reputation on earth.

In our pay-attention-to-me world, it's nearly impossible to hold the world's attention for long. Thankfully, you don't have to. You are free from that exhausting burden when you know that the entire Trinity—Father, Son, and Spirit—have their eyes turned in your direction all day long. So rejoice today! You are known and loved by God himself.

Good or bad advice?
Pastor Matt Ewart

Life can be complicated, and some decisions put a lot at stake. It's during those times that you often turn to the advice of others.

Our biggest challenge today is not finding advice. Countless books, podcasts, and digital articles are at your fingertips at any moment. Our biggest challenge is determining which advice is good and which advice is bad. Thousands of years ago a king named Rehoboam, son of Solomon, learned this the hard way.

Rehoboam was given some excellent advice from the elders who served under his father. Unfortunately, he opted for some bad advice from his peers, and the result was that he split an entire nation in two. (You can read about his story in 1 Kings 12.)

Your decisions today might not have the potential to split a nation, but you do have the potential to change the world for the people around you. So how do you discern between bad advice and good advice?

One rule of thumb is to stay focused on eternity. Thankfully Jesus got that right. While on the Mount of Transfiguration, where it seemed that heaven had come down to earth, Peter gave Jesus some earthly minded advice: **"Lord, it is good for us to be here"** (Matthew 17:4). Peter wanted Jesus to stay there. But mindful of eternity, Jesus pushed on toward the cross for you.

Good advice won't always point you in the easy direction. The best advice will focus on goals and principles that are mindful of the eternity that God has in mind for you.

Make us bold to pray
Pastor David Scharf

Which of these scenarios best describes your relationship with God?

Scenario #1—The scene is a courtroom. God, the judge robed in black, takes his seat. The guards lead you, the prisoner, into the room. You see your judge, and your heart is filled with fear. There's a good reason you're fearful. This judge needs to pronounce the sentence for your crimes!

Scenario #2—The scene is a courtroom. God, the judge robed in black, takes his seat. You are a young child who enters the room and makes your way through the seats filled with spectators. You run up to the judge and whisper something into his ear. The judge reaches into his pocket and gives you a piece of candy, and you exit in a happy mood. You have no fear of the man robed in black. After all, the judge is your father.

Which scenario best describes your relationship with God? Here is the difference maker: Jesus. Without Jesus, scenario #1 is our fate. With Jesus, scenario #2 is the better description. Think about that today. When the disciples asked Jesus to teach them to pray, Jesus said, **"This, then, is how you should pray: 'Our Father in heaven'"** (Matthew 6:9). Jesus became the prisoner and took your sentence so that you can approach the judge without fear and call him Father. And he wants to hear from you, his child. Call on him often today!

Delayed wrath
Pastor Jon Enter

Why doesn't God stop bad people from doing bad things? There you are, trying to do the godly thing, towing the biblical line, and you become the collateral damage of others' evil. It's not fair. When that happens, it's easy to wonder what happened to God's justice.

Don't you wish God would stop them dead cold in their tracks? Well, maybe not dead dead. But at least stop them? He did in the Bible. Where's that power against evil now?

What if every time evil happened, God brought the atomic elbow of his judgment? Like, if you yell in anger at the driver who cut you off, your car breaks down, costing you $532. If you tell a lie, a tooth falls out. You'd curb those wrong actions fast. But your change would be done out of fear of God, not faith in him. That's not the relationship he wants with you. God explains why he delays his wrath: **"For my own name's sake I delay my wrath. . . . I hold it back from you so as not to destroy you completely"** (Isaiah 48:9). God delays because he's a God of mercy who desires to show love.

Second Peter 3:9 reveals that God **"is patient with you, not wanting anyone to perish, but everyone to come to repentance."** God delays his wrath so unbelievers who do wrong and Christians who do wrong come to repentance and experience his powerful grace.

God delays his punishments. Thank God he does!

Do nothing when you need to
Jason Nelson

When I couldn't work because of disabling back pain, I learned a difficult lesson. Sometimes we just need to do nothing. I still feel guilty about doing nothing. When I was growing up, if we sat on the couch too long my mom would say, "Can't you find something to do?" That became the voice of God in my head. I memorized it. **"I must work the works of him that sent me, while it is day: the night cometh, when no man can work"** (John 9:4 KJV). God and my mother had the same expectation of me. Find something to do.

Like many of you, I operate with a sense of urgency. "Let's get going." I won't apologize for being driven. It was my way of being dedicated. I didn't appreciate that God also built rest into the rhythm of Christian piety. Not just any old rest, but a Sabbath rest; a time-out to think about God. **"Tomorrow is a day of rest—a holy day dedicated to the Lord"** (Exodus 16:23 GW). For me, even a Sunday off was a chance to work at something else when we got home from church. And I usually made my children work at it with me. Now I see that they don't know how to rest either.

I don't think I can be rehabilitated. **"There remains, then, a Sabbath-rest for the people of God"** (Hebrews 4:9). I guess I'll just rest in heaven.

Loved by our Father
Pastor Mike Novotny

Years ago Ernest Hemingway wrote a story about a Spanish father and his son Paco who had a falling out, causing the boy to run away from his home to Madrid. Eventually, the father went to look for his son, wanting to reconcile and be with him again. So he took out an ad in a local newspaper. It read, "Paco, meet me at Hotel Montaña at noon Tuesday. All is forgiven. Papa." When that Tuesday arrived, Paco's father went to the hotel to see if his son still wanted his love. There gathered at the hotel were eight hundred young men, all named Paco!

What those Pacos all wanted, Jesus is giving away. He came as the perfect Son who was willing to die in our place so that everyone who trusts in him would have a forgiving and gracious Father. The words spoken at Jesus' baptism are true for us too: **"And a voice from heaven said, 'This is my Son, whom I love; with him I am well pleased'"** (Matthew 3:17). Our Father, due to the death of his Son, calls us his sons and daughters. He is no longer angry or indifferent but, rather, "well pleased." His face is shining upon us and smiling with grace toward us.

Life gives us few guarantees. We don't know if our neighbors will be nice, our families will be functional, or our bodies will avoid breaking down. But we can rely on this single glorious truth—All is forgiven. We are eternally loved by our Father in heaven.

You get the gold
Linda Buxa

In 2018, for the first time in 20 years, the U.S. women's hockey team earned a gold medal. Now, I'm a sap for just about any gold medal ceremony—and have been since my childhood heroes Mary Lou Retton and Dan Jansen stood on that platform. But as the women's hockey team put their arms around each other and loudly sang the national anthem, I realized just how much more fun teams seem to have on the podium than those who stand by themselves.

Then I realized that *this* is what life as a Christian is like. Well, should be like.

Sometimes life feels like a grind as you slog through your daily chores, kind of like the hours of training you never see Olympians put in. But you aren't alone. You are on a team, a team that prays for you, holds you accountable, listens to your confession, brings you meals when you're sick, hurts when you hurt, and celebrates with you in the good times.

Your team of fellow Christians is even better than an Olympic team because Jesus has already won the gold medal for us. Now, thanks to faith in him, we know that **"there is in store for me the crown of righteousness, which the Lord, the righteous Judge, will award to me on that day—and not only to me, but also to all who have longed for his appearing"** (2 Timothy 4:8).

That will be the best gold medal ceremony ever.

Bounce cuz you're blessed
Sarah Habben

What did I bring to church this week? My kids. My purse. Pens for sermon notes. A mop for the rain that had dripped through the aging church roof.

On the surface I looked squeaky clean.

What else did I bring? A frowny face because my kids were annoying me. Distracted fingers that reached for my phone instead of the Bible in those minutes before church. Apathy about uncapping my pen for another sermon about stewardship. An eye roll over the unpatched roof.

Just beneath the surface, I looked pretty icky.

Satan is fine with me schlepping to church with my grudges, my smartphone, and my cynicism. But King David reminds me why I should actually *bounce* into God's house: **"Enter his gates with thanksgiving and his courts with praise. . . . *For the Lord is good and his love endures forever*"** (Psalm 100:4).

The truth is that my heart isn't automatically set to "thanksgiving." Like an old car on a winter's day, my heart needs some TLC in order to run properly. Before I roll out of bed on a Sunday (or any day), it helps me prepare my heart by opening my Bible and reading a verse or two. I see myself through God's eyes: a sinner once barred from his presence; now busted free by God's grace in Jesus. From my pillow it helps me to pray, "My Savior-God, you deserve my applause. Fill me with thankfulness as I worship and serve you today."

Try it with me. We can bounce cuz we're blessed.

Of little importance
Jason Nelson

Here's a rainy day activity. Go to a resale shop and buy an old globe. Put seven billion dots on it. Distribute them around the globe. Each dot represents one person on earth. Can you find your dot? No? Me either. Now slingshot your globe into an infinite universe and zoom way out. Can you find your planet? No? Me either. Do you feel small? Me too. Sometimes we need to feel small because it magnifies our worth to God. I'm okay with being of *little* importance to him. Being of little importance to God is like being the only thing important to God.

God is very detail oriented. **"Every hair on your head has been counted."** We are one of the details. So, **"don't be afraid!"** (Matthew 10:30,31 GW). God pays more attention to our well-being than we pay to it ourselves. He must say to himself, "I can't believe he's going to eat that."

He is especially good at protecting us from things we don't see coming. I survived four deer and one telephone pole crashing into my vehicles. I've been shocked but not electrocuted. He gave me a safe landing when I fell from the top of an extension ladder. I wonder how many other times he extended his almighty arms and kept me safe. My guardian angels must have their own support group. I hope they can hear me praise the Lord. Let all of us little people praise the Lord.

From complaining to praising
Ann Jahns

Have you ever noticed how we like to complain incessantly about the weather? Is it because it's inoffensive fodder for small talk? "The humidity must be 1,000 percent today!" Or, "Seriously? A snowstorm on Easter?" Or is it because it's something we have no control over, so we don't have to work at fixing it?

Just like us, God's Old Testament people, the Israelites, sure liked to complain—except they didn't complain about a freak Midwest snowstorm in April or the correlation between the humidity and a bad hair day. Even though God had performed miracle after miracle to spring them from their slavery in Egypt and then provided for their every physical and spiritual need, they still whined to their leaders: **"If only we had died by the Lord's hand in Egypt! There we sat around pots of meat and ate all the food we wanted, but you have brought us out into this desert to starve this entire assembly to death"** (Exodus 16:3). Silly, ungrateful Israelites!

But, wait. I'm no better than the Israelites. God has showered me with blessing upon blessing. He has even given me blessings of which I am completely unaware. And how do I repay him? I whine about everything from the weather to my circumstances to the political climate to the government leaders he has put in charge of me. Can you relate?

Let's all pray for strength to guard our thoughts and words today. Let's turn complaining into praise and ingratitude into awe for all God has provided for us.

What to do when someone sins against you—Part 1

Pastor Mike Novotny

When someone's sin hits you like a stone, hurting you deeply, there are four things you can do. Here's the first—You can try to forget. That's what people say, right? "You need to forgive and . . . forget." That sounds like a nice Pinterest post, but is that idea biblical?

I searched the Bible and learned that the word *forget* is used 64 times. Guess how many have to do with forgetting about someone else's sin? Zero. In fact, "forgive and forget" could be a guilt-inducing, danger-producing way to live. If you have to forget to truly forgive, how many of us could ever do it? How could we forget the source of those scars that came from our ex's abuse, our dad's addiction, or the cruel words from some cruel classmates?

In addition, if we forgot every sin, how would we know who are the fools and wicked souls whom God warns us about in Proverbs and in Paul's letters?

No, the truth is that you can forgive, even if their sin is impossible to forget. (More on this in the days to come.)

Today, as you try to forgive what you can't forget, remember the unique forgiveness of God. He once promised, **"I will forgive their wickedness and will remember their sins no more"** (Jeremiah 31:34). This is the new covenant (the one-sided promise) that comes to us at the cross and at the cost of Jesus' blood.

The all-knowing God is certainly not forgetful, but somehow (thank you, Jesus!) he chooses to remember our sins no more.

What to do when someone sins against you—Part 2

Pastor Mike Novotny

When someone's sin hits you like a stone, hurting you deeply, there are four things you can do. Here's the second—You can get them back. You can pick up the stone and throw, making them hurt just like they hurt you. That might feel like the right thing to do, but vengeance won't work.

Just ask Samson and the Philistines. In the Bible book called Judges, the Philistines threatened to kill Samson's wife, so Samson killed 30 of their men. So the Philistines killed Samson's girl and her dad. So Samson picked up that stone and covered the rocks with Philistine blood. So the Philistines picked up that stone, bribed Samson's girlfriend, captured their rival, and gouged out his eyes. So blind Samson picked up that stone and tore down the temple where the Philistines gathered to mock him. They died. He died. Everyone died. The end.

No matter how ugly or bloody it got, the score was never settled.

You won't settle the score either. If you make them hurt, it won't help. Hearts don't heal like that. In fact, once your stone is thrown, they'll pick it up and throw it right back. Perhaps that's why Jesus taught: **"You have heard that it was said, 'Love your neighbor and hate your enemy.' But I tell you, love your enemies"** (Matthew 5:43,44).

If you want more pain, then make them pay. But if you prefer peace, choose the path of forgiveness. Just like Jesus chose to forgive you and give you peace with our Father above.

july 29

What to do when someone sins against you—Part 3

Pastor Mike Novotny

When someone's sin hits you like a stone, hurting you deeply, there are four things you can do. Here's the third—Get bitter. Bitterness is when you pick up the sin that hurt you and hold on to it. You don't throw it back in vengeance but instead curl your fingers around its edges, going through the ugly event in your mind, re-telling the story of your pain to anyone who will listen. But that bitterness will destroy you.

My first job involved hours and hours (and hours) of Weedwhacking at a golf course. I'd gas up the tank, grip the handle, and pull the trigger until the fuel ran out. But by the time my shift was done, my hands could barely move. I had held on to the Weedwhacker's handle for so long that my fingers were stuck in that position.

Bitterness is like that. The longer you hold on to that stone, the harder it is to let it go. Hebrews warns, **"See to it that . . . no bitter root grows up to cause trouble and defile many"** (12:15). Bitterness is a root that produces toxic fruit. It leaves you stuck—troubled and defiled. Getting bitter never makes it better.

So, friend, let that stone alone. Pry open your fingers with prayer, and let the past go. Ask the Holy Spirit for help (he wants to!). Ask your Father to remind you of your own forgiveness. Ask Jesus to help you love your enemies.

Just like he loved you when you were his enemy.

What to do when someone sins against you—Part 4

Pastor Mike Novotny

When someone's sin hits you like a stone, hurting you deeply, there are four things you can do. Here's the final option—Forgive. You don't have to forget, but God calls us to forgive.

What exactly is forgiveness? It's the daily choice to let the stone alone. You don't forgive once and for all anymore than you make the choice to be patient once and for all. No, that stone is always there at your feet, which means every day, every moment, with every trigger, every memory, you have to make a choice to let the stone alone. To trust that God will take care of the justice. To believe that God knows what happened and his path, free from bitterness and vengeance, is the best way to be healed.

Once your hands are free of their sins, they are open to pray, to bless, and to reach out in reconciliation. Peter wrote, **"Repay evil with blessing, because to this you were called so that you may inherit a blessing"** (1 Peter 3:9).

I think I know where Peter learned that from. Jesus didn't repay us for our evil but instead blessed us by his blood. His calling was to love us, forgive us, and save us. His choice to let all of our sinful stones alone means that we have an inheritance in heaven, a clear and constant view of the face of our Father.

I know forgiveness can feel impossible. So fix your eyes on the cross where God makes the constant choice to let those stones alone, to forgive you.

What to do when someone sins against you—Part 5

Pastor Mike Novotny

In 2018 Botham Jean was sitting in his own apartment when the unthinkable happened. Amber Guyger, a police officer, entered Botham's apartment, mistakingly believing it was her own and assuming Botham was a burglar. She shot him, ending his life. Thirteen months later, when Guyger was sentenced to ten years in prison, Botham's brother, Brandt, took the witness stand to speak: "I hope you go to God with all the guilt. . . . I forgive you. I love you just like anyone else."

Brandt then asked the judge, "Can I give her a hug?" Once granted, he leapt out of his chair and met Amber in the middle of the courtroom. She collapsed into his arms, and he embraced her for an entire minute (!) and spoke words of forgiveness into her ear.

Such shocking grace should move you, but it shouldn't surprise you. After all, that's what the gospel says every day: **"When** [Jesus] **suffered, he made no threats. . . . 'He himself bore our sins' in his body on the cross"** (1 Peter 2:23,24). Jesus didn't threaten to get us back for our sins. Instead, he handed everything over to God and suffered so that we could be saved.

Then, on Easter morning, Jesus asked his Father, "Can I give them a hug?" Once granted, he leapt out of the grave and spoke grace into our ears, not just for a minute but for every minute of all eternity.

That's why we love Jesus. He forgives the worst of us and the worst in us!

August

From the rising of the sun to the place where it sets,
the name of the Lord is to be praised.

Psalm 113:3

august 1

People pleaser
Pastor Matt Ewart

If you believe that Jesus lived and died for you, one of the ways you show it is by loving and serving the people around you. But if you aren't careful, the service you show to others can become a trap. Here's how it happens.

The approval of others is something that everyone wants naturally. Approval is positive feedback that lets you know that you are doing something right. You fit in. You belong. You are needed.

But if you aren't careful, you can begin to live for other people's approval. You become dependent on the approval of others to the point where your emotional well-being is tied to their opinion of you. And no matter how well-intentioned the other people are, you are setting yourself up for a trap.

Proverbs 29:25 says, **"Fear of man will prove to be a snare."**

If you live for the approval of others, you're setting yourself up for failure. It's partly because you'll become exhausted by trying to please everyone around you, and it's partly because people are unable to give you the level of approval that you need.

So here's something to keep in mind. Today, like every day, you will have opportunities to reflect God's love by serving others. Remember what God's love is all about. He approves of you in Christ. He declares you his loved child. And what God declares about you is so much more important than what people might think about you.

It's a God thing
Jason Nelson

"King Belshazzar gave a great banquet. . . . Suddenly the fingers of a human hand appeared and wrote on the plaster of the wall" (Daniel 5:1,5). This was disturbing and put a damper on the celebration. The king wanted to know what it meant. He sent for Daniel who had a **"keen mind and knowledge and understanding, and also the ability to interpret dreams, explain riddles and solve difficult problems"** (verse 12). Daniel interpreted the writing on the wall because the Spirit of God was on him and Daniel had a very good sense of history. He recognized a God thing when he saw it.

We may never achieve Daniel's level of clairvoyance. But we can develop spiritual insight and discern the hand of God in our lives. God wants us to see him at work, even in the most troubling times. And he wants us to credit him for getting us through them. **"Ascribe to the Lord, O families of the peoples, ascribe to the Lord glory and strength! Ascribe to the Lord the glory due his name"** (1 Chronicles 16:28,29 ESV).

Next time you think you see a God thing, make a note of it on your calendar. Document what occurred. Do a little cause/effect analysis. Predict how you think it will all play out. If you make this a spiritual habit, you will see the hand of the Lord. The days of your life are filled with God things.

Where forgiveness begins

Pastor Mike Novotny

Have you ever seen the musical (or read the book) *Les Misérables*? It is, in part, about a convict named Jean Valjean who refuses to forgive the legal system that sinned against him, leaving him broke and broken. In his bitterness, Valjean decides to steal some silver candlesticks from a kind priest who showed him only love. The police catch him and are ready to bring the hammer of justice down on his head, but the priest defends Jean, claiming the candlesticks were a gift. Stunned, Valjean stares as the priest draws close to his ear and says in a low voice, "Jean Valjean, my brother, you no longer belong to evil, but to good. . . . I withdraw [your soul] from black thoughts and . . . I give it to God." I won't ruin the rest of the story, but I will tell you that this absurd forgiveness changes Jean Valjean.

It changes us too. Like that priest, Jesus has shown us grace. When justice would have locked us up in hell, far from God, Jesus leans in close and whispers, "I forgive you. I bled to buy you back and give you to God." Paul writes, **"In [Jesus] we have redemption through his blood, the forgiveness of sins"** (Ephesians 1:7).

Meditate deeply upon that gospel truth. God, for the rest of your life, will never get you back. He will never treat you as your sins deserve. He will always love you.

That kind of forgiveness never leaves a soul the same. Just ask Jean Valjean.

What's your angel story?
Pastor David Scharf

I can't tell you that it was an angel for sure. I'll find out in heaven. When my mother was a little girl, she vividly remembers running down the sidewalk, planting her foot on the curb, and launching herself into the street just as a car suddenly came whipping around the corner. She remembers feeling like she was picked up and placed back on the curb. But when she looked around, there was no one there. Was it an angel? Maybe.

Do you have an angel story? A story where the only logical conclusion is that God sent an angel to help you? God says through his psalmist, **"He will command his angels concerning you to guard you in all your ways"** (Psalm 91:11). This means that whether we know of a story or not, we all have angel stories! God promises that it's true! I'm convinced that one of the joys of heaven will be to hear all the ways that God protected us with these powerful creatures without us even knowing.

Just think of that today. Perhaps an angel will hold back a tree limb from falling when you're under it or cause a deer to trip so that it passes just behind your car instead of in front of it. We may never know those things in this life, but this I know: God will continue to provide angel stories in your life. You have his Word on it!

Hold out your hands!

Ann Jahns

My dad was an amazing gift giver. Oh, the joy I'd feel when he would return from a trip and say the magic words: "Close your eyes and hold out your hands!" I'd screw my eyes shut and squirm in anticipation, palms open, ready to receive his small token of love. I knew it would be a gift I would treasure.

But as adults, sometimes we're afraid to close our eyes trustingly and hold out our hands, aren't we? We're afraid of being vulnerable, afraid of what might be placed there. Maybe someone has hurt us, and we're wary of getting burned. Maybe we had a father who never gave us a good gift, or maybe we never even knew a father's love. Maybe we had a mother who withheld her affection, or maybe we even had another adult in our lives who hurt us in ways we don't want to speak about.

But God our heavenly Father won't hurt us. He invites us to close our eyes and hold out our hands, palms open, to receive his good gifts. In fact, **"every good and perfect gift is from above, coming down from the Father of the heavenly lights, who does not change like shifting shadows"** (James 1:17).

Even those who love us most will hurt us sometimes. In a beautiful contrast, we never have to worry about how God feels about us. He will never withdraw his gifts of love and forgiveness and eternal life. Go ahead—hold out your hands, unafraid, and receive God's good gifts.

Back to basics
Linda Buxa

I've been going to church since I was born. I went to a Christian grade school, high school, *and* college. Plus, for much of my adult life, I've written thoughts about God for thousands of people to read. And yet . . . sometimes I skim over parts of the Bible that are hard. There are so many stories and lessons that don't make sense.

It's easy to get confused about some of God's words and then worry about knowing (or understanding!) it all.

Fortunately, a part of the Bible that's incredibly clear reassures us. First John 3 says we have confidence before God and receive from him anything we ask because we obey his commands and do what pleases him. God's command is to believe in the name of Jesus Christ and to love one another.

So when you're confused about faith, get back to the basics:

One: Believe in Jesus.

Two: Love others as he commanded.

Three: Pray confidently.

This reminder isn't only for us when faith seems to get confusing; it's also a humbling reminder when we're tempted to get arrogant because we think we have it all together. This simple list gets us back to basics when we get discouraged by how often we fail.

Please don't think I'm encouraging you never to tackle the hard parts of the Bible. We should mature in our faith by growing in knowledge and understanding. Even as we do that though, we keep it simple: Believe in Jesus. Love others. Pray confidently.

Faith's foothold
Sarah Habben

My friend Roman was a rookie warden in the 1960s, training for mountain rescue in the Canadian Rockies. A farm boy, he'd never climbed before. In time, Roman's instructor, Mike, decided Roman was ready for a vertical cliff face called the Chin. Roman and Mike angled up the cliff, looking for holds on two-inch ledges. High above the cars on Highway 16, Roman found himself hanging from three holds—unable to move up or down, filled with terror.

"Mike," he managed, "I think I'm in trouble."

Mike quickly maneuvered below him. He grabbed Roman's boot, pressed it into a toehold, and said, "You're okay now." And he was right. Roman made the summit. But he told Mike, "Never again. Next time you might not be there to help me."

"When I said, 'My foot is slipping,' your unfailing love, Lord, supported me" (Psalm 94:18).

The psalmist was slipping too. He was focused on his troubles and the wickedness in the world. Anxiety dislodged his faith. Who of us hasn't felt our insides drop when we watch the news and read the headlines, when we look for evidence of God in the face of so much evil?

God took the psalmist's faith and pressed it into the toehold of his promises, into the firm support of his unfailing love.

If your faith is hanging by its fingernails, leave the hamster wheel of your troubles. Open your Bible. Let the unfailing love of your Savior-God reanchor your faith.

He'll *always* be there to help you.

The math of forgiveness

Pastor Mike Novotny

Here's a story that Jesus *almost* told—There was a man who owed a king 100 silver coins. The king, knowing the man couldn't pay the debt, smiled and said, "I forgive your debt, all 100 coins." The forgiven man left, ecstatic over the king's forgiveness . . . until he ran into a neighbor who also owed him 100 coins. He demanded payment, causing the man to beg for mercy. Unlike the king, however, there would be no forgiveness. When the king heard what the man had done, the man who had just been forgiven *that very amount*, he was furious.

Do you recognize that tale? It resembles a parable Jesus told. Except for one little detail. In Jesus' actual story, the first man wasn't forgiven just 100 silver coins but instead **"a man who owed** [the king] ***ten thousand bags of gold* was brought to him"** (Matthew 18:24). The debt was not silver but gold. Not 100 coins but 10,000 bags. It's hard to perfectly crunch the numbers, but some scholars suggest that the man owed the king $7,000,000,000 and was owed around $12,000.

Why did Jesus choose those numbers? Perhaps he knew we could never truly forgive unless we realized how much we have been forgiven. Not a silver coin or two but billions of dollars, paid in full at the cross.

If you're holding on to bitterness toward someone, take some quiet time with Jesus. Think deeply about how often and how completely you have been forgiven. Then you'll be ready to forgive.

Like a swarm of bees
Jason Nelson

Animate things like bees, birds, and youth soccer teams demonstrate swarming behavior. They move en masse one direction and then in another in response to some kinetic murmuring felt by all of them. It is a natural law written large by the Creator of all things. If we had a God's-eye view of the earth, we would see that even all of humanity can move like a swarm of bees. That is why God had the confidence so say, **"Let all the earth fear the Lord; let all the people of the world revere him"** (Psalm 33:8). God wants the whole world to move in his direction.

Do you remember how Christians became a swarm? The risen Savior commissioned his ragtag band of followers to take the gospel throughout the world. People heard the good news, saw the signs and wonders of God, put it all together, and believed in Jesus in increasing numbers. The gospel still has tremendous influence in our world. There are a couple billion staunch believers in Jesus and countless others who appreciate him and his teachings. This is a pretty good track record for the Jesus movement. And it only took a couple thousand years to get this far. Jesus doesn't always get the credit, but he is the reason for every act of decency and love that people express to one another. Let the swarming continue. When the bees break out of the hive, it's on!

You *can* grow!
Andrea Delwiche

What are the characteristics of people who live with God here on earth and in the world to come? Good question.

If you read the short five verses of Psalm 15 (please, go ahead and read them right now!), you get an answer, a description of a child of God who is beginning to function the way she or he was made by God to function. This isn't about some sort of checklist to get to heaven. Rather, this list shows how people who belong to God conduct themselves as they grow in grace and live seeking after God.

But after looking at the list, you may think, "This way of life doesn't describe how I act on a daily basis. Will I live with God in the end?"

Be comforted by these words: **"My grace is sufficient for you, for my power is made perfect in weakness"** (2 Corinthians 12:9). God has us covered in forgiving love. But who, having experienced this love of God, would not desire to work with him? Change *is* possible in this life. It *is* possible to grow in grace and godly living and to live unshaken in the Lord.

As we strive to live following the blueprints for living designed for us by God, we taste the joy of living with him, not just in eternity but experiencing fellowship with him right now.

The gift of repentance

Pastor Mike Novotny

Do you love repenting? That word might bring some uninspiring pictures to mind. Perhaps an angry preacher thumping his Bible or a street corner Christian with a scowl and a threatening sign.

But repentance is more beautiful than you might assume. The word in the Greek language means, "to change your mind." Whenever you change your mind and agree with God, you are officially "repenting." So when you reorder your life so God is the center of your universe, the glorious sun around which the planets of your time, your finances, your words, your career, your relationships, and your sexuality orbit, you are repenting. You're simply agreeing that God deserves to be your first and your best.

I won't lie to you—repentance is costly. When you change your mind about something, it leads to a change in behavior. You might have to give up a short-term pleasure or humble yourself and apologize for something you said. However, those sacrifices are small compared to being on the same page as God.

John the Baptist, famous for calling people to repentance, was once described in this way: **"John exhorted the people and proclaimed the good news to them"** (Luke 3:18). It was good news to give up something as small as sin in order to be with God himself.

Is there anything you need to repent of today? anything that's taken over God as your greatest passion? Change your mind and agree with the God who has taken away all of your sins. You won't regret it.

God's way is the best way
Andrea Delwiche

Who is the expert you rely on? Whom do you call on when you need someone to show you the best way to live?

The writer of Psalm 16 arrived at an answer to these questions: The Lord is his expert and guide. His life experiences have proved that it is the Lord who is wise and who sets the best path forward.

Listen to his realization and his submission to the Lord: **"I say to the Lord, 'You are my Lord; I have no good apart from you. The Lord is my *chosen* portion and my cup'"** (verses 2,5 ESV). When he looks at all the ways he can choose to live his life, he realizes that he *wants* to submit to the Lord's guidance, protection, and plan. The rest of the psalm reads like a list of all the benefits that come from choosing the Lord's way. It's an overflow of richness!

There are lots of people who tell us how to solve our problems. Only God's way is proven. Take time to pray and think. Do you really believe that God's good way is the best way? Do you *want* to believe this about God but struggle to actually believe that it's true?

Sit in the quiet and ask the Lord to help you be honest with yourself and with him. He loves and forgives you. He will always respond with his Spirit to a heartfelt request, "Lord, I *do* want to choose your guidance above everything else. Please help this be my reality!"

august 13

The best friends ever
Pastor Matt Ewart

People are kind of like Lego bricks. You have a finite number of pegs that allow you to connect in meaningful friendships with other people.

Maybe you feel some emptiness in your life and wish you had another friend. Or maybe as you look at your friendships, you feel like you could use a better friend. But who?

Something Jesus said transformed the way I think of friendships. I always thought that a best friend was someone who improved the quality of my life. But I was wrong. Here's what Jesus said:

"My command is this: Love each other as I have loved you. Greater love has no one than this: to lay down one's life for one's friends" (John 15:12,13).

Jesus did much more than just improve the quality of your life. He changed the direction of your life. He saw the direction you were headed, so he intervened lovingly to change your eternity.

That's what best friends do. Good friends improve the quality of your life, but a best friend will improve the direction of your life.

The best friend you could have is a Christian who knows you well enough to see where your life is headed and loves you enough to intervene when necessary. A best friend is able to take the eternity-changing gospel and apply it to everyday decisions you face.

Sometimes the first step to finding that kind of friend is being that kind of friend to someone else.

How do I forgive?

Pastor Mike Novotny

Years ago I got into a rather unloving exchange with a fellow Christian. The tension had been growing for months, so we met face-to-face to figure it out. As we talked about what God would want us to do—just love—she closed her eyes and gave a slow nod: "I know . . . I know . . ." I sighed, because I knew exactly how she felt. As a Christian, I wanted to let it go and choose to love her as the Bible commands. But it can be so hard to get the truth of the Word into the emotions of your heart, the thoughts of your mind, and the words of your lips.

Have you felt that too?

If so, Jesus wants to help. That's why he taught us to pray, **"Father . . . we also forgive everyone who sins against us"** (Luke 11:2,4). Our Savior knew how hard forgiveness would be, so he directs us to the source of supernatural power. When you feel like you can't, talk to the God who always can!

But look at what Jesus said first: **"Forgive us *our* sins, for we also forgive everyone who sins against us"** (Luke 11:4). "First, Father, forgive us our sins. Forgive me mine." Forgiveness starts not with you forgiving them, but with God forgiving you. And he has! And he is! And he will!

So when forgiving them seems impossible, remember to pray to your supremely capable and shockingly forgiving Father.

The Savior of poor sinners

Pastor Mike Novotny

When Jesus was baptized, the Holy Spirit came down like a dove. Do you know what that means? In the Bible, doves are connected to all kinds of things—beauty, life after judgment, the ability to fly away from danger—but the #1 use of the dove in the entire Bible is for . . . sacrifice. In the book of Leviticus, doves are mentioned nine times as sacrifices for sins, especially among poor people who couldn't afford a lamb or a goat.

Isn't that incredible news? If you're like me, you don't have that much to offer God. What in the world would we give him to make up for all the sins we've committed? How many prayers would we have to pray or dollars would we have to donate to make it right? Thank God it doesn't work like that. Because Jesus is the dove. He dies for the poorest of sinners and the biggest of strugglers. We don't have to wonder if we're good enough for God or hope we don't end up in hell. No! We have Jesus, who died and rose not just for above-average people but for the poor and the lowly, for me and for you.

Look at Jesus and rejoice at the Spirit's reminder: **"When all the people were being baptized, Jesus was baptized too. And as he was praying, heaven was opened and the Holy Spirit descended on him in bodily form like a dove"** (Luke 3:21,22).

The beauty of God's presence

Andrea Delwiche

My family and I recently camped at the foot of a mountain in Glacier National Park. In the morning, when I stepped out of my tent, I was eager to sit with my coffee and soak in the beauty. I wanted to watch mountain goats following their personal paths across rocky ledges and then turn my eyes above the peak and look for eagles soaring. I wanted to be present in that moment so that it would stay with me the rest of my life.

The closing lines of Psalm 17 remind me of that feeling. The psalmist has spent his life on a journey of trust and faith with the Lord. He has followed the path of the Lord, and it's worked for him. His **"steps have held to** [God's] **paths"** and his **"feet have not stumbled"** (verse 5). He has learned the beauty of God's ways and memorized what God's faithfulness looks like. He loves the Lord so much that he says, **"When I awake, I will be satisfied with seeing your likeness"** (verse 15).

Is this peace possible for people like you and me? Simply, yes. We too can live interwoven with the Lord and his likeness. How? As we spend loads of time dwelling in his Word and listening to his voice and living in Christian community with others, he will become ever-present to us.

Even better than a stunning mountain scene, we can begin each morning in a good place as we dwell in God's presence.

The bridge that brings peace
Ann Jahns

Are you afraid of bridges—like the gigantic marvels of steel that span two parts of land? Or how about the rickety rope kind in adventure movies that disintegrate as the main character frantically races over them?

In reality, there's a legitimate phobia of bridges; it's called gephyrophobia. Maybe you suffer from it, causing you to forgo adventurous hiking or causing your sweaty palms to tightly clutch the steering wheel as you nervously drive over a large body of water.

There's one bridge that should provoke no anxiety in us—in fact, it's crucial in our relationship with God. Because of our sin, we are separated from God by a barrier—a gaping chasm that we can't cross. We simply can't keep all of God's laws perfectly to stand in his holy presence.

But Ephesians 2:13-15 declares, **"In Christ Jesus you who once were far away have been brought near by the blood of Christ. For he himself is our peace, who has made the two groups one and has destroyed the barrier, the dividing wall of hostility, by setting aside in his flesh the law with its commands and regulations. His purpose was to create in himself one new humanity out of the two, thus making peace."** Because Jesus was sinless and paid for our sins with his life, his cross is the bridge that brings us peace with God.

Gephyrophobes, fear no more. We all can walk with confidence across the bridge built by the cross of Jesus—the unshakeable and incorruptible bridge that leads to eternal life with God.

Helping boys become men
Jason Nelson

In the 90s, I was a regular on the church basement seminar circuit. One of my presentations was entitled, "Helping Boys Become Men." It drew nice crowds, but I don't think I did a good job because it's still a very confusing issue. Back then it seemed simple enough to reinforce stereotypes like men were from Mars, not Venus, and that boys should be plugged into a kind of masculinity they could acquire by imitating the big males in their world. Throw in a dash of savagery and a BB gun and you're good to go. Well, it isn't that simple. You could end up with a cartoon character and not a man.

Dear God, what makes a man? You do. Manhood goes deeper than having external plumbing and the physiology to donate sperm. Manhood develops out of the heart of what God wants to see in all of humanity: **"The Lord looks down from heaven on all mankind to see if there are any who understand, any who seek God"** (Psalm 14:2). Real men can be lots of different things, just like real women can. What does God ultimately want to see in men? What is God looking for from his sons? **"A man who loves wisdom brings joy to his father"** (Proverbs 29:3). Tough boys can become good men. Gentle boys can become good men. All boys can become good men. Good men seek God and grow up in his wisdom and grace.

Is peace possible?

Pastor Mike Novotny

I love how realistic the apostle Paul is. While teaching on sin, forgiveness, and reconciliation, he wrote, **"If it is possible, as far as it depends on you, live at peace with everyone"** (Romans 12:18). Paul is pushing us to do everything we can to reconcile with those who sin against us. But notice that phrase, "if it is possible." Sometimes it isn't possible, in this life, to fix what sin has broken.

Think of what infidelity might do to a marriage. Even Jesus recognized that the damage could lead to divorce (Matthew 5:32). Or think of what gossip might do to a friendship. Solomon knew such sins might separate close friends who are no longer eager to share their deepest struggles and secrets (Proverbs 16:28).

That's important to know. While we strive to forgive everyone who sins against us (Luke 11:4), it might not be possible to reconcile every relationship. That doesn't mean we're bitter or vengeful. It simply recognizes there are other factors involved. It's like a runner after a car accident. She might not be able to sprint like before, despite the work of rehab.

Thankfully, however, Jesus' forgiveness is perfect. Because of the cross, living at peace with God is always possible, no matter how ugly the sin or long-lasting the consequences. While we might struggle to trust the people who've hurt us, we can always trust that Jesus has helped us, giving us a perfect relationship with our Father. No distance. No separation. Just God with us until the day we see him face-to-face.

On the run
Pastor Jon Enter

"Jonah ran away from the LORD and headed for Tarshish . . . to flee from the LORD" (Jonah 1:3). Jonah ran from God and went the opposite way than God commanded. Often we make the story of Jonah about a big fish, but it's actually about big forgiveness.

What are you running from or worried about? Jonah's story is our story too, minus being digested in the belly of a swimming taxi for three days. This story is about God going after Jonah and us to bring big forgiveness.

When Jonah turned left toward the sea when he should've turned right toward Nineveh, his heart must've yelled out, "I shouldn't be doing this." But he did.

Where has your conscience and faith yelled out, "I shouldn't be doing this"? It often takes more work to avoid responsibility than fulfill it, yet you and I go the wrong way again and again.

When we say, "I shouldn't be doing this," God says, "Then I'm going to do something." God sent Jesus. Jesus didn't take a wrong turn; he didn't avoid responsibility. Jesus did what Jonah refused to do. Jesus marched right into this world, right into the hearts of those who are hurting, to bring peace.

Truthfully confess, "God, I ran away from you. Please forgive me." And he will. And he has. Why? The fury of God's wrath over sin struck Jesus on the cross so that you are free and forgiven and refocused in life.

Defiance and acceptance

Pastor Jon Enter

When Jonah ran from God, buying a one-way ticket away from Nineveh, he put himself and everyone on that ship in danger.

Who have you hurt with your defiance of God?

When Jonah sailed away from responsibility, God wouldn't let him get away with sin. God's perfect. He can't let sin go unpunished. If someone is unwilling to confess, God will confront.

God will not stop coming after you, not to destroy you but to restore you. That happens through confession, admitting failures without excuse. That's what Jonah finally did. He admitted his guilt, being moved from defiance to acceptance of what he did.

"'Pick me up and throw me into the sea,' he replied, 'and it will become calm. I know that it is my fault that this great storm has come upon you'" (Jonah 1:12).

God lovingly sends storms when you sin. How is that loving? If he didn't, you'd march from him toward hell, so he sends storm after storm to show that path leads to destruction. When you repent, he will relent.

What are you not confessing?

Stop running. You can't outrun God. You can't outrun his grace. God is pursuing you to save you from yourself and eternal consequences. There's an ache in your heart to change. Be changed. Be a Jonah. Go from defiance to acceptance in repentance, and watch what God does next!

But that's tomorrow's devotion. When Jonah hits the water, God responds. God restores. How? It's a whale of a tale!

Rescued but responsible

Pastor Jon Enter

The longest anyone has held his or her breath underwater is 22 minutes. Impressive! How long did Jonah hold his when he was thrown overboard? Most people can only last two minutes or less. This means God had to ACT to save Jonah!

"The LORD provided a huge fish to swallow Jonah, and Jonah was in the belly of the fish three days and three nights" (Jonah 1:17).

At my house, we have this Precious Moments picture of Jonah. He's sitting in a living room inside the belly of the fish. Smiling. Relaxing. Sipping tea. No! He was submerged in stomach bile that was eating away at his skin and getting in his eyes. He likely didn't sleep. For three days he endured that unique hell, but it was better than literal hell. He was rescued but still responsible.

We sometimes think that when God forgives us it should make life easy. God's forgiveness heals our relationship with him, but there's still the need to repair our relationships with others. When life doesn't get easy after we confess, we tend to blame God. But it's not his fault; the mess is ours.

Who have you hurt or strained your relationship with? Go talk to that person and confess.

It'll take work. It'll bring pain, but there will be gain. You will gain true peace when you work to reconcile with others. You're forgiven by God. Seek forgiveness from those you've hurt. When you do, that's when true peace prevails!

Refocused but resistant

Pastor Jon Enter

Did you know there are only four verses in the book of Jonah that talk about the big fish swallowing him? This story isn't about a big fish; it's about God's big forgiveness. Jonah experienced that forgiveness when he was conveniently yet grossly vomited onto the shoreline. Jonah was pointed right at Nineveh, but he felt they didn't deserve to receive God's love. **"To Jonah this seemed very wrong, and he became angry"** (Jonah 4:1). Forgiveness was great for Jonah but not for others. He was refocused on God but resistant to following God.

The devil is good at getting us to be disgusted by how God gives grace, as if God forgiving those we deem super sinful somehow devalues the forgiveness he gives us. It doesn't! Don't look down on someone because he or she sins differently than you. All sin destroys our relationship with the Almighty. Look up to God, thanking him that his grace is universal, unstoppable, and can heal anything you've ever done wrong.

Jonah had it wrong. God's big forgiveness didn't get weaker by giving it to the people of Nineveh. God's grace proved its worth, value, and validity by blasting away the sins of an entire city dedicated to evil.

When you see people a bit rough around the spiritual edges, don't look down on them. Pray for them that they might know what you know . . . God has big forgiveness for all sinners. We've been treated better than we deserve! Let's treat others the same.

When sin tears people apart

Pastor Mike Novotny

I find Paul's words to the Romans as challenging as they are beautiful: **"If it is possible, as far as it depends on you, live at peace with everyone"** (12:18). While it takes two people to live at peace, Paul urges us to do everything in our power to restore the relationships that sin has broken.

How do you do that? In Romans 12, Paul points to a few vital truths. First, don't be proud. One percent of the time, like in cases of child abuse, sin is one-sided. But the other 99 percent of the time, two sinners are involved in the situation. *She escalated it . . . but I might have started it. He threw this massive stone in our marriage . . . but I threw a thousand small ones first.* Living at peace starts with humility, with owning our part and confessing, not excusing, our sin. So don't let your hurt take away your humility.

Second, love them. Bless those who persecute you. Rejoice when they celebrate. Overcome the evil they did by doing good. Use your hands not to pick up the sinful stones they threw at you but to serve and love them. That might not guarantee healing, but it's God's best path forward.

Those steps remind me of Jesus. So humble that he chose the cross for us. So loving that he loved his enemies. So committed that he didn't just forgive us; he reconciled us to God! He did everything possible to live at peace with us for ever and ever. Amen!

Faith lessons from a Fitbit
Linda Buxa

I'm sporadic about my Fitbit. I wear it but don't care if I reach that arbitrary 10,000 steps to earn the "Sneakers" badge. Sometimes I forget to wear it. (Is there an "Are you sure you're alive?" badge?)

My husband, on the other hand, is faithful and diligent. He gets his 10,000 steps each day—even if he has to pace inside our house. He's earned the "Great Wall of China" badge.

My faith life (and I'm guessing yours too) often resembles these extremes. Sometimes we grab our phones instead of our Bibles. We complain about blessings and grumble about opportunities to grow. We intentionally look the other way when given opportunities to serve. We expect to get an "Are you sure you're even a Christian?" badge.

On other days, we're faithful and diligent. We read our Bibles, pray, look for the good works God prepared for us to do, thank him for blessings, and see how he works through challenges. We might expect the "Great Christian" badge.

God sees it differently because he's not looking at what you do; he's looking at what Jesus has done for you. Jesus paid for the times you're sporadic, and he gives you all the credit for the 100 percent of the time he was faithful and diligent. **"Therefore, since we have been justified through faith, we have peace with God through our Lord Jesus Christ"** (Romans 5:1,2).

Thanks to Jesus, we get the "Peace with God" badge. That's the only badge that matters.

The pressure is off

Pastor Mike Novotny

In November 2019, social media giant Instagram decided to hide the number of "likes" each posted picture received. Instead of revealing that 73 people liked his picture and 102 people liked her picture, Instagram took out the number. Why the change? Instagram CEO Adam Mosseri explained, "The idea is to try and depressurize Instagram, make it less of a competition."

Fascinating, isn't it? Instagram realized how dangerous (and completely natural) it is to compare your life to the lives of others.

John the Baptist had an even more helpful way to deal with the obsessive comparison disorder in his heart. When some of his disciples panicked as the crowds gave their attention to Jesus, **"John replied, 'A person can receive only what is given them from heaven'"** (John 3:27). John had little interest in comparing blessings because he believed that a person could only get what heaven decided to give.

What a relief! You and I don't have to waste our time comparing our family, our job, our home, our car, our body, our platform, our grades, our stats, our income, or anything else to our neighbors' situations. Instead, we can receive the one and only life that God has given to us and use it for his glory.

So, child of God, the pressure is off. You don't need to have any other life than the one you have. Today is not a day to compare but, rather, a day to thank God for his grace and use every blessing he has given to reflect his unfailing love.

Pursuing happiness

Jason Nelson

When the founders of America declared independence from England, they listed "the pursuit of happiness" as one of the reasons. They argued we were given this right by God. They couldn't guarantee we would always be happy. They did declare we have a right to try. Nice. What a blessing to live in a nation that values human happiness! But it's a negotiated happiness. We have a constitution and laws that set limits on our happiness because each of us has a dubious power to destroy another person's happiness.

Our best happiness accrues to us when we make God happy. **"To the person who pleases him, God gives wisdom, knowledge and happiness"** (Ecclesiastes 2:26). We will never be happy if we alienate ourselves from God. The pursuit of happiness starts with pleasing him. Have you ever heard anyone say, "I'm making myself miserable because I keep doing the right things"? Doing the right things is an enormous source of personal satisfaction.

So is bringing joy to others. God's happiness, other people's happiness, and our own happiness are fraternal triplets. They are related in a way that bonds humanity with the divine. We are free to put an unforced smile on the face of a child, senior citizen, or anyone in between through our acts of kindness. My fellow Americans, **"I know that there is nothing better for people than to be happy and to do good while they live"** (Ecclesiastes 3:12). Pursue all the happiness you can get.

This same Jesus . . .

Pastor David Scharf

I once read a story about a woman who couldn't recognize anyone once that person left the room and came back in. She couldn't even recognize her own family! A reporter asked her if it was scary to pick up her girls from the mall. Her answer was astounding: "Not really. They know who I am."

Jesus ascended into heaven to rule all things for your good. He is preparing a place for you, and he will come again to take you to heaven. When Jesus returns again, will you recognize him? Just think of how many different depictions of Jesus' likeness you have seen. There are hundreds from every culture and time in history! The truth is that we don't know what he looks like. Will we recognize him? On one hand, we'll have no problem recognizing him. He'll be the One to whom every knee is bowing on the Last Day!

However, just as comforting is the truth the angel shared with the disciples at Jesus' ascension: **"This same Jesus, who has been taken from you into heaven, will come back in the same way you have seen him go into heaven"** (Acts 1:11). Even if we don't know what he looks like, what a cool thing to know that it doesn't have to concern you. The One who lived and died for you, this same One, will return. Don't worry! He knows who you are!

august 29

Jesus reconciles with real sinners
Pastor Mike Novotny

There's a difference between forgiveness and reconciliation. Forgiveness is when you make the daily choice not to get back at the person who sinned against you. You refuse to hurt him because he first hurt you. But reconciliation goes a step further. It restores, reunites, and rejoins separated people. If you're like me, you know that forgiveness is hard but that reconciliation is even harder!

That's one more reason why I adore Jesus. After his friend Peter sinned against him, denying that he even knew who Jesus was (Luke 22:60), our Lord made sure to reconnect with Peter after the resurrection. **"Follow me!"** Jesus invited him, just as he had three years earlier, long before Peter's epic failure (John 21:19). It would have been pure grace for Jesus to forgive Peter and then end their friendship. But it was grace on top of grace (on top of grace!) for Jesus to welcome Peter back to the table and call him his follower and friend.

Isn't that wonderful? When you sin, even in embarrassing ways, Jesus does more than forgive you. He refuses to let you wander through life alone, forgiven but far from him. Instead, Jesus reconciles with you, draws you close, and assures you that you are still his follower and friend. While true reconciliation might be rare in our broken world, it is the promise that the gospel makes to you. Believe it and enjoy that promise today!

Welcome home
Sarah Habben

My family made two big moves in three years. Just when we were getting our feet on the ground, we had to adjust all over again. It made me feel a bit like a dandelion yanked out by the stem.

That feeling of rootlessness doesn't only accompany an address change. Maybe your friendships don't go much deeper than a "like" on Instagram. You wonder, *"Who cares about me?"* Your neighbors are strangers you wave to on trash day. You wonder, *"How do I fit into my community?"* Your work demands your time and energy and gives so little feedback. You wonder, *"Who values me?"* Your family is fractured. You wonder, *"Where do I belong?"*

The Old Testament prophet Moses, displaced his whole life, must have asked those questions. Here's his beautiful conclusion:

"Lord, *you* have been our dwelling place throughout all generations. Before the mountains were born or you brought forth the whole world, from everlasting to everlasting you are God" (Psalm 90:1,2).

Our rootless hearts have a home in God. That everlasting home puts our short lives into perspective. God is eternal—nothing like the dandelion fluff of our tiny, shifting desires, our worries about present or future. He's the very opposite of our mortality. But he's also the *answer* to our mortality. His Son fought sin and Satan and death to deliver us safely into God's everlasting arms. We stand in the light of God's favor. We are loved. We are valued. We belong.

Welcome home.

The hill we died on
Jason Nelson

Christianity is at a crossroads. Some churches have planted their flags on the hills they're willing to die on. They'll stand firm where they've always stood. Members are bound by long-standing procedural and social behaviors and are unlikely to change them. Other churches are ending their self-imposed lockdowns and stepping out with good news. They're engaging the world through social media, by modernizing the worship experience, and by starting ministries that change people's lives for the better. This is uncharted territory for them. But they are excited to go there.

Christianity will always be at a crossroads because an ever-changing world needs Jesus. Remember, there is one hill that we all died on. It is Calvary. On Calvary, we died to ourselves and **"in Christ all will be made alive"** (1 Corinthians 15:22). Our devotion to Jesus evolves out of the churning of repentance and renewal. We are always in a cycle of killing off our old inadequacies and coming back to life in new, God-pleasing ways. God's mercy on us releases the power of God's grace in us. We can initiate new directions for ourselves and for the church.

If you are a church leader, please help us choose the right road. More than anything, we come to church to see Jesus. We need to experience his love on a personal level. We want to follow him as best we can and lead others to him. You may need to reinvent yourself to help us do that. You are at a crossroads too.

September

Whatever you do, work at it with all your heart,
as working for the Lord, not for human masters.

Colossians 3:23

New open door
Pastor Jon Enter

Culture shifted. Absolute truth died. There's a new norm. Your truth is your truth. Someone else's truth is their truth. Everyone wins. Everyone gets a trophy.

The greatest offense today is telling someone their truth is wrong and you're right. To believe Jesus is the only way to heaven and the Bible the only absolute truth is offensive.

So how do you live confidently and express your faith?

This is one of the greatest open doors to the gospel! Be like Paul. When he was in Athens, the people there believed in many false gods. Rather than complaining about their culture, he used it. Paul found a statue with the inscription: "To An Unknown God," and then he connected them to Christ (see Acts 17:22-34).

In today's culture, no one can tell you your personal truth is wrong. So . . . tell your truth, the truth of how God's love gives you peace, how the power of God did the impossible for you. Tell others about Jesus by sharing how Jesus' mercy gives you confidence to face each day. They'll listen if you don't tell them they have to believe it themselves. And you can't make them believe anyway. That's the Spirit's job. Your job is to plant the seed of the gospel.

So share your story, which is God's story. Tell others how you've seen God's power and God's presence in your life. And after you share that truth, pray the Spirit will work on their hearts to see the truth that God loves them too!

Test him

Linda Buxa

My college-aged daughter was stressing about money. The deposits were due for two study abroad opportunities, and things were tight. When her paycheck arrived, she realized putting ten percent of it into an offering plate would be $50. She wrestled with it, and ultimately decided she didn't want be stingy with God. She gave the offering—and then prayed God would somehow help her earn the additional $100 she needed for a financial cushion.

The *very* next day a friend reached out and said, "I want to work where you work. If you refer me, do you get a bonus?"

I bet you're not surprised to hear that the company's referral bonus is $100. She called to share the amazing news and said, "Mom, God didn't have to answer me right away, but he did."

Seeing God provide for her was a reminder of his commitment: **"'Bring the whole tithe into the storehouse, that there may be food in my house. Test me in this,' says the LORD Almighty, 'and see if I will not throw open the floodgates of heaven and pour out so much blessing that there will not be room enough to store it'"** (Malachi 3:10).

God doesn't actually need my daughter's $50; he simply wants her heart, her trust, her faith. He wants her to know that everything she has—not just that ten percent—is actually his for her to manage and that he will provide.

That's what he wants from you too. Test him in this.

Every day—you are blessed

Andrea Delwiche

"You, Lᴏʀᴅ, keep my lamp burning; my God turns my darkness into light. With your help I can advance against a troop; with my God I can scale a wall. As for God, his way is perfect: The Lᴏʀᴅ's word is flawless; he shields all who take refuge in him" (Psalm 18:28-30).

Do you ever read Scripture out loud as a conversation between you and the Lord? Try rereading the words from this psalm out loud right now.

If you're just beginning your day, God bless you. If you've reached a hard point of your day, God bless you. If you're at the end of the day and lying in bed perhaps exhausted or fearful as you contemplate tomorrow, God bless you.

Try reading these words out loud again.

Can you picture the Lord protecting the flame of his lamp and tipping it toward you to help you light your *own* lamp so that you can see in the darkness? Can you picture the Lord ready with his strong hands to help you vault over the wall that confronts you? Can you dwell in the assurance of these words: **"As for God, his way is perfect"**?

Slow your thoughts. Take time to breathe. Read these words again. Carry them into whatever challenge you're facing. **"As for God, his way is perfect: The Lᴏʀᴅ's word is flawless; he shields all who take refuge in him."**

May you be blessed.

The healing business
Jason Nelson

From the start, Christians have been in the healing business. **"Jesus called his twelve disciples to him and gave them authority to drive out impure spirits and to heal every disease and sickness"** (Matthew 10:1). Healing proved Christ's love and that he was something special. The healing we do today fits a slightly different definition.

healing [hee-ling] NOUN 1. the process of making or becoming sound or healthy again.

Healing takes love and something special. It's good work for Christians. Saint Basil started an early hospital in the Byzantine Empire back in the 4th century. Christians in medieval Europe started hospitals and universities. Today, Christians sponsor a variety of health, education, and social service ministries. I'm seeing individual churches get back into the healing business. They deploy the expertise of members and invite people from the community to come and be healed.

Church support groups help grieving people cope with sadness and divorced people overcome bitterness. I know of a small-town church giving free haircuts to the rural poor, which boosts their self-respect when they look in the mirror. Nurses are providing screenings to people who don't see the doctor often. Financial planners are teaching money management so folks know what to do with it if they get some. Churches offer food, shelter, and compassion to the homeless and displaced. The possibilities to prove Jesus' love are endless. What are you qualified to do that would help people? Join a good church, and get into the healing business.

A battle worth fighting
Pastor David Scharf

"You have to pick your battles." In other words, there are some things that are either just too small to worry about or battles you'll never win, so don't even try. When it comes to this physical life, it's sometimes good advice.

Nevertheless, when it comes to our spiritual lives, it's terrible advice, even deadly. A battle with sin, any sin, is a battle worth fighting. And you know what? It's tiring. Look at your soul. Does it have bags under its eyes? Are you worn out from the struggle? Listen to what your Savior tells you today: **"Come to me, all you who are weary and burdened, and I will give you rest. Take my yoke upon you and learn from me, for I am gentle and humble in heart, and you will find rest for your souls"** (Matthew 11:28,29).

What makes us tired is what we're yoked to. Are you yoked to your spouse, career, your own mortality, your kids? Do you see what Jesus is saying? He wants you to realize that you are yoked to him. He wants you to know that he has won eternal rest for your soul because he paid for every sin on the cross, including the one you struggle with. You may lose battles against sin, but because of Jesus, you have already won the war. It's a battle worth fighting!

What kind of aroma are you?

Ann Jahns

Everyone has a favorite aroma. What's yours? Is it freshly mown grass or crisp, line-dried laundry? Is it warm chocolate chip cookies or a steaming loaf of bread straight from the oven? How about the downy crown of a newborn's head?

On the flip side, what's your least favorite aroma? Is it the outside garbage can in the dead of summer or your son's sweaty football pads, uniform, and cleats after they fester in the trunk of your car all weekend?

Good or bad, an aroma permeates everything. I know this involves science regarding molecules that's beyond my understanding, but simply put, an aroma winds itself in, around, and under everything near it. It has the power to either attract or repel.

In an interesting metaphor, the book of 2 Corinthians urges us to be the attractive aroma of Christ to the world around us: **"But thanks be to God, who always leads us as captives in Christ's triumphal procession and uses us to spread the aroma of the knowledge of him everywhere. For we are to God the pleasing aroma of Christ among those who are being saved and those who are perishing"** (2:14,15).

Unbelievably, when Jesus returned to heaven after he rose from the dead, he entrusted the work of spreading his gospel message to us stinky, sinful human beings. What a privilege. What a responsibility. All of our words and actions are to be an enticing aroma that attracts others to Christ.

What kind of aroma are you?

september 7

God's operating manual
Andrea Delwiche

"The decrees of the LORD **are firm, and all of them are righteous. They are more precious than gold, than much pure gold; they are sweeter than honey, than honey from the honeycomb"** (Psalm 19:9,10).

What's your view of the guidelines and commands set down by God in Scripture? Are they a mixed bag, some of them reasonable and others out of touch with today's world? Do you feel guilty when you "break a rule" and yet secretly feel that it can't be helped in this day and age? Would you describe God's guidelines as **"more precious than gold"** and **"sweeter than honey"**? Are you somewhere in between?

As Christians, we may have absorbed the idea that God's commandments and guidelines are his way of hammering us. We may also hammer ourselves or others with God's commands, in ways that aren't Christ-like at all. God's love and God's wisdom are trampled under guilt and anger toward God, other people, and ourselves.

But perfect love guides God's every interaction with you and me. Perhaps it's more useful to think of God's guidelines as an operating manual written to keep the human heart, mind, and body in top working condition. God is our wise designer and loving Father. He knows what the human soul and body need to live a life that works.

Lord, let me see love in your every word. Grant me insight and help me extend your love to others, especially those who seem, in my eyes, to disregard your ways. Amen.

Everything is fleeting, but GOD is forever

Pastor Mike Novotny

For 157 straight Sundays, I wore the same blue, checkered, button-up shirt to church. I'm not exaggerating. A creature of habit I must be, because I loved wearing that shirt. Sadly, however, the beautiful blue checks started to wear thin, and my treasured church wear ended up in the garbage can.

According to Solomon, that is how life **"under the sun"** works (Ecclesiastes 1:14). All the things of earth, even the things we treasure, are temporary. **"Everything is meaningless,"** Solomon lamented, which was his way of saying that nothing lasts all that long (Ecclesiastes 1:2). Not just clothes, but friends, family, comfort, control, praise, productivity, money, and health all come and go, no matter how hard we pray for them to endure. This reality is why we worry so much about tomorrow. We might lose something we love.

This, by contrast, is why I adore GOD. Our GOD is eternal. He is everlasting. He endures forever. While anything might leave us and anyone could forsake us, GOD has promised: **"Never will I leave you; never will I forsake you"** (Hebrews 13:5). The good news is not that GOD is loving or forgiving or merciful, but that he is eternal. That means his love and forgiveness and mercy endure forever.

In the days to come, I want us to appreciate the eternal nature of GOD. In a world where everything is fleeting, GOD's presence is the one thing we can always rely on. That truth is enough to give us true peace.

september 9

Friendship is fleeting,
but GOD is forever
Pastor Mike Novotny

The other day I paged through my grade school yearbooks. Besides the questionable clothing choices and baffling hairstyles, I was struck by a simple fact—I haven't seen those people in years. My dearest friends from those days are now distant memories.

That's how most friendships work, right? Friends come and friends go. You get close and then drift away. The dorm, the job, or the team brings you together, but then the busyness of life pulls you apart. Even friendships that survive the decades are threatened by the grim realities of Alzheimer's and unavoidable funerals.

This, by contrast, is why I adore GOD. Jesus, GOD in human flesh, once said, **"I have called you friends"** (John 15:15). Instead of merely being our Savior or our King, Jesus is willing to also be our Friend. The Friend who gets what we're going through (Hebrews 4:15). The Friend who cares about our anxiety (1 Peter 5:7). The Friend who will be there forever, since he is risen from the grave (Matthew 28:10,20).

I don't know if you have good friends or battle loneliness, but I do know this—Christians are never alone because the eternal GOD calls us his forever friends.

Praise is fleeting, but GOD is forever

Pastor Mike Novotny

I have a special email folder labeled "Encourage-ment." Whenever a kind, thoughtful word comes my way, I drag that message into that folder, saving it for a rainy day when my critics are many and my motivation is miniscule.

If you've ever been encouraged, you know the emotional power of praise. Perhaps you can even re-member the exact words your father or professor or coach spoke to you all those years ago. "Well done, son!" or, "You really impressed me!" are sentences that we save in a special folder in our hearts.

The problem, however, is that praise is fleeting. Few people pay attention to our efforts or bother to say anything nice at all. You can work your tail off for months and receive nothing more than your required paycheck. You can change a dozen diapers a day and get zero thanks. You can be a good neighbor, a dedi-cated volunteer at church, or a selfless spouse and hear crickets (or critiques of what you failed to do well).

This, by contrast, is why I adore GOD. The eternal GOD, in sheer mercy, not only forgives us in Christ but dares to praise the good works that we do. Even if our efforts are the smallest things done for the "least of these" on earth, King Jesus will one day shout, **"Well done,"** words that will echo throughout eternity (Mat-thew 25:21).

So when people forget to praise you (or notice you at all), remember the GOD who always sees and whose praise endures forever.

Romance is fleeting,
but GOD is forever

Pastor Mike Novotny

As much as I would love to say that the teenage me was saving my heart for Kim (my wife), the truth is that I was romantically pathetic. A six-month-old could have counted how many dates, girlfriends, and total kisses I had before my high school graduation (that is, zero). I learned, the hard way, how uncertain romance is.

That's true for all of us. Meeting "the one" is no guarantee. Convincing that one to commit their life to you is unpredictable too. Even those of us who do exchange vows with the one we love have no idea if that love (or our spouse's life) will last for very long. Commitments come and go. Vows are sometimes kept, sometimes broken. Even the best marriages end with one brokenhearted spouse at a funeral.

This, by contrast, is why I adore GOD. The eternal GOD vows to give us eternal love. Psalm 136 puts this truth on repeat: **"His love endures forever"** (verses 1 and 2 and 3-26!). Your dating life might be nonexistent, but your GOD's love endures forever. Your boyfriend might move on, but your GOD's love endures forever. Your girlfriend might choose your best friend, but your GOD's love endures forever. Your fiancé might get cold feet, but your GOD's love endures forever. Your wife might grow tired of marriage, but your GOD's love endures forever. Your beloved husband might pass away, but your GOD's love endures forever.

When love doesn't last, run to the infinite, bottomless, enduring, and everlasting love of the eternal GOD.

Family is fleeting, but GOD is forever

Pastor Mike Novotny

Pastor Mark Jeske, the original Time of Grace pastor, once told me that I needed to be intentional about parenting in the early teenage years. If memory serves, he said, "Mike, you think you have until they're 18, but you don't. Soon they'll have jobs, friends, and so much going on that you'll barely see them." Pastor Mark encouraged me to make the most of the time I have with my pre-job, pre-car, pre-phone daughters.

Essentially, his words are a reminder of a larger truth—family is fleeting. Some of us want kids but can't find someone to have kids with. Others find that someone but struggle to conceive. Those who are blessed with babies learn, just like *everyone* says, that "they grow up so fast." One day you're packing a diaper bag; the next you're unpacking at their first apartment.

This, by contrast, is why I adore GOD. The eternal GOD is the Father of the family that endures forever. Through the death and resurrection of Jesus, we have been gifted a perfect Father, a protective big brother (Jesus), and countless siblings in Christ. In fact, no matter what your biological family life is like, Jesus taught you to pray, **"Our Father . . ."** (Matthew 6:9), a reminder that your spiritual family is forever.

Earthly families, even the best ones, are temporary. Thank GOD that our Father in heaven is eternal.

Money is fleeting, but GOD is forever

Pastor Mike Novotny

I just made the mistake of looking at my checking account. $6.85 for bathroom supplies at the grocery store. $0.93 for gas station coffee. $23.73 for new clothes from Kohl's. $114.49 for life/disability insurance. $36.00 for the YMCA. $129.78 for Aldi. $21.00 for a local burger joint. Here's the worst part—that list was only *some* of the charges from the last 48 hours!

Money is fleeting. Proverbs remind us: **"Cast but a glance at riches, and they are gone, for they will surely sprout wings and fly off to the sky like an eagle"** (23:5). We work so hard to earn and save money, but then our expenses suck every dollar and cent out of our accounts. One day you have money in the bank; the next you're asking friends to wait before they cash your checks. It's hard, even in the First World, to feel secure about your financial situation.

This, by contrast, is why I adore GOD. The eternal GOD has promised his people eternal riches: **"Christ is the mediator of a new covenant, that those who are called may receive the promised eternal inheritance"** (Hebrews 9:15). We have eternal riches that are guaranteed to endure. The promise of GOD's presence, of greater worth than an armored truck full of gold, is an inheritance that no uninsured driver, company downsizing, or market crash can touch.

In other words, no matter what your net worth or your credit score, you are and always will be spiritually rich. Because GOD endures forever.

Productivity is fleeting, but GOD is forever
Pastor Mike Novotny

After 16 years of marriage, I know exactly what makes my wife happy—productivity. If you've never met Kim, you should know that she is a smart, organized, disciplined, humble-but-hardworking, box-checking woman. She loves to get stuff done, a passion that is a HUGE blessing to me, her coworkers, and our children. So when Kim gets stuff done, she is happy. And when life gets in the way of her list, she's not.

That's the frustrating part about life, isn't it? You intend to do this, but then that happens. You have plans to finish up these things, but then those things (or those people) interrupt you. Just when you're in the groove, the phone rings, the emergency email rings, and the urgent text buzzes. Productivity is always one emergency away from exploding. Even if we get today's list done, there's always another list waiting for us tomorrow.

This, by contrast, is why I adore GOD. The eternal GOD always gets his to-do list done. As the all-knowing GOD, he is never surprised by the events of life. As the all-powerful GOD, he never runs into a situation he can't take care of. As the eternal GOD, he never runs out of time to finish up his tasks.

Paul wrote that the GOD who saved us by his grace **"created** [us] **in Christ Jesus to do good works, which God prepared in advance for us to do"** (Ephesians 2:10). GOD has a list of good works for you to do. They might interrupt your plans for the day, but that's no reason to panic. Just remember that while our productivity is fleeting, GOD's is perfect. That truth can make all of us, even Kim, extremely happy.

Success is fleeting, but GOD is forever

Pastor Mike Novotny

One of the worst parts about being a middle-aged runner in the 21st century is that you know you're getting slower. Thanks to the data on my running app, I have objective data to prove that I'm slowing down. It's very possible that my greatest athletic success is completely in the past.

The temporary nature of success is a frustrating part of life, isn't it? We never truly know if our grades will get better (or worse), if our church will need extra chairs (or have enough pew space for people to lie down), or if our business will make money (or close its doors). Success is fleeting, uncertain, and anything but guaranteed. This can be a hard truth to swallow as you enter the final decades of life.

This, by contrast, is why I adore GOD. The eternal GOD never has to live off of his past success. No, GOD was glorious to Moses, Isaiah, and John in the past; is glorious to every soul that seeks him in the present; and will be glorious to every eye that sees him in the future. **"Jesus Christ is the same yesterday and today and forever"** (Hebrews 13:8).

That is gloriously good news. The best part of our lives—being with GOD, not earthly success—is the one thing that will never change. Yes, the young runner might pass us by, the old ways of business might not work, and our church's biggest attendance might already be in the books; but with Jesus we still have a thrilling future because our GOD is forever!

Health is fleeting, but GOD is forever

Pastor Mike Novotny

Unless my doctor is lying to me, my body isn't getting any better. My 6'3" frame has compressed to 6'2" (on a good day), a bad sign for my curling spine. The jokes about how atrociously I eat yet how impressive my cholesterol is are no longer quite as funny now that the cholesterol is a concern. And here's the kicker—this week I strained a back muscle . . . playing ping-pong!

Have you been there? Are you living proof of Paul's belief that our bodies are in **"bondage to decay"** (Romans 8:21)? Do your joints find it harder to wake up in the morning? Has your mind given up its ability to memorize names, faces, and Bible passages? Do you need "readers" to unfuzz these words or hearing aids to grasp the pastor's message? Age, in a thousand ways, is our enemy.

This, by contrast, is why I adore GOD. The eternal GOD who flexed his muscle at the Red Sea and had the power to raise his Son from the grave still has enough strength to fight against your every spiritual enemy. There is no challenge you're facing, no temptation you're denying, and no demon you're resisting that he's not strong enough to overcome.

Paul urges us, **"Be strong in the Lord and in his mighty power"** (Ephesians 6:10). So don't fret if age is taking its toll on you. Your strength will never fade if your strength is the eternal GOD.

Comfort is fleeting, but GOD is forever

Pastor Mike Novotny

"Can I put on my comfies?" That question is asked nearly every night in my home. When Kim or I come home from work, we ache for that moment when we can change out of the teacher/pastor clothes and put on the stretchy pants and fuzzy sweatshirts. Few things feel better than feeling comfortable.

One of the problems with life is that it's rarely comfortable. From uncomfortable shoes to uncomfortable situations to uncomfortable conversations, it's rare that we can truly relax and let things go. If Jesus called people to **"take up their cross"** and follow him, we probably shouldn't expect a stretchy-pants kind of life (Mark 8:34).

This, by contrast, is why I adore GOD. Because GOD is offering us eternal comfort. One day, very soon, Jesus will return and every uncomfortable moment will be over. The discomfort of death will pass. The wincing of pain will be gone too. The reign of discomfort will end, and Jesus will make all things new (Revelation 21:4,5). Even now, our Savior invites us to **"be still, and know that I am God"** (Psalm 46:10).

Can you even fathom it? When we see Jesus, we will put on eternal comfort, happiness that will never end. Bodily aches and relational pains will be locked in the past. Our forever future will be one of rest, relaxation, and indescribable comfort. Few things—not even stretchy pants—could feel better than that!

Control is fleeting, but GOD is forever

Pastor Mike Novotny

I learned from a local doctor how common it is for teenage girls to cut themselves. Self-harm might seem like odd behavior, but the doctor's reasoning made sense: "They want something they can control." Many young women are dealing with parents they can't control (will they divorce?), friends they can't control (will they share my secrets?), and a future they can't control (will the college accept me?); so they turn to something they have total control of.

I've never been tempted to self-harm in that way, but I do understand the frustration of feeling out of control.

Do you lose sleep thinking about the things you can't control? Does anxiety consume you when you don't know the future of your career, your chemo results, or your children's choices? In a broken world, our fleeting ability to control things is frustrating.

This, by contrast, is why I adore GOD. The apostle Paul once said of our Savior, **"By the power that enables him to bring everything under his control . . ."** (Philippians 3:21). Note the word "everything." There's nothing you're dealing with that's out of Jesus' grasp. Instead of turning to self-harm, we can turn ourselves to the Holy One who has everything under his control. Whether it's wonderful or painful, Jesus has your whole world in his hands and uses it to draw you closer to GOD.

Friend, there's no reason to fear, no matter how helpless you feel. The eternal GOD has things completely under control.

Rockin' to the oldies

Jason Nelson

My apologies to any of you who don't have oldies yet. You will. I think often of my former students who are trapped in my mind the way they looked in the '70s, '80s, '90s, and '00s. *Nice hair!* I know they don't look that way anymore. I know that aging is stalking them and they have changed. I'm not sure if we would recognize each other if we ran into each other on the street. Aging catches up with all of us. That's why we get to a point in life where we enjoy a little trip down memory lane.

When my wife and I are forced to accept the ravages of aging, we say to each other, "We had our turn to be young and beautiful." Hearing an old song makes it seem like it was just yesterday. But a look in the mirror reminds us it wasn't yesterday. That's why I don't go to class reunions. I don't want to hear an old friend ask, "Oh, buddy, what happened to you?" I don't want to land in the ER because I busted out my best dance moves one last time. I'll do my rockin' where no one can see me. And I'll remember God's promise: **"Even when you're old, I'll take care of you. Even when your hair turns gray, I'll support you. I made you and will continue to care for you. I'll support you and save you"** (Isaiah 46:4 GW).

What are we *for*?
Jason Nelson

We Christians often state what we're against. That way of arguing is called polemics. It's taking others down by picking apart their belief systems. Sometimes we need to object when people are wrongheaded. Other times we are forced to defend ourselves when people object to us. That is called apologetics. We are quick to defend our faith. And if we are convinced that we are in a hostile environment, we become Christian minutemen and women ready to discharge our duties and become offensive and defensive.

I don't think we need to be either of those things very often if we are prepared to do the work of evangelists. The Bible teaches us to win people over with the love of Jesus. No one is argued into heaven. Anyone can engage in combat. That's just making noise. We distinguish ourselves when we show people a better way. Isaiah spoke eloquently of the work of an evangelist (Isaiah 61). He said it's when we proclaim good news to the poor. When we bind up the brokenhearted and free the captives from their guilt. It's when we are willing to comfort all who mourn and bestow on people beauty instead of ashes. It's when we anoint folks with the oil of joy and wrap them up in a garment of praise instead of dumping on them in a spirit of despair. I don't think people will want to argue with us if they are experiencing the Lord's favor.

I'll be happy when . . .

Pastor Matt Ewart

I'll be happy when I'm done with school. I'll be happy when I'm married. I'll be happy when I have kids. I'll be happy when the kids leave the house. I'll be happy when I get a job. I'll be happy when I retire.

I'll be happy when . . . ?

As I think about it, I say those words a lot more than I realize. I often let my present happiness be determined by a future condition that might not even happen. And as I pause to think about it, why would I make my happiness depend on an uncertain condition in the future? I think my personal and emotional well-being are too important to chance on something like that.

More than that, God points to the conditions for my happiness as far different: **"Consider it pure joy . . . whenever you face trials of many kinds"** (James 1:2-4).

Let's try this out. See if you can say this next sentence out loud: I'll be happy when I face difficulties that complicate multiple areas of my life at the same time.

The older you get, the more you realize that it was during the difficult seasons of life that God grew you the most. It's when you were stretched thin that he made your faith more resilient and your purpose more determined.

Perhaps "when" has been an unnecessary obstacle to the joy and happiness right in front of you. Let God set the conditions for your happiness. He says that even in difficult times, he is working out something good.

Remember, you are blessed

Andrea Delwiche

When did you last contemplate the blessings you've received from God? Have you thought about it like this psalmist? **"Surely you have granted him unending blessings and made him glad with the joy of your presence. For the king trusts in the Lᴏʀᴅ; through the unfailing love of the Most High he will not be shaken"** (Psalm 21:6,7).

Do you realize that God's face is turned toward you with love and attention? His blessing is present even when you forget or turn your attention away.

As followers of Jesus, we are conduits of God's blessings to other people. When I forget that I *am* blessed, I may wound people rather than bless them. This makes life so hard for those around me! At such times I'm wronging them in a twofold sense. I rob them of the joy God intends them to experience, and I'm not extending additional blessing to them as followers of Christ.

I desire to live a life of peace flowing from God's deep love and blessing. I want to contribute to this blessing in the lives of others. When we live in God's peace, we are not shaken, even when the world around us is rocked to its core.

Holy Spirit, I've been blessed eternally. Bathe me in an awareness of the blessing and love I receive from you. Assist me as I try to remember my own blessedness and try to bless others. Help me be more consistent. Let me grow and reflect your light so that blessing shines out from me to others. Amen.

Unstoppable

Jason Nelson

Let's say you're a contestant on *Jeopardy*. One of the categories is "The Bible." Right in your wheelhouse. When it's your turn, you get your swag on and say, "Alex, I'll take 'The Bible' for $1,000." It's a DAILY DOUBLE! You risk it all. The clue is, "A wise man." You confidently ask, "Who is Solomon?" Alex says, "No, I'm sorry. The correct question is, "Who is Gamaliel?" You try not to look dumbfounded but think to yourself, "Gamaliel? Never heard of him."

Gamaliel was a respected rabbi and leader of the Jewish Sanhedrin when Christianity was in its infancy. The teachings of Christ were misunderstood. The apostles were healing many, and that made the Pharisees jealous. They wanted to kill this thing in its cradle. Gamaliel spoke up: **"Leave these men alone! Let them go! For if their purpose or activity is of human origin, it will fail. But if it is from God, you will not be able to stop these men; you will only find yourselves fighting against God"** (Acts 5:38,39).

And here we are proving Gamaliel right. The apostles never stopped teaching the good news of Jesus. Christianity spread from one person to another, from house church to house church, from nation to nation, continent to continent, from their millennium to ours. Jesus is from God. We are living proof that when something is from God, no one can stop it. Now it's our turn to keep it going.

Be ready

Pastor Jon Enter

As a Christian, you'll stick out when you don't bash Jessica in office gossip, when you don't mock Randy's new fashion disaster, when you don't join the guys at the gentlemen's club because true gentlemen don't go there.

You can simply say, "I'm not comfortable with that." And then be ready. Someone might say, "Why?" And you can be like Peter.

Peter was a pastor who learned personally from Jesus basically every day for a couple of years. He gives this guidance: **"Always be prepared to give an answer to everyone who asks you to give the reason for the hope that you have. But do this with gentleness and respect"** (1 Peter 3:15). Notice Peter doesn't say be ready to pick a fight. There are times for that. That's reserved for times when people are unapologetic in sin. But in this case, when someone's engaged you by asking why you live the way you live, don't be confrontational. Share the reason for the hope you have. Tell that person why you live differently. The answer is Jesus.

Jesus changes everything. His death on a cross changes everything. His conquering the grave changes everything. His preparing a place for you in heaven changes everything. Because of Jesus' incredible love, you value what Jesus values.

Guess what else Jesus values? Jesus values the person who asks you, "Why?" So be ready to tell about the hope that you have. Be ready to tell about Jesus.

They use Jesus against us

Jason Nelson

Maybe Jesus was having a bad day when he told a story where the hero was a dishonest manager. Maybe he felt discouraged by what he was up against when he said, **"Worldly people are more clever than spiritually-minded people when it comes to dealing with others"** (Luke 16:8 GW). Spiritually minded people can be easy marks for dishonest, worldly people.

This is our original sin: We put ourselves first. This is the power of the gospel in us: We don't like that about ourselves. Jesus calls on us to rise above self-interest, and he showed us how to do it. For his sake, we don't want to act out of self-interest. So, when the dark side wants to manipulate us, it appeals to that desire in us. It twists our logic into a pretzel to convince us that by acting in its interests, we are really rising above self-interest. Follow me?

That's how disreputable causes get our money. They tell us if we give it to them, we are rising above self-interest. That's how dishonest politicians get our vote. They tell us if we vote for them, we are rising above self-interest. That's why we sweet-talk others. That's how vulnerable souls get into all kinds of trouble. I'm sorry to say this, but children of light can learn something from the world. We need to be as shrewd as the people in it. We shouldn't be scammers. We just need to wise up.

Be an ambassador
Pastor Jon Enter

I was once called the Ambassador of New Ulm, Minnesota. Are you impressed? I was a teenager working a fast-food drive-through. I told a customer enthusiastically about some sights to see in my hometown. My excitement gave him excitement to explore the city. Ambassadors promote what's great about their city/country so others want to see it.

Two thousand years ago, a pastor named Paul wrote to Christians in Corinth and encouraged them: **"We are therefore Christ's ambassadors, as though God were making his appeal through us. . . . Be reconciled to God"** (2 Corinthians 5:20).

As Christ's ambassadors, you promote Jesus' love so others want to experience it. Too often, Christians are viewed as people who are AGAINST things. We're anti this. We reject that. It's true that we're set apart by God to live differently. But it's better to be known for what we're for. We're for Jesus. We're for forgiveness. We're for life being different, having meaning, having peace through Christ. That's something to be excited about. That's what others are yearning for, whether they realize it or not.

Be an ambassador for Christ. It's easier to live your Christian faith when your focus is living FOR something rather than AGAINST something. Live for God.

People will notice. Proclaim the joy you have being reconciled to God, having your life restored into a right relationship with Christ. May your excitement in God's grace be used by the Spirit to connect other people's lives to Christ.

Rich

Sarah Habben

For years my husband and I took a perverse pride in *not* owning a cell phone. We reasoned that everyone else had one, so if we broke down on the highway, eventually someone would pull over. A couple years ago, we finally joined the smartphone crowd. I love my humble Android. Directions, pictures, music, books, friends, facts . . . all in the palm of my hand.

What can't you live without? Your smartphone? Your big-screen TV? Your bed (said my 13-year-old)?

Such treasures we have! But when do treasures become treacherous? Jesus warns us: **"Do not store up for yourselves treasures on earth, where moths and vermin destroy, and where thieves break in and steal. But store up for yourselves treasures in heaven. . . . For where your treasure is, there your heart will be also"** (Matthew 6:19-21).

When a tool with a limited lifespan becomes your biggest treasure, watch out. If you can't possibly be happy until your current iPhone or paycheck is replaced with the bigger, better version, watch out. You're flirting with discontent and its cousins: envy, worry, greed. A quest for material wealth can so easily drag us into spiritual poverty.

What's the remedy? To turn in repentance to our Savior who gave up everything so we might be rich. Not 401(k) rich. But rich as we await an inheritance no money can buy: a pain-free, sorrow-free, joy-filled eternity. And rich in generosity as we use our fleeting earthly blessings to share this sure hope of our hearts.

I need a heart transplant

Linda Buxa

Whenever I hear people say, "Follow your heart," I kind of want to scream. I'm not trying to offend you if you've ever said that. It's more because that advice makes me take an honest look at myself, which is not something I really enjoy.

You see, deep down I know what a dope I really am. Left to my own devices, I'll put my subjective interests and comfort first. I'll strategize and rationalize and do my best to cover up my flaws. You probably know that's true about you too.

This shouldn't be a surprise. After all, the truth is that **"out of the heart come evil thoughts—murder, adultery, sexual immorality, theft, false testimony, slander"** (Matthew 15:19).

The big problem is that, on our own, we can't do anything to change our hearts. They're separated from God by our failures and sins and selfishness.

That's where, thankfully, God stepped in to change our situation. He sent Jesus to live for us and to die for us and to live again to defeat death forever. When we're baptized and believe in Jesus, God promises, **"I will give you a new heart and put a new spirit in you; I will remove from you your heart of stone and give you a heart of flesh"** (Ezekiel 36:26).

Thanks to him, we never have to follow our own hearts ever again. We get to follow God's heart.

Your faith family tree

Ann Jahns

People have always been fascinated with tracing their genealogies and filling in the leaves on their family trees. There's something comforting about knowing where you came from and the history of the people who helped you get there.

As intriguing as tracing our biological genealogies is, I think it would be even more interesting to trace our faith genealogies. Who first shared Jesus with you? Was it a parent or another relative? or a friend or coworker or teacher? Many of us grew up in families where faith was not a priority. It was not a given that our parents or grandparents faithfully took us to church or led us by the hand to Sunday school. Perhaps no one read devotions to us at home or prayed with us at bedtime. So maybe God placed someone else in your life who shared with you the hope you have in Jesus.

Thankfully, we can trace our faith genealogies back thousands of years to God's people in the Old Testament. In Psalm 78:5,6, it says that God **"commanded our ancestors to teach** [his laws] **to their children, so the next generation would know them, even the children yet to be born, and they in turn would tell their children."**

So who first shared God's love with you? Thank that person today if possible. Because of his or her deep love for you, God's grace, and Jesus' sacrifice on the cross, you will enjoy eternity in heaven.

Who can you share God's love with today? Go on—you can be a leaf on someone's faith family tree.

Jesus walks with you
Andrea Delwiche

"The LORD is my shepherd, I lack nothing. He makes me lie down in green pastures, he leads me beside quiet waters, he refreshes my soul. He guides me along the right paths for his name's sake. Even though I walk through the darkest valley, I will fear no evil. . . . Surely your goodness and love will follow me all the days of my life, and I will dwell in the house of the LORD forever" (Psalm 23:1-4,6).

Psalm 23 is comforting and a witness to God's faithfulness at life's end. It's also so much more. We *live* in the valley of the shadow of death. Each day brings threats to us and those we love. The valley of the shadow is our home address while we walk this earth.

But here's a great thing. It doesn't matter. Because we also walk with the One who passionately loves us and searches every day to bring us pastures of renewal for our bodies and souls. And so the valley of the shadow is also a place of growth and green grass.

He knows what this place is like—he's walked through the same valley. It was his home address too. But he also knows that this is the beginning, not the end for us, and he gives us rest and good things that help us grow more like him even through disaster.

To what green pasture or quiet water is Jesus leading you? *Oh, Lord, let me live into your offered rest!*

October

All Scripture is God-breathed and is useful for teaching,
rebuking, correcting and training in righteousness.

2 Timothy 3:16

Who is Jesus? Our Prophet!

Pastor Mike Novotny

On the Sunday before Jesus' death, there was a question echoing off the massive stones of the temple—"Who is this man the crowds are praising?" Here was the answer—**"This is Jesus, the prophet from Nazareth in Galilee"** (Matthew 21:11).

Do you break out in praise because Jesus is a prophet? You would if you remembered what a prophet is. In the Greek language, a prophet is someone who hears from God and then "speaks out" the truth. So when this passage says that Jesus is "the prophet," it means that he always speaks the truth about your life.

In a way, that truth hurts. I'm guessing you like being judged for your critical words, called out for your selfish attitude, and corrected for your lazy behavior as much as I do. Everything in us wants to hire our inner lawyer and find some technical reason why our actions weren't that bad. But prophets speak the truth, which is exactly what Jesus is doing when he calls us selfish sinners.

But in another way, that truth helps. Because Jesus, the prophet, speaks the truth about grace. He says that through his blood we are part of God's family. We are forgiven. We are loved. We are cherished. We are filled with his Spirit. We are going to be okay.

That's good news. Because Jesus isn't just a person. Jesus is our Prophet.

Who is Jesus? Our Priest!
Pastor Mike Novotny

In 2014 a gunman opened fire at a military base in Texas, tragically murdering three people. But there would have been more if it hadn't been for Danny. When the shots first rang out, military personnel crowded behind a closed door, but the door wouldn't lock. That's when Danny Ferguson ran to the door and held it shut so the shooter couldn't get inside. Before he left, the frustrated gunman fired at the door, killing Danny, making him a sacrifice who saved many lives.

That heroic strength reminds me of Jesus. Before sin broke down the door and separated you from God forever, Jesus set up his strong cross, unwilling to budge, even if it cost him his life. **"He sacrificed for their sins once for all when he offered himself"** (Hebrews 7:27).

I have to imagine that the survivors from that military base thank God for the sacrifice that gave them life. In the same way, let us wake up each day with gratitude, knowing that today we have life with God through the cross of Christ. There is no breaking news that can separate us from his amazing love. There is no critic or bully who can change our status as redeemed, treasured, and cherished children of God. There is no devil strong enough to bust down the cross-blocked door and snatch us out of our Savior's hand.

That's good news. That's what it means when we say that Jesus is our Priest.

Who is Jesus? Our King!

Pastor Mike Novotny

Have you ever read the Old Testament book of Zechariah? (It's okay to be honest.) Zechariah isn't quite as famous as Philippians, is it? But it's worth your time. If you ever wonder if you're going to make it through this life, if you'll conquer your struggles and habits and shame and fears, if you feel like you're losing the fight to hopelessness and exhaustion, then read the book of Zechariah and remember what it means that Jesus is your King.

"Rejoice greatly, Daughter Zion! Shout, Daughter Jerusalem! See, your king comes to you, righteous and victorious, lowly and riding on a donkey, on a colt, the foal of a donkey. . . . He will proclaim peace to the nations. . . . As for you, because of the blood of my covenant with you, I will free your prisoners. . . . The LORD their God will save his people on that day as a shepherd saves his flock. They will sparkle in his land like jewels in a crown. How attractive and beautiful they will be!" (Zechariah 9:9-11,16,17).

I told you! Zechariah is a worthy read! It reminds you that King Jesus is righteous (he never does wrong), victorious (he conquers your sin), and lowly (he's humble enough to listen to you and die for you). He proclaims peace to you (no matter what your race/nation), sets you free (from sin, death, and hell), and makes you as beautiful as a sparkling jewel in a crown.

That's good news. That's what it means when the book of Zechariah says that Jesus is our King.

october 4

On being the favorite
Jason Nelson

One of the nicest things anyone ever said about me was that I was the favorite. We don't hear that very often, and it's a hard thing to accept. Showing favoritism is generally frowned upon even by God. **"My brothers and sisters, believers in our glorious Lord Jesus Christ must not show favoritism"** (James 2:1). Showing favoritism can cause problems if it leads to treating some people better than others. But being the favorite is empowering! It's thrilling! It's motivating! It means that someone we admire thinks we're special. It takes a very gracious person to convince you that maybe you really are the favorite. You never want to let that person down.

I gave each of my children many opportunities to be my favorite. All of my grandchildren are my favorites, and I spoil them to prove it. I've been married to my favorite wife for over 40 years and never wanted a different one. And you are my favorite readers.

God shows favoritism to all of us. He said, **"Out of all the peoples on the face of the earth, the Lord has chosen you to be his treasured possession"** (Deuteronomy 14:2). He convinced us to believe in him and that we are his dearest treasures. He does great things in each of our lives because we are special to him. We live each day with shameless awareness of his undeserved love, and we just can't thank him enough.

A joyful welcome
Andrea Delwiche

"You are a hiding place for me; you preserve me from trouble; you surround me with shouts of deliverance" (Psalm 32:7 ESV).

The joyful deliverance described by David in this psalm comes after a time of separation from God. The Lord waited to deepen his relationship with David while David increased the separation from the One who loved him perfectly.

Separation from God causes agony—physical and spiritual. Earlier in the psalm David speaks of his body wasting away. His strength is dried up like in the heat of summer. Lethargic, lifeless, despondent—cut off from his power source.

When he finally acknowledges his wrongdoing and turns to God, the welcome is deafening. God's comfort for David isn't just quiet, soothing words but shouts and glad cries. Picture a baseball player returning to the dugout after a home run or a child running up to a grandparent. God is enthusiastic and all-encompassing in his joy.

What's true about God's embrace of David is true for you as well. Jesus' stories are full of references to God's longing for his distant children—a father runs to greet his lost son, angels rejoice over a sinner who repents, and Jesus' own plaintive words: **"How often I have longed to gather your children together, as a hen gathers her chicks under her wings, and you were not willing"** (Matthew 23:37).

And know this. When you return to God, there is no scolding or shaming. He will not give you a cold shoulder or remind you of your failings. He will welcome you. Instantly.

october 6

Jesus is worth the hype
Pastor Mike Novotny

During the collectibles craze of the late 1980s, I realized that if my brother and I hadn't opened his original Star Wars toys, they would have been worth tens of thousands of dollars! That's why, when Star Wars released a new line of figures in the early 90s, I bought them by the dozens, stored them carefully in boxes, and waited for the riches to come rolling in. Apparently, however, I wasn't the only kid investing in action figures. The market was flooded with collectors like me, increasing supply and decreasing demand. Decades later, after moving my collection multiple times, I sold the entire lot at a garage sale for a shamefully low price. Despite my audacious dreams, those toys weren't worth the hype.

Life is a lot like that. When you're little, you assume that getting your own car or setting your own bedtime or making five figures will produce instant happiness. Even as we age, we assume marriage, having kids, or retiring will be all we need; but earthly blessings rarely live up to the hype.

Thankfully, our God is better than anything this world offers. Jeremiah wrote, **"[God's] compassions never fail. They are new every morning; great is your faithfulness"** (Lamentations 3:22,23). As the years go by, our spiritual investment in God only increases in value. Every morning adds to his mercy, and every evening adds to his faithfulness.

Friend, you will never regret the time you spend thinking about God. In a world of uncertain investments, our eternal Father is absolutely worth the hype.

You're in a competition
Pastor Clark Schultz

It's amazing to see Olympic athletes compete. It's breathtaking to watch them perform in their events. But how did those athletes get to that point? By eating Twinkies and Cool Ranch Doritos (the best Dorito flavor there is)? No. They took advantage of every effort they had to train and to get stronger, mentally and physically.

"Make every effort to enter through the narrow door" (Luke 13:24). When Jesus told a crowd of listeners to "make every effort," he was saying the same thing. The original Greek word ἀγωνίζομαι *(anonidzomai)* speaks of working hard, as if you're in a competition. So is Jesus advocating we go out and work on our balance beam routines? No. He's letting us know that we're in competition with the devil, the world, and our own sinful self. There are voices that whisper to us that God's Word is outdated; do what feels right; you don't need to listen to parents, boss, or pastor. We need to make every effort to be in the Word so we can ignore those whispered temptations.

The fact that you're reading this now shows you're making an effort. After you finish, start thinking of what your next option to grow in the Word will be. Small group? Women's Bible study? Family devotion? Let's be clear; we're not "earning" our way to heaven. That's only through Jesus.

Our goal is to be strong in his Word, and that will give us the balance needed in the competition of life.

After the feasting
Christine Wentzel

What do you suppose happened after the feasting for the lost son's return? In Jesus' parable in Luke chapter 15, we learn it wasn't a happy time had by all.

According to our definition of fairness, we can understand the anger and resentment by the older sibling who saw his fool of a brother being welcomed home like a king and given more riches. Who can't relate to following the rules and not "seeing" any reward?

"His father said to him, 'My child, you're always with me. Everything I have is yours. But we have something to celebrate, something to be happy about. This brother of yours was dead but has come back to life. He was lost but has been found'" (Luke 15:31,32 GW).

What does all that worldly wealth for both brothers mean in terms of eternal life?

To those faithful children of the Father, consider the riches of protection, safety, comfort, provision, growth in faith, and love both now and in eternity. Extend that wholesome goodness to the returned lost child who still feels the shame of a corrupted past. Teach him or her godly contentment and the joy of living in a Christ-like community.

To those once-lost children, your sins along with the guilt and shame are forgiven—your second chance is made possible by the blood of Christ. Ask the Holy Spirit to strengthen your faith. Take the next returned child under your wing and demonstrate abiding joy over their eternal homecoming!

Triggers and truth are tricky

Pastor Daron Lindemann

Your Facebook post isn't liked as much as you want, so it triggers feelings of low self-worth and failure. Adjustments to routines trigger anxiety. Health concerns trigger fears.

Have you ever pushed a button on your screen and nothing happens? So you push it harder, again and again! You keep pushing it, holding it down. Triggers aren't meant to be held down. They are one-time shots to get your attention.

Dig into these psalm verses for three key actions when it comes to triggers: Reaction. Reassurance. Response.

"Hear my cry, O God; listen to my prayer. From the ends of the earth I call to you, I call as my heart grows faint; lead me to the rock that is higher than I. For you have been my refuge, a strong tower against the foe. I long to dwell in your tent forever and take refuge in the shelter of your wings. For you, God, have heard my vows; you have given me the heritage of those who fear your name" (Psalm 61:1-5).

The psalmist is aware that his heart is faint, weak, and lonely. These are reactions to experiences. But he doesn't keep crying. He lets go of the trigger and holds onto the reassurances of God, who is his refuge, rock, and strong tower. This leads to his responses: calling to God, vowing obedience, and praising God's name.

Instead of letting your triggers continue to make choices for you, by faith make choices about your response based on God's truth.

You have the right words
Pastor David Scharf

"I just don't know what to say." How many of us have had that thought when someone challenges God's truth? Before Jesus sent them out, the disciples wondered the same thing. Jesus reassured them, **"Do not worry about what to say or how to say it. At that time you will be given what to say, for it will not be you speaking, but the Spirit of your Father speaking through you"** (Matthew 10:19,20).

If called on to defend your faith, do you have the right words to speak? The reformer Martin Luther stood before the most powerful man in the world, Emperor Charles V. He was commanded to retract his writings on the Bible, writings that highlighted the Bible's teaching that we go to heaven by God's grace alone because of Jesus and what he has done. Yet Luther didn't need to worry. All he needed to do was let God fight the battle with God's own powerful Word. We can do the same, even in the face of persecution.

Luther wrote in his hymn "A Mighty Fortress Is Our God": "Though devils all the world should fill, all eager to devour us, we tremble not, we fear no ill; they shall not overpower us. This world's prince may still scowl fierce as he will. He can harm us none. He's judged; the deed is done! One little word can fell him."

One little word of God is more powerful than all the attacks of the devil. You have the right words!

Faith up close

Pastor Mike Novotny

I love seeing faith up close. A while back, I received a kind invitation from the wife of a dying man. She correctly guessed that her husband was getting close to the end of his earthly road, so she invited me into their living room to share some encouragement and offer some prayers.

But I was, by far, more blessed that day. In that living room, I saw their faith up close. Death didn't scare this man or his bride. While she understandably wondered/worried about life as a widow, neither of them doubted where he was going (heaven) or how he was going to get there (Jesus). In their own words and in their own way, each of them expressed their rock-solid confidence in the Savior who had done everything to give them the hope of eternal life. They embodied the definition from the Scriptures: **"Now faith is confidence in what we hope for and assurance about what we do not see"** (Hebrews 11:1).

Sometimes we miss those up-close glimpses of faith. We forget how the Holy Spirit has connected real souls to a real Savior, defeating our fear of death and planting our feet on promises that cannot be shaken.

You don't have to wait until your final days to see faith like that. Ask a Christian friend about her hope. Ask your pastor if he fears death. Ask your grandchild if he knows he'll be with God. You might get a chance to see what I saw that day—the beauty of faith up close.

Paying the fine
Linda Buxa

As I was checking out my books at the library, I dug in my wallet. The librarian asked, "Are you getting the money to pay your $0.20 fine?"

I replied, "I sure am." After all, I wanted all the benefits of the library without any of the guilt of a fine.

"It's always the people who have a $0.20 fine who pay, and the ones with the $80 fine don't," she laughed.

Admittedly, a $0.20 library fine is a pretty small thing, and the consequences of returning your library book late are minimal. But a relationship with God isn't like the library. The consequences of the most minor infraction are eternally serious: **"Whoever keeps the whole law and yet stumbles at just one point is guilty of breaking all of it"** (James 2:10).

With God, though, I can't just dig in my wallet and pay him for my sins. I can't do enough good things to make up for even the smallest bad thing I did, because even one sin separates me from him.

That's why God sent Jesus, because I can't fix it, and neither can you. We needed someone to pay the fine for our sins. And Jesus did all of that, all for us. Now we get all the benefits of a relationship with God with none of the guilt.

P.S. If you have an $80 library fine, talk to your librarian. Many will forgive late fees and welcome you back. Just like Jesus does every day.

Build me up

Sarah Habben

I tell my kids that people are like building blocks. Our words can build them up or knock them down. When conversations with a sibling take a negative turn, I sometimes start singing an oldie: "So build me up (*build me up*), Buttercup . . ."

It's easy to recognize negative patterns in our children's interactions. But those very same patterns can gnaw at the foundation of our adult relationships, weakening the base, chipping away its beautiful design.

Maybe it's your marriage. After the euphoria of courtship and honeymoon, you got so comfortable that you started taking your spouse for granted. Contempt wasn't far behind. The person you once saw with such starry eyes now seems . . . less than. Unwelcome thoughts fly into your mind and out of your mouth like popcorn in a pot with no lid.

Or maybe it's your roommate, a parent, a coworker. You're in danger of knocking down your relationship one eye roll or one sarcastic comment at a time.

Our Savior died for those sins. And he empowers us to regard others as he does—not with contempt but with a craftsman's loving eye. **"Do not let any unwholesome talk come out of your mouths, but only what is helpful for building others up according to their needs"** (Ephesians 4:29).

Stack a new brick. Acknowledge that differences aren't bad. They add flavor. They challenge us. They remind us that there's a place and purpose for us all in God's kingdom.

God knows

Pastor Mike Novotny

If my research is right, there are 8 billion sparrows on earth, and God knows every feather on every flying creature. In addition, there are 7.8 billion people on earth, and God knows every hair on every head (including the clump stuck in your brush!). Jesus once said, **"Are not five sparrows sold for two pennies? Yet not one of them is forgotten by God. Indeed, the very hairs of your head are all numbered"** (Luke 12:6,7).

The fact that God knows everything about everything is why we fear him. Because God knows what goes on in your mind. God knows the words you typed into your phone . . . and then backspaced because they were so bad. God knows what you say on the car ride after church. God knows how you treat the people under your roof, no matter how much religious art hangs on your walls. God knows.

Which is why God knows that we need grace. Jesus continued, **"Don't be afraid; you are worth more than many sparrows"** (Luke 12:7). The reason we don't fall apart with fear of what God knows is because God has given us worth. When Jesus, the Lamb who was slain, erased your sins, he made you worthy to stand in God's presence. The God who counts every bird and every hair stopped counting the reasons why you shouldn't be with him. Instead, his face shines on you and is gracious to you.

What a gift! What a God!

I promise
Pastor David Scharf

How many promises have you made in your lifetime? How many have you broken? You've probably made enough promises to realize that they get broken all the time. Sometimes we're afraid because others have hurt us with their dishonest words. Sometimes we're skeptical of the promise because of the one promising or simply because the promises made seem too good to be true. Can you ever really feel comfortable believing someone when they give you their word?

What about when God makes promises? *"Go ahead, Peter, step out onto the water. . . . Abraham, your 90-year-old wife will bear a child. . . . My dear child, I have forgiven your sins. . . . Out of the billions of people who walk the face of the earth, I have you in my sights. . . . I love you. . . ."* Are you ever afraid that God will change his mind and not keep his promises? You're not alone. So did Peter. So did Abraham. Then what's the answer? The answer is to look at the cross and remember who God is. He's the One willing to suffer and die to save you. The answer is to remember Jesus' words: **"For no word from God will ever fail"** (Luke 1:37). The answer is to look at his track record for Peter, for Abraham, and for you. Not one failed promise—ever!

Our Lord will keep every word he has spoken, including your eternal life in heaven. After all, he promises it.

The earth is the Lord's

Andrea Delwiche

Sometimes I need to be reminded who this world belongs to. Sometimes it seems that it belongs to everyone except me; people whose ideas of how to live life are diametrically opposed to my own. Sometimes I think the world belongs to me, and I would like everyone to think the way I think and act the way I act.

But **"the earth is the Lord's, and everything in it, the world, and all who live in it; for he founded it on the seas and established it on the waters"** (Psalm 24:1,2). The earth is the Lord's, and all that is in the earth is also the Lord's. This is unequivocally good. He founded it. He established it. He knows what makes it function successfully, and he loves all the creatures who dwell in it; even those who don't love and appreciate him, or me. He loves those whom I don't love and appreciate. All people are safe and treasured in his hands.

This is a comfort when I feel alienated. It's a reminder when I feel authoritarian. It gives perspective in those hours and days when everything is falling apart and I can't grasp the loose ends much less braid it all back together.

The earth is the Lord's. I belong to the Lord. You belong to the Lord. Because this is true, you and I are safe in the Lord's hands.

Why I love Baptism

Pastor Mike Novotny

Do you ever stop to thank God for your baptism? Do you have your baptism date marked on your calendar and your annual baptism party planned?

According to Paul, you should, because Baptism is one of the greatest gifts you have ever received. "[God] **saved us through the washing of rebirth and renewal by the Holy Spirit, whom he poured out on us generously through Jesus Christ our Savior"** (Titus 3:5,6). Notice that language. God saved us "through the washing," a reference to Baptism. I might say, "The lobby is through that door," which means that you use the door to get to the lobby. Here Paul says, "Salvation is through Baptism," which means you use Baptism to get saved. What a gift!

There are other ways for Jesus to save you. Perhaps you were saved through the Word in a conversation or personal devotion or pastor's sermon and were baptized afterward: **"He chose to give us birth through the word of truth, that we might be a kind of firstfruits of all he created"** (James 1:18). Or maybe you were like me and God first saved you through the washing, and the teaching followed to put grace on top of grace. In either case, Baptism is one of a Christian's greatest blessings.

This is why our church claps at Baptisms. Even though many of us came from less emotional church upbringings, we decided that Baptism was too beautiful for serious faces. We smile and cheer and celebrate with the angels. Why? Because we believe Paul's words. God saved us through the washing.

God always answers
Christine Wentzel

The news headline read, "Answered prayers!" Does that well-intentioned declaration really testify to the completely awesome work of God? Or does it lead someone to question why his or her prayers "weren't answered"?

We Christians say it all the time for good reason. We are ecstatic over divine love coming to our rescue. It's fuel for our faith. It's validation to our witness. It's proof of God's personal care in our lives.

But for a fellow Christian who is struggling in his or her wait (and even the unbelieving public watching us under a microscope), we can testify that the fuel, validation, and proof also come with a closed door or a command for patience. God does his best work behind the scenes of our understanding.

"Then you will call on me and come and pray to me, and I will listen to you" (Jeremiah 29:12).

Let's have the headlines read, "God always answers!" This is a statement of our sure hope that God hears every single prayer from his children. He answers every one with a yes; no; or, "I have something better." It's the yeses we crave, because we think we know what's best, especially when in crisis mode. But if we truly trust that only God knows best, that he is passionately invested in our well-being, then we will rest in his "silence" with the support of our family and friends.

The meaning of meaningless words
Pastor Daron Lindemann

Is there such a thing as a meaningless word? Words like *emergency* or *winner* demand much more attention than words like *asparagus* or *follicle*.

But the word *asparagus* could answer the question, "Which of the items on this plate is laced with rat poison?" That gives it much more meaning.

Sarcasm. Harsh criticism. Gossip. Angry arguing. Wrong words don't just hurt others. They hurt the ones who speak them. We are polluted by our own noise pollution.

To change how you speak, Jesus doesn't give you speech lessons or stick duct tape over your mouth. No, Jesus changes your heart. He fills it with his grace, his righteousness, and his words of love.

Here's how he did that. First Peter 2:23 talks about the enemies of Jesus torturing and crucifying him: **"When they hurled their insults at him, he did not retaliate; when he suffered, he made no threats. Instead, he entrusted himself to him who judges justly."**

Jesus didn't argue with his enemies or even curse them, but he prayed to his Father to forgive them. On the cross, he spoke saving words to a condemned thief and caring words to his mother. These words forgive and save you too. They mean Jesus loves you and is teaching you God's language.

Texans can detect my Midwestern accent that gives away my roots and identity. Likewise, people will be able to tell that your identity is rooted in Jesus when you love him and use his words.

Waiting on us

Jason Nelson

God must fold his everlasting arms across his chest and lean against a pearly fence post just waiting for us to try. We have a mindset to **"wait for the Lord"** (Psalm 27:14). Patience is a good thing, I guess. That's until it becomes an excuse for underperforming in life. We can rationalize that God must not be ready to bless us. So it's his fault if we fall short. Hoorah for us for waiting on him. But that can become spiritualized laziness. I think more often than not, God is waiting on us to do something: to work harder, to act smarter, to just do something. **"Does he speak and then not act? Does he promise and not fulfill?"** (Numbers 23:19). The answer is no.

Long ago, God issued the open-ended matching grant challenge: **"'Test me in this,' says the Lord Almighty, 'and see if I will not throw open the floodgates of heaven and pour out so much blessing'"** (Malachi 3:10). God is waiting on us. And he is more than generous. It doesn't matter if the currency of our effort is elbow grease, money, or ingenuity. He's not picky. When we go all out for him, he gives back even more than we bargained for. People who try are blessed. Businesses that try are blessed. Ministries that try are blessed. God's middle name is grace, and he will bless you if you try just a little. Just think of what could happen if you try a lot.

What measurement system do you use?

Andrea Delwiche

"No king is saved by the size of his army; no warrior escapes by his great strength. A horse is a vain hope for deliverance; despite all its great strength it cannot save. But the eyes of the LORD are on those who fear him, on those whose hope is in his unfailing love, to deliver them from death and keep them alive in famine" (Psalm 33:16-19).

How do you measure your importance? Probably not by the size of your army or the wealth of your horse stables. Perhaps not even by your physical strength. But most of us have ways of gauging our relative strength and importance when it comes to other people: cars, position in our company, disposable income, cultural awareness, the bands we listen to, our witty conversation, how well we are known in the social circles that are important to us—maybe our church or civic organizations. We may look at others and rank their strength and worth in comparison to our own. Sometimes we seem to come out ahead. Other times we feel sure that we fall short.

Here's a different measurement system to try. Hold all you have—or don't have—up to the Lord as an offering of love. Give it all to him—strengths and weaknesses. Stop checking to see how you (or someone else) measures up. Instead, fix your gaze on Christ.

He keeps you physically and spiritually, in feast or famine, success or failure. As an integral individual in his kingdom, you are a great treasure. He delivers you and delights over you right now and always.

Jesus stands with you
Pastor Jeremy Mattek

Young Peyton got into a fight with his sister. He was the instigator, and his mom made him stand in a corner in a time-out. While he was in the corner, his mom took a picture of him and posted it online, not because she wanted everyone to see what a crummy kid he was but because of who went to the wall and stood there with him. Dash, the family dog, walked over, sat down on the floor right next to Peyton, and didn't move until Peyton was done serving time for his punishment.

The Bible tells us the story of Jesus and a Samaritan woman. He certainly knew who the woman at the well was and that she had tried unsuccessfully to satisfy the thirsts of her heart with adultery and sinful pleasure. In the same way, he knows everything about our lives we'd prefer to keep hidden and every place we go looking for satisfaction.

Yet he didn't move when she came walking in his direction. He sat right next to her at that well and gave this woman's thirsty soul the Water of Life: **"Everyone who drinks this water will be thirsty again, but whoever drinks the water I give them will never thirst"** (John 4:13).

But he didn't just stand by her side. On the cross he took the punishment that he didn't deserve. Now she and all who believe in him have a forever home in heaven.

The true cost of following Christ

Pastor Mike Novotny

Jesus wasn't a fan of fine print. When someone from the crowds wanted to follow him, Jesus didn't get out a glossy brochure with all the blessings of believing. Instead, he admitted the true cost of being a Christian.

"When Jesus saw the crowd around him, he gave orders to cross to the other side of the lake. Then a teacher of the law came to him and said, 'Teacher, I will follow you wherever you go.' Jesus replied, 'Foxes have dens and birds have nests, but the Son of Man has no place to lay his head'" (Matthew 8:18-20). Even though this teacher of the law was ready to follow "wherever" Jesus went, our Savior still wanted him to know how hard that "going" might get.

Jesus wants you to know that too. Being a Christian will cost you. Letting go of control and letting Jesus be the Lord of your life (your schedule, your sexuality, your checkbook, your body, your worldview, your everything) will make you more uncomfortable than a homeless man without a pillow.

So why would you become (or stay) a Christian? Because Jesus is worthy. He is a treasure, a pearl of great price (Matthew 13:44-46). He is the Lamb of God who takes away your sin (John 1:29). Following Jesus is the only way to get to God (John 14:6).

Be honest with yourself about how much Jesus will cost you. But make sure to remember all that Jesus promises you. He is worthy! Jesus is worth it!

Jesus feels your pain
Pastor Jeremy Mattek

Gerdi was invited to spend a weekend with her college friends, but she didn't want to go. She had breast cancer, had lost all of her hair, and felt embarrassed to be in public or have her picture taken with her friends.

After wrestling with the decision, she decided to buy a wig, hoping no one would notice. When Gerdi arrived at the meeting place, she noticed something about her friends. They didn't have any hair on their heads! Not even a wig. The other women had met at a hair salon earlier that day and had their heads completely shaved so that Gerdi wouldn't be the only one without hair.

What kind of friends do such a thing? The best kind. The ones who are more concerned about being there for someone who is hurting than worrying about embarrassment.

Jesus knows you need a friend like that too. That's why Jesus showed up at the cross wearing thorns on his head—and not just the ones that pierced his skin. The ones that pierce your heart with guilt. The ones that make you feel weak, worthless, and broken. **"Surely he took up our pain,"** the Bible says, **"and bore our suffering"** (Isaiah 53:4).

He did this to show you and me that we will always have the very best friend who's determined to stay by our sides through everything.

Goodbye, garbage
Sarah Habben

An article in the news told how early one spring morning, Chris White found garbage strewn across the front of his farm. As he turned over one soggy box, he found a shipping receipt. So White decided to give the culprit's garbage back. He packed the trash into his truck and drove to the address on the receipt. The man who answered the door denied everything . . . until White presented the shipping receipt. What could the accused do in the face of that evidence? He sheepishly admitted his crime and unloaded his garbage from White's truck.

Our guilt over sin has a way of heaping up. It stinks. We try to dispose of it in all the wrong ways—by heaping blame on others, by excusing ourselves, by drowning it in alcohol or numbing it with drugs or an overly busy schedule. But as long as that guilt bears a receipt with our names, it will always come back to haunt us.

Enter Jesus. He didn't shrink from our stinking garbage of sin. He loaded it on his own back and took it to the cross. He died under its burden; he paid our fine. **"As far as the east is from the west, so far has he removed our transgressions from us"** (Psalm 103:12).

Our resurrected Lord won't ever come knocking at our doors to give back our guilt. Satan has no evidence to wave in our faces. Why not? Because Christ blacked out our names on those sins and entered his own.

Our garbage is gone. Only gratitude remains.

octoben 26

Give God the glory
Andrea Delwiche

Imagine you're introducing God to a friend who's never heard of him. How would you make his reputation "great" in the eyes of the other person? Where would you begin? What would you say?

What glory is due the name of the Lord in your life? Make a list. Where has God done great things to support you? Where has he protected you, provided for your daily needs, built you up? Where have you seen examples of God's beauty or provision? How would you describe your relationship with God to another person?

Have you payed attention to the signs and glory of God in the natural world? Have you noticed and praised God for a powerful thunderstorm? for the brilliant colors of the trees in fall? the bright blue of a lake? a full moon?

Perhaps you could find Psalm 29 in your Bible, take some time in creation, and start a list. **"Ascribe to the Lord, you heavenly beings, ascribe to the Lord glory and strength. Ascribe to the Lord the glory due his name; worship the Lord in the splendor of his holiness"** (verses 1,2).

Give God the glory. When we notice these things and praise God for them, we're offering God the praise he deserves. We're also establishing in our own hearts a record of God's goodness.

We have no problem complimenting the faithfulness of a good friend. We can do the same in our relationship with God. We can give God thanks and praise and bear witness to others about his faithfulness and grace.

Endless mercy

Pastor Mike Novotny

There's a song that we love to sing at our church called "His Mercy Is More." Written in 2016 by Matt Papa and Matt Boswell, the lyrics remind me of the height and width and depth and length of the love of Jesus. Take a moment to look up the song. Beautiful, isn't it?

The authors of that song shared the inspiration for the lyrics. They came from a sermon preached by a famous sinner you might know—John Newton. Newton, a former slave ship captain and the writer of the hymn "Amazing Grace," once said to his congregation, "Let not [your sin] discourage you. For if God casts out none that come to him, why should you fear? Our sins are many, but his mercies are more." Beautiful, isn't it?

But Newton didn't invent the idea of God's mercy outnumbering our sin. He was inspired by another notorious sinner, the apostle Paul, who penned, **"But where sin increased, grace increased all the more"** (Romans 5:20). Beautiful, isn't it?

But Paul wasn't sharing an original thought. He was just summarizing what Jeremiah said through his scribe: **"Because of the Lord's great love we are not consumed, for his compassions never fail. They are new every morning"** (Lamentations 3:22,23). Beautiful, isn't it?

Thank God for mercy, passed down through the ages and spoken to us!

Only one door
Pastor Clark Schultz

My wife and I are building a home. If you've ever done the same or even remodeled, you know there are many choices to be made. What flooring do we get? What color should the dining room be? The hardest choice for us involved choosing the type of doors we want. Our choices were many: four panel, six panel, solid oak, pine. We just needed something solid enough to withstand the pounding they'll take from three little boys.

When it comes to our eternity, how many choices of doors are there? ONE! And the door is Jesus. **"Make every effort to enter through the narrow door"** (Luke 13:24).

Jesus says that he is the door, and he is the only way to heaven. Others will say if you do good works, pray, fast, or do other good deeds that those will get you access to heaven. Nope! One door.

Jesus, who lived a perfect life for you and died in your place, made death a door to heaven. Your heavenly home awaits. Thank you, Jesus, for taking all the guesswork out of our eternity. When it comes to your heavenly home, one door is all that's needed—Jesus—and that's as solid as it gets!

Jesus is more painful
(and glorious) than you thought

Pastor Mike Novotny

During a recent trip to Jerusalem, I had this romantic idea for a morning run: Get up early; run from my hotel up the Mount of Olives; and watch the sunrise over the places where Jesus lived, died, and rose for me.

But I had no clue how hard that would be. To get to the finish line, I had to plunge into one valley and climb out of it. Then I had to repeat the process, a 997-foot elevation hike that left my lungs gasping for oxygen and my thighs begging for mercy.

That experience reminded me of something Jesus often said: **"Whoever wants to be my disciple must deny themselves and take up their cross and follow me"** (Mark 8:34). Following Jesus is more painful than a Jerusalem run. It's more like denying some of your deepest urges. It's more like taking up a cross.

Prioritizing Jesus in all you do will be agonizing. If the selfish part of your heart doesn't scream like my burning legs, the people around you might. Following *every* command *all* of the time is never easy. So please don't be too romantic about this journey with Jesus.

Yet please don't forget he is worth it. To be with Jesus is to be constantly loved, completely forgiven, absolutely accepted, unconditionally cherished, and eternally safe. At the end of my run, I saw the sun come up, and it was breathtaking. And at the end of your life, you will see something infinitely better—the face of God!

Nothing is more glorious—and more worth it—than that.

october 30

The day I became Jesus
Linda Buxa

A friend of mine who is a makeup artist needed people willing to let her do makeup testing. I signed up immediately. She warned me it wasn't going to be pretty—because she needed to practice what Jesus' lacerations and wounds might have looked like. She painted, sprayed, glued, and rubbed to make it look gruesome. Throughout the morning, my arm was transformed from that of a Caucasian woman to that of a Jewish man.

I couldn't help but think over and over: *This should have been me.* I've known that my whole life, but this was the first time I saw it. Because of my sin, I should have suffered, been whipped, beaten, crucified, forsaken. Then I should have died and descended into hell—and stayed there.

But I didn't. All because **"God made him who had no sin to be sin for us, so that in him we might become the righteousness of God"** (2 Corinthians 5:21).

I became like Jesus for pretend for one day, but he became me—and you—for real, taking our real punishment for us. He had real nails in his hands, real gashes on his arms, real bruises, real dirt, real drops of blood.

And then he really rose from the dead after three days, transforming us from enemies of God to children of God. To the righteousness of God.

Turn 'em loose
Jason Nelson

I've looked behind the curtains in a number of religious organizations. The people at the top seem preoccupied with pulling the levers so they can keep all the munchkins in line on the same rigid road. Eventually, the word gets out that the church is a confining place to work. I have a suggestion for ecclesiastical authorities. Send a memo to the people you supervise. Tell them, "We trained you. We trust you. You know what it's all about. Do what you think is best." Then don't have any meetings for about five years and see what happens. I say turn 'em loose. **"Because of God's immense generosity and grace, we don't have to dissect and scrutinize every action to see if it will pass muster"** (1 Corinthians 10:23 MSG).

Churches are competing with every other industry to recruit young talent. How would we attract the best and brightest if we posted our openings on CareerBuilder? *"Enterprise with eternal consequences will pay you a modest salary to play it safe."* Or, do we want smart, ambitious, and creative leaders? Do we want followers or forerunners? Would your church have hired John the Baptist?

One of my mentors told me, "The most unfair thing you can do is treat everyone the same." We are not all the same. And we shouldn't expect the same things from each other. Let's give each other permission to kick the flying monkeys off our backs and do what we think is best.

November

Give thanks to the Lord, for he is good;
his love endures forever.

1 Chronicles 16:34

The existential question
Jason Nelson

I'm going out on a limb, and I'd like to take you with me. I think it's time we shed the worn-out exoskeletons of two divine institutions. I don't know what post-partisan democracy or post-denominational Christianity might look like. But each could emerge as something prettier than what we are looking at now.

God wants us to organize our lives around church and state. They are necessary spheres of influence and seem to have the same sickness. The most partisan and parochial operatives drive wedges between people to keep their own in camp and win over a few defectors. They make distinctions among people where few differences exist. Divide and conquer is not a strategy Jesus taught. Those are marks of a slippery devil, a winner-take-all culture, and insecure egos. What happens to us if this disease is left untreated and goes to its inevitable conclusion? That is the existential question.

If you disagree, then prove me wrong. Hamlet was mistaken. It's not conscience that makes cowards of us all. It's self-preservation. That's the sin of tenured bureaucrats. There's no give in them anymore. But they need us more than we need them. Listen to Paul: **"Do nothing from selfish ambition or conceit, but in humility count others more significant than yourselves. Let each of you look not only to his own interests, but also to the interests of others"** (Philippians 2:3,4 ESV). Putting others first is what makes church and state indispensable.

Lost and found
Sarah Habben

Some years ago, "Lost" posters appeared in my city picturing a homely looking dog named Sidney. A woman vacationing in Mexico had rescued Sidney after the stray was hit by a car, paid for her vet bills, and nursed her back to health. Then the woman flew Sidney to her home city and found a willing owner. But 12 hours after moving into her new home, Sidney ran away. The original woman offered a reward, and it grew as the months ticked by . . . to a whopping $10,000. Seven months later and 60 miles away, Sidney was finally found. She was lurking around the shed of someone who threw her a hot dog every once in a while.

How does the story end? The woman, the rescuer, paid the reward . . . and adopted that unpedigreed pooch herself.

Sidney's story is ours. We may as well hang a "Lost" sign on our souls. Apart from our God, we have no worth. Even when we know and taste his love, we often skitter from his will. We prefer to live by our sinful instincts, hoarding our resources, abusing our bodies, gorging on unhealthy pastimes rather than seeking God's banquet of mercy.

But like Sidney, we've been rescued at great expense. Not $10,000 but our Savior's priceless blood and perfect life. He loves us despite ourselves. He calls us to himself in his Word. He rejoices to adopt us as his own.

"Christ also suffered once for sins, the righteous for the unrighteous, to bring you to God" (1 Peter 3:18).

We can rally around Jesus
Linda Buxa

I live in a politically diverse state. This is a bad thing because it means we get an abundance of political commercials that try to sway our vote. This is a good thing because it means we live next to and work with and talk to people who disagree on government policies, but we can rally around our love of the same football team, cheese curds, and the first 40-degree spring day.

Mind if I'm honest? Sometimes it feels like the citizens of God's kingdom behave worse than the citizens of my home state. We get all riled up about all sorts of issues and forget that we can rally around our love of Jesus—and Jesus' love for us.

This was happening back when the early Christian church was forming, and they needed to be reminded: **"For the entire law is fulfilled in keeping this one command: 'Love your neighbor as yourself.' If you bite and devour each other, watch out or you will be destroyed by each other"** (Galatians 5:14,15).

Now, I'm not suggesting that we ignore all of our differences. After all, one of the reasons that the letter to the people in Galatia was written was to hold believers accountable lovingly. Still, today is a good day to pause and remember to love one another, to pray for *all* the people who believe in Jesus, to defend them, and to speak well of them.

Won't you be my neighbor?
Pastor Clark Schultz

Tom Hanks saw some Oscar buzz for his portrayal of PBS TV icon Fred Rogers. Today's children identify more with the tune to *Daniel Tiger's Neighborhood.* But back in the day, it was "a beautiful day in the neighborhood." While wearing a red sweater and a pair of sneakers, Mr. Rogers would ask the viewers, "Won't you be my neighbor?" Being a Methodist minister, one would like to think Mr. Rogers asked that question based off Jesus' parable of the good Samaritan. Jesus told this parable to an expert in the law who had asked, **"And who is my neighbor?"** (Luke 10:29). The religious rulers like this man tended to only love and care about people in their inner circle.

This is why in Jesus' parable the priest and Levite walked on by the hurt man without helping him. The only help came from an enemy to the Jews. Jesus wants us to think about how we treat our neighbors. Do we show love to the person sitting alone at lunch? Do we join in the jokes at another's expense? Do we judge those who dress differently than us? God's law is simply summed up like this: Love God and love others as you love yourself.

We often tend to love our inner circle and ourselves more. Thankfully Jesus is the best neighbor ever. He showed love by taking our place on a cross and taking our sins on himself.

This love is what motivates us to say, show, and sing to all, "Won't you be my neighbor?"

Follow first—the hardest part of Christianity

Pastor Mike Novotny

If someone asked you the hardest part about being a Christian, what would you say? Here's what Jesus said: **"Another disciple said to him, 'Lord, first let me go and bury my father.' But Jesus told him, 'Follow me, and let the dead bury their own dead'"** (Matthew 8:21,22). This disciple seemed committed, but "first" he wanted to bury his father. Jesus' blunt answer was, "I want you to follow first."

That's the hardest part about being a Christian. Anyone can say he or she loves God, cares about the poor, agrees with forgiving others, and sees the value of faith. But the real question is what comes *first*. When you love God but also love something God forbids (like too much wine), what comes first? When you care about the poor but also have plans to invest, get a boat, and buy a new phone, what comes first? When you want to forgive in general but you don't want to forgive that specific person, what comes first? When you see the value of faith but that faith is messing with your Sunday plans, what comes first?

Be honest today and ask yourself what tends to come first in your life. What do you think about first? spend money on first? spend time on first?

The First Commandment is not just about believing in God. It's about loving, trusting, and putting God first in everything you do. That's the hardest part about following Jesus.

He insists on being first. Which is why you need to read tomorrow's devotion . . .

november 6

Follow first—the best part of Christianity
Pastor Mike Novotny

Yesterday I told you the hardest part of Christianity—Jesus commands us to prioritize God, to follow *first*. Today I want to tell you the best part of Christianity. It's hinted at in the word *follow*.

If my dictionary is correct, *follow* means, "to go after a person or to be near a person." In this case, therefore, to *follow first* means to be near Jesus. In case you don't know the beauty and glory of Jesus' name, let me explain.

Jesus is everything our hearts need. We long to be loved, and Jesus is the definition of love. We crave being safe, and Jesus has rescued us from every eternal danger and secured our place in heaven. We ache for a faithful friend, and Jesus is the friend of sinners. We grasp for something solid, a rock in the storms of life, and Jesus is the rock of our salvation. We need a king, someone who is in control and cares about his people, and Jesus is the King of glory. We need the Bread of Life, food for our souls, and Jesus is just that. **"Do not work for food that spoils, but for food that endures to eternal life, which the Son of Man will give you"** (John 6:27).

Many people are intimidated by the priorities implied in Jesus' invitation to follow first. But please don't miss what that same invitation promises. A person like you gets to be with a Savior like him.

That's the best part of Christianity.

An unknown future in the hands of a known God

Pastor David Scharf

Some describe the future as peering into the deep unknown. Anything can happen! Do you agree that no one can know how something will work out in the end?

In the most important ways, you *do* know the end. You know that you're God's child and he will guard your faith through his Word and sacraments until the day that he calls you to his side in heaven. So, in the most important way possible, you do know.

It's the less significant earthly future that we struggle with. Not knowing the future can be scary! We don't know how long our jobs will last, how long we'll have to spend with family on this earth, or how anything will turn out in this life specifically.

But God does. He says, **"'I know the plans I have for you,' declares the Lord, 'plans to prosper you and not to harm you, plans to give you hope and a future'"** (Jeremiah 29:11). Notice what God says in this passage: "*I* know the plans I have for you," not "*You* know the plans." And we may be thinking, "Well, it sure would be nice if he let us in on those plans!"

But if the One who sent his only Son to die for me knows and controls my future, then that's enough for me. Entrust an unknown future to a known God!

Actively seeking God

Andrea Delwiche

Where would you like to step out into a new adventure with the Lord and yet are held back by fear or lack of belief in what the Lord can do *for* you and *in partnership* with you? Is there a place in your life where you have a desire to serve and to live into your purpose in Christ but you feel unqualified or unfit?

Perhaps the words of Moses as the Lord called *him* into service from the burning bush could come from our own lips: **"Pardon your servant, Lord, I have never been eloquent"** (Exodus 4:10). Or we might add, "I'm not qualified or smart enough or talented enough. Please send someone else."

But, as Psalm 27 reminds us, it's God himself who is our light and salvation and strong place. He provides the power and inspiration. We have nothing to fear. **"The Lord is my light and my salvation—whom shall I fear? The Lord is the stronghold of my life—of whom shall I be afraid? My heart says of you, 'Seek his face!' Your face, Lord, I will seek"** (Psalm 27:1,8).

In fact, the news gets even better. Not only can we trust God as our light and salvation; we can actually move more deeply into relationship and friendship with him by *seeking him*.

As we do this, worries about success or failure cease. We live for God. His light and wisdom guide us and make us suited for whatever adventure he brings our way.

Developmentally able
Pastor Mike Novotny

Many years ago a woman named Tina would show up at church with her mother. Tina was in her mid-40s, but due to some cognitive disabilities, she communicated like a young child. Her frequent smile was a joy to those who met her, even if a PhD was probably not in her future.

One service, during those heavy weeks leading up to Easter, I was preaching bluntly about our sin. How bad sin is. How much it turns God's stomach. What we deserve because of it. But Tina wouldn't have it. Before I could get to the good news, Tina turned to her mother and whispered (loud enough for the pastor to hear!)—"But, Mom, Jesus died on a cross!"

What faith! Yes, my sin is bad. Yes, my life isn't good enough to earn a spot in heaven. Yes, all have fallen short of the glory of God, myself included. But Jesus died on a cross! There is more to our spiritual story than honest efforts at improving our prayers, empathy, and generosity. Our story ends with Jesus, crucified for every sin and raised so that the worst of sinners wouldn't have to live with shame.

"For the wages of sin is death, but the gift of God is eternal life in Christ Jesus our Lord" (Romans 6:23). Tina would love how fast the apostle Paul got to the second part—But the gift of God! But we have life! But Jesus died on a cross!

Listen to Paul and Tina. They're right. Thank God!

Stepping in to save the game
Linda Buxa

In the National Hockey League, an emergency goalie must be available for every game. I don't think many people knew about this rule until February 2020 when the Carolina Hurricanes' regular goalie and their backup both got hurt. The Hurricanes knew they'd probably lose, but the game had to go on. The call went up to the media room for 42-year-old dad David Ayres to suit up and step in. He made eight saves and helped the Hurricanes defeat the Toronto Maple Leafs.

What's interesting is that Ayres is actually a practice player for the Toronto Maple Leafs. That's right; Ayres was called on to help the other team win. He did his job.

Because our mistakes and sins separate us from God, we were on an opposing team—and there's no way we could win. Because God knew that—and because he is a God of mercy—he called on Jesus, who was sitting in the throne room of heaven, to suit up in human flesh and step into our world. Jesus willingly did that. He came to earth to be on our team; he played for us and secured the outcome for us. He did his job. Now we get to celebrate his hard-fought win and give God all the credit.

"Thanks be to God! He gives us the victory through our Lord Jesus Christ" (1 Corinthians 15:57).

You have what it takes

Pastor Daron Lindemann

The joy of a couple becoming pregnant is soon replaced with morning sickness. Then pregnancy tiredness. Then a baby convinced that the world revolves around her. "What did we get ourselves into?" they wonder wearily.

Over the years, they are blessed with three more children, a rescue dog, and some goldfish. After the kids graduate, the empty nesters look back with pleasant appreciation. "How did we manage all that?" they sigh with grateful smiles.

What are you facing today that seems overwhelming? Do you have what it takes to do it well? Someday you'll look back on it and see it as Jesus sees it now. You will sigh with a grateful smile and say, "How did I do that?"

Jesus will say, **"Well done, good and faithful servant!"** (Matthew 25:21).

How can you do it? Today's overwhelming task or broken relationship or controlling addiction or dead-end job. Do you have what it takes? Yes.

If Jesus tells you that you're faithful, that means you need something to be faithful with. Something to be responsible for. Something he gives you.

Jesus equips you with everything it takes to do everything he asks. Be faithful with these gifts. Be as good as Jesus, in his grace, is equipping you to be.

Now read Matthew 25:14-30. Compare and contrast the two servants who receive the affirmation, **"Well done,"** to the **"wicked, lazy"** servant. The faithful servants see their task as God's work. Do you?

So deep

Sarah Habben

Snorkeling in the Caribbean Sea is like snooping on a weird and wonderful metropolis. The classy, the clownish, the fat, the flat, the finned, and the flippered all slip between currents and mingle among the coral. What imagination God invested in that underwater world! And for what audience? So much of it is unseen by human eyes! During the years that I snorkeled in one small corner of that sea, I always had some version of the apostle Paul's exclamation going through my head:

"Oh, the depth of the riches of the wisdom and knowledge of God! How unsearchable his judgments, and his paths beyond tracing out!" (Romans 11:33).

What makes *you* say those words? An undeserved second chance? A blow that became a blessing? Paul's jaw dropped when he considered God's plan of salvation, one that germinated among the Jews but blew across the oceans to grace every nation: God became a man. Though innocent, he bore our guilt. Though eternal, he died. Though dead, he rose again in power. Paul was a master of theology, but when he tried to put words to God's wisdom, he wasn't splashing through a shallow puddle. He was pulling hard beneath the ocean's surface to get a better view of some wonder—and he found himself out of breath and out of his depth.

The next time you're tempted to question God's hand in your life, remember that God's ways are no less marvelous because we can't properly grasp them. Simply praise God for his bottomless wisdom and love.

God is in control
Pastor Mike Novotny

One of the scarier parts of my life is realizing how much is completely out of my control. Like my daughters. My wife and I work hard to disciple our kids—to teach, encourage, correct, and model the Christian faith, but we can't control what our girls believe or how they behave. I can bring them to church, but I can't make them meditate on God's Word. I can tell them to say, "Sorry," but I can't make them mean it. I can beg them to only like boys who love Jesus and love like Jesus, but I can't control what happens at school.

I am not in control. That reality tempts me to freak out. Maybe it tempts you too.

But it doesn't have to. Because the One who is in control is the One who loves you more than you can imagine. "[God] **raised Christ from the dead and seated him at his right hand. . . . And God placed all things under his feet**" (Ephesians 1:20,22). I love how "all things" are under Jesus' feet. The same feet that were pierced to prove his immense love for you now rule over the very situations that you cannot. They are not going toe to toe with Jesus. No, they are under his feet, completely under his control.

So take a deep breath. Remember that Jesus has it handled. That's the good news of worshiping the Savior who is in control.

november 14

When you can't, he can
Pastor Mike Novotny

There comes a time in your life when you can't. Despite all your efforts, you can't control a situation in your family or you can't solve a problem with your health or you can't work things out with your siblings. The *USS Independence* is sinking, and you simply can't.

But God can! That's what Matthew learned the day when **"[Jesus] got up and rebuked the winds and the waves, and it was completely calm"** (Matthew 8:26). Can you even imagine this? Jesus wiped his groggy eyes, lifted his divine voice, and shook a commanding finger at the storm . . . and it listened! From grown men screaming for help to a silence so still you could hear Matthew's breath. "Why are you so afraid?" Jesus can!

Please don't forget that. While we might not know God's will or understand his timing, we do know his power. So we can pray, "God, you can bring a good friend into my life today. You can save this marriage, even this marriage, this year. You can change my unrealistic expectations. You can give me peace on unproductive days. You can make my pet sins a part of my past. You can give me the faith to forgive him. You can transform me into a patient parent. You can overcome this addiction. God, you can cure cancer. You can defeat depression. You can leave doctors dumbfounded. You're God! You're the omnipotent, all-powerful, can-do-anything God who can calm any storm."

Pray with boldness as you keep the faith that God can.

It's right in front of you
Pastor Clark Schultz

In our home the following can be heard, "Honey, where's the ketchup?" Or one of our boys will shout, "Mom, I can't find my shoes!" My wife will come along, open the refrigerator, and in a millisecond pull out the ever-so-elusive ketchup bottle and simply respond to my son, "You're literally standing on your shoes." As we stand their mystified as to how she does that, she says, "The answer is right in front of you."

When we look at the world around us, we can agree it's sometimes a hostile environment for Christians. There is failure to see Jesus as the priceless treasure. The apostle Paul's time was no different. Rome and the Jewish leaders appeared to be in power. Christians were offered to lions for sport. What hostility have you faced for being a child of God?

God's Word is the dynamite that convicts the guilty conscience. It's also the cool salve that heals our broken hearts and assures us of sins forgiven. **"So do not be ashamed of the testimony about our Lord or of me his prisoner. Rather, join with me in suffering for the gospel, by the power of God"** (2 Timothy 1:8).

As Paul reminds Timothy, it's not a loss to spend your life in the service of the gospel. The real loss is not to have the gospel. Leaders and governments come and go, but the Word endures forever. By faith in Jesus, so will we. Yes the answer is right in front of you! It's Jesus!

Cumulative effect

Jason Nelson

I was cleaning out some files and read things I wrote decades ago. Yikes! I would never say stuff like that today. I reiterated conventional wisdom because I had an amateur's command of life. I scratched the surface by quoting "experts" and slinging jargon around like word hash to give the impression I knew what I was talking about. Now I would have to eat some of those words. Yuck!

Life makes us reconsider things. The longer we live the more things we'll need to reconsider. It's good to reconsider things in light of God's Word and with a tested faith. That's a mental habit of disciples who finally get to a point that they know what they don't know. **"Who is really wise? Who knows how to explain things? Wisdom makes one's face shine, and it changes one's grim look"** (Ecclesiastes 8:1 GW).

When the ride gets rough, it's the lightweights who are thrown off. You'll see panic on their faces. They don't have the gravitas to stay in the saddle because they haven't paid their dues. Wise people flash wry smiles because this isn't their first rodeo. They've been bucked off before. They've been neck deep in manure and know from experience that this too shall pass. They can explain to others how it will pass because they've learned some lessons in life. One lesson I've learned is don't write down what you think you know in permanent marker.

Public confession
Christine Wentzel

It's one thing to repent of our wrongdoings to our all-powerful, all-knowing, and all-present God. In light of this, it kind of makes it a bit easier to drop the excuses and come clean. We can approach our Father, penitent and wrapped in our white robes that were purchased by his Son, Jesus Christ, for the forgiveness of all sins.

On the other hand, it seems a daunting task to express our sins to our peers. This part of being in a Christian community is an important faith-building activity. It's through this kind of intimate sharing that we draw closer to one another in our common struggles. However, we also know not all is fair in love and war. In the community of saved sinners, we are careful about confessing our sins for fear of judgment. It's quite easy to cherry-pick them and kick the "worst" under the rug.

"Therefore confess your sins to each other and pray for each other so that you may be healed. The prayer of a righteous person is powerful and effective" (James 5:16).

Let's ask the Holy Spirit to help us share our weaknesses with one another so we can build up our strengths prayerfully. The ransom the accuser once demanded for each of our lives was paid in full.

Things will be better
Pastor Jeremy Mattek

"The angel said to the women, 'Do not be afraid. . . . He has risen from the dead and is going ahead of you into Galilee. There you will see him'" (Matthew 28:5,7).

When the women left the tomb that Easter morning, they hadn't seen Jesus with their eyes. In other words, they lived by faith. They left the tomb believing the promise the angel gave them.

Galilee was almost a hundred miles from where they were that day, but do you know when they actually saw Jesus? About ten seconds later Jesus appeared to them. I bet that was a nice surprise! They moved forward in faith, and the reality that God gave them turned out to be better than they were expecting.

And your reality will be too. I'm sure you've thought about what it will be like to be in heaven, what it might feel like to never hurt or feel weak again. I'm sure you've thought about what it will feel like to hug your loved ones when you see them again. Those are happy thoughts. But the reality will be far better than you could ever imagine. God doesn't tell us *when* we'll see these things. I know that sometimes it seems we're still a hundred miles away. He only promises that we *will* see them.

So don't be afraid of whatever in life is making it hard to wait for things to be better. The risen Jesus is proof that your wait will be worth it!

God's path
Andrea Delwiche

It's possible to believe that Jesus is my Savior from sin and that he has given me eternal life and yet spend my days ignoring the way he has set for me to live.

I ignore the basics of the Ten Commandments. I make excuses and fail to love my neighbors. I don't follow God's plan to **"let the word of Christ *dwell* in** [me] **richly"** (Colossians 3:16 ESV) so that I can learn from the Lord and from other Christians to live in thankfulness and joy.

These are dark days. These are, in many ways, hard days. As Christians, we know that better days are coming, but these days on earth are precious and meant to bless us and others as well. So how, in the midst of job loss, illness, boredom, fatigue, loss of purpose, do we make the most of and excel in our earthy walk?

"Show me your ways, Lord, teach me your paths. Guide me in your truth and teach me, for you are God my Savior, and my hope is in you all day long" (Psalm 25:4,5). The One who saved us from a life curved in upon itself and opened our lives to his glorious plan has some pretty good ideas for how we can live for him and others in this life as well.

How do we discover this path? We ask the Spirit for guidance and then read the example that Scripture sets before us. It's God's roadmap for a hope-filled, joyful life here on earth as we walk toward the hereafter.

Only Jesus saves

Pastor Mike Novotny

One day a retired pastor told me a sad story. Years earlier, when he had just arrived at a new congregation, he decided to visit the elderly members of the church, many of whom were close to death. During his visits, he asked them a vital question: "If today was the day God ended your life, are you sure you'd go to heaven?"

The answers were almost entirely, "Yes!" But when the pastor asked them to explain their confidence, his smile faded at their replies. "Because I've paid my dues, Pastor." "Because I went to church all my life, Pastor." "Because I helped build the church where you preach, Pastor." Time after time, these "Christians" thought they could cover up a lifetime's worth of sins with the good works written on their spiritual resumes.

That simply isn't true. So before your day of judgment comes, let me remind you of the foundation of the Christian faith: **"For it is by grace you have been saved, through faith—and this is not from yourselves, it is the gift of God—not by works, so that no one can boast"** (Ephesians 2:8,9). We are saved (rescued from the danger of hell), not by our works so that we can make some deathbed boast but rather by grace. By the wonderful gift of God's undeserved, promised love for us. By Jesus—crucified and risen. Because only Jesus saves.

So if someone asks you about the day you die, please don't start your answer with, "Because I . . ." Remember grace and begin with, "Because Jesus . . ."

His eye is on the sparrow

Pastor Mike Novotny

Back in the spring of 1905, a songwriter named Civilla Martin and her husband became friends with Mr. and Mrs. Doolittle, two devout Christians who lived with serious health complications. Mrs. Doolittle had been bedridden for two decades, and her husband, unless God intervened with a miracle, would be bound to a wheelchair for the rest of his life. Yet the Doolittles didn't mope through their final years. In fact, those who visited them left their home inspired by their joy. One day, Civilla's husband asked the couple how they could be that hopeful when they lived with that much pain. Mrs. Doolittle, quoting Jesus, expressed her faith: "His eye is on the sparrow, and I know he watches me."

That wonderful woman knew our Savior's promise: **"Are not five sparrows sold for two pennies? Yet not one of them is forgotten by God. . . . Don't be afraid; you are worth more than many sparrows"** (Luke 12:6,7). That promise is true for you too. God knows what pain you're going through. He hasn't forgotten one moment of it. He is using it for his glory and for the church's good, so you have no reason to be afraid.

Mrs. Doolittle's faith inspired Civilla to write her famous hymn "His Eye Is on the Sparrow" (you should Google it right now!). I pray that our Savior's words inspire you to sing your own song of praise. Don't be afraid! God knows what you're carrying today. And he says that you're too important to him to forget about it.

Let your body be joyful!
Andrea Delwiche

How do you do with outward expressions of joy? Can you imagine doing as David suggests in Psalm 30? Turning from wailing (which is very much a bodily reaction) to dancing (also a bodily reaction)? **"You turned my wailing into dancing; you removed my sackcloth and clothed me with joy, that my heart may sing your praises and not be silent. Lord my God, I will praise you forever"** (Psalm 30:11,12).

Our Creator gave us each a body that is equipped to express both grief and joy. These bodily reactions help us grieve and celebrate with God and with our fellow women and men.

What does joy look like? Think of the contagious happiness of a puppy—the full-body wriggles and joy spasms when it sees a beloved person. Think of the unguarded enthusiasm and bodily expression of a small child with an ice cream cone or a birthday present. Think of an adult celebrating a touchdown from a favorite football team.

This same emotion can be channeled into our worship of God. As we grow closer to the Lord and experience his joy, we can relax into our bodily reactions to his love. We can let down our guard and by his Spirit overflow with gratitude that is not childish but *childlike*.

Does this seem daunting? Try something simple—read the psalms out loud, using your voice to express the emotions the psalmists describe. Are there other ways to integrate your whole self in your worship of God?

Grace gets the last word

Pastor Mike Novotny

Do you know the very last thing that Jesus said to his disciples? While the Bible doesn't record the exact words, we get the gist of it in Luke chapter 24: **"While [Jesus] was blessing them, he left them and was taken up into heaven"** (verse 51).

Don't you love the word *while*? *While* Jesus was in the very act of blessing them, of promising them something good in God's name, he was taken back up to heaven. His final words were not, "Don't you boys make me come back down here!" Nor were they, "Peter? Peter, are you listening? I am keeping my eye on you." Instead of warnings or threats, Jesus' final words were a blessing. Grace got the last word.

That is how God operates. Yes, his Word is filled with plenty of warnings regarding sin and the reality of hell. But for the disciples of Jesus, for those of us who have been brought to saving faith in our Lord, the last word is grace. Our Savior may have to call us out for some pattern of behavior, but his last word is mercy. The devotion or sermon or conversation might convict, but the last word is love. Our Father might discipline his beloved children with a rebuke, but that's never where the conversation ends.

Because Jesus didn't leave us with a curse. He left us with a blessing. Grace gets the last word!

I love her bald

Jason Nelson

My wife always had beautiful hair. It was long and blonde and full. She was a perfect example of the apostle Paul's and my cultural bias regarding feminine hairstyles: **"If a woman has long hair, it is her glory"** (1 Corinthians 11:15). But chemotherapy changed that for her. Of all the side effects of being treated for cancer, losing her hair hurt her the most. She didn't have to say it. I could see it on her face. She dreaded going out in public in her wig or wearing one of those telltale, little chemo hats because she didn't want to deal with people's reactions. I told her before it happened, while it was coming out, and after it was gone that it didn't matter to me. I love her just as much. And every day I kissed the top of her adorable, smooth, round head.

There are gender inequities I will never understand. I've lost a lot of my hair, and no one ever asked me about it. People haven't told me stories of their uncle's courageous battle with alopecia. I never received a sympathetic hug from another hairless man. No one ever tried to encourage me by saying, "Don't worry; it'll grow back." They know it won't, so they leave me alone. But it's different for girls. There are lots of things that are different for girls, and the most honorable thing I can do as a man is recognize it.

Remember to be thankful

Pastor David Scharf

The pilgrims, remembered for the first Thanksgiving dinner, developed an interesting custom. They would place five kernels of corn on each empty plate before bringing out the Thanksgiving feast. Why? They never wanted to forget to be thankful. You see, before the first harvest in the New World, things were so bad that they had to ration food at a rate of five kernels of corn per person per day. How far they had come! Rather, how far God had brought them! This helped them remember to be thankful for God's gifts. Similarly, God encouraged the Israelites: **"When you have eaten and are satisfied, praise the Lord your God for the good land he has given you. . . . Remember the Lord your God"** (Deuteronomy 8:10,18).

How will you remember to give thanks? Perhaps you could be reminded of God's physical gifts by placing five kernels of corn on your plate like the pilgrims did. But might I suggest you go a bit deeper? To better appreciate God's greater gifts, you could place a black napkin (to represent "dirty") on each plate at the table. Why? To lead you to remember that as you remove that napkin from your plate and fill your plate with good things, so God has removed the dirtiness of your wrongs by dying on a cross and has now filled your plate with every promise of his love and protection! This amazing gift of salvation far outstrips all the kernels of corn in the world!

God came near

Pastor Daron Lindemann

One of my spiritual mentors reminded me of this shift: There is a difference between faith in the outcome I am dictating to God and faith in God himself.

Faith in God's character. Faith in who he is. Faith that he is good all the time. Faith that he is never scared or confused. Faith that he's not playing a game of chess with me. Faith that he is forgiving even when I don't feel like it. Faith that he knows what is best for me even when I don't. Faith that he is my friend. Faith that he became human to save us.

"You came near when I called you, and you said, 'Do not fear'" (Lamentations 3:57).

When you are overcoming fears with faith, it is faith in a personal, relational Savior. A real being. Not faith in an idea or a hoped-for place of happiness. Those are slippery.

Evaluate your prayer life. Don't be afraid to ask God for the impossible. Then have faith more in his character and person than the impossible coming true.

Consider your worship life. Give it a boost by adjusting your expectations. Rather than worshiping as a consumer whose needs must be met, worship as a friend of God who is delighted to spend time with him.

Calm your fears. Catch yourself spinning in mental circles of what if this or that, and instead ask, "What if God truly keeps his promises to me?" And he does. In person.

Thanksgiving memoir

Jason Nelson

"I thank my God every time I remember you. In all my prayers for all of you, I always pray with joy because of your partnership in the gospel from the first day until now, being confident of this, that he who began a good work in you will carry it on to completion until the day of Christ Jesus" (Philippians 1:3-6).

Paul's letter to the Philippians is a memoir of thanksgiving. It's filled with expressions of love and appreciation for people who meant the world to him. The Philippians expressed their faith generously and humbly. They sent Paul money when he needed it because they were deeply concerned for him. But that wasn't the only reason for Paul's gratitude. Paul recognized that serving them made him a better man. He speaks here as one of them. He brought them the gospel, and they set an example for him. It was Christian community at its best. So Paul could confide in them: **"For to me, to live is Christ and to die is gain"** (Philippians 1:21).

It always takes some kind of remembering to produce any kind of thanksgiving. We can remember lots of things and be thankful for them. But our best remembering is about people. Our best thanksgiving is for people we love and long to see because we share a life that is worthy of the gospel. I may not know you, but I will thank God every time I remember you.

31 kings conquered by God

Pastor Daron Lindemann

Boom!

Years ago when I attended baseball games at Miller Park in Milwaukee, cheering on the Brewers, every time they hit a home run there would be a loud cannon blast. Boom!

I think it was actually some kind of fireworks, not really a cannon, but it sounded like one. It was percussive, and I could feel it in my gut. It was loud, even if I anticipated it and covered my ears. It got my attention. Boom!

One by one, God's Word in Joshua chapter 12 names the mighty, renowned kings of old that Joshua defeated on a mission from God. Like Sihon and Og.

Boom!—31 times, 31 home runs for God. Boom! Boom! Boom!

God wants your attention. Who's in charge here? Who's ruling this world and its nations and governments? Not the kings. Not the rulers. Not the governments. God is.

The end of the chapter concludes, **"thirty-one kings in all"** (verse 24).

As presidential tweets are interpreted and political parties bully each other for election priority. As drug cartels infiltrate government powers and lobbyists manipulate government policy. As nations around the world fight in civil war and our own nation struggles to find the nationalistic pride we once had. Boom!

This chapter in Joshua is a reminder. None of this ultimately controls what happens in our world.

Our saving God rules over it all. Say that 31 times today: "My saving God rules over it all."

Culture of comparisons

Pastor Mike Novotny

We live in a culture of comparisons. That thought hit me while watching Thanksgiving football last year. I noticed that when the TV flashed through the pictures of the starting lineups, they didn't just have the guys' names, positions, and alma maters. They also had a comparison. This receiver is the 27th best in the NFL. This linebacker is the 19th out of whatever at his position. Think about that—These guys are the 1 percent of the 1 percent, men who worked and trained and hustled to become professionals and then NFL starters, yet what do we still do with them? We compare.

That's our culture, right? More than ever before, we compile the data, run the numbers, spit out the analytics, and compare everything. Height, weight, income, impact, sales, speed, square footage, everything. But when the numbers aren't in your favor, that comparison can crush you. It can make you feel worthless, unimportant, and unnecessary.

Thank God that our Father isn't into comparisons. Rather, he uniquely knits us together in our mothers' wombs (Psalm 139:13). He determines the specific times and places where we should live (Acts 17:24-28). His Spirit blesses us with gifts that our neighbors lack (1 Corinthians chapter 12). For God, there are no apples-to-apples comparisons with people, because every human is unique in the grand plan of the kingdom of heaven.

So let culture do its thing. You, however, remember these life-giving, pressure-reducing words: **"You knit me together in my mother's womb. I praise you because I am fearfully and wonderfully made"** (Psalm 139:13,14).

In the presence of your enemies
Pastor Mike Novotny

Are you surrounded by people who aren't all that nice? Maybe a neighbor who is grouchier than Oscar from *Sesame Street*. Or a mother who can't resist criticizing you in every conversation. Or the heartless commenters who forget that digital words still hurt. Or a spouse who never seems happy with you, no matter how hard you try.

If so, I want you to remember the apostles. After Jesus returned to heaven, the apostles returned to a city filled with their enemies. The same church leaders who lied about Christ and the same soldiers who pounded the nails into the cross were still running the show in Jerusalem. Yet here is how the apostles felt: **"They . . . returned to Jerusalem with great joy. And they stayed continually at the temple, praising God"** (Luke 24:52,53).

How could they feel like *that* while living *there*? Because they were blessed by the Savior who sits at the right hand of God (Luke 24:51). They believed that the King of the universe loved them, was with them, and would work out everything for their good.

After this devotion, you're going to "return to Jerusalem" too. You'll go back into a world that isn't always nice to you. But that doesn't have to take away your joy because you have exactly what the original apostles had—forgiveness through Jesus, the presence of the Spirit, the plans of your Father.

To quote singer Taylor Swift, "Haters gonna hate." But that doesn't have to stop your joy. Through Jesus, you are a child of God!

December

But when the set time had fully come,
God sent his Son, born of a woman,
born under the law, to redeem those under the law,
that we might receive adoption to sonship.
Galatians 4:4,5

God knows what's best
Pastor Clark Schultz

"I quit!" says our five-year-old when trying to do his math assignment. Sadly he's inherited his father's dislike for math. Do you sometimes look at God's gift of prayer in a similar way? If you don't get the answer you like, do you say, "I quit!"?

God answers prayers with no, yes, and wait. But sometimes we pray the equivalent of this: "God, give me patience and give it to me right now!"

Here's a thought though. Maybe God has something better in mind for you. Imagine a small child who sees something he wants in the mall, something that was never intended for a child his age. Sure it would be fun, but he would end up hurting himself and making a mess. When the child hears no, he immediately goes into a meltdown, crying, "I thought you loved me?" What the child doesn't know is that his parents had planned to go to a local toy store to let him pick out a toy to play with at the park they were picnicking at.

When we pray, God may not give us what we want, but he promises to hear and answer every time. **"Before they call I will answer; while they are still speaking I will hear"** (Isaiah 65:24). And he always has something better in mind. Trust him. Trust the Father who sent his Son for you! He does love you! He loves math too, so I've been told ☺.

The only word I need on my tombstone
Pastor David Scharf

Sin is like walking down a hill. Every step we take makes it more difficult to return. How far down the hill are you today? Sometimes our sin crushes us so greatly that we can't imagine being on top of the hill again, even after we hear these words from God: "I forgive you in the name of the Father and of the Son and of the Holy Spirit." Can it really be true?

A prostitute found Jesus at a Pharisee's house. Though uninvited, she went in anyway with a jar of perfume. She wet his feet with her tears, kissed them, and poured perfume on them. What do you suppose Jesus did? Jesus did what Jesus does. He gave her what she needed, not just for this life but for the one to come. **"Then Jesus said to her, 'Your sins are forgiven'"** (Luke 7:48). It *is* true.

Not far from New York City is a cemetery with a grave that has just one word on the tombstone: "FORGIVEN." There's nothing else. No name, no date of birth or death, no word of praise for the departed, just the one word, "FORGIVEN." What other word could you need?

We can't walk back up the hill. Jesus had to come down to save us on the cross. But he did that to be able to seat us with him in heaven. Now *FORGIVEN* is the only word you need on your tombstone.

What makes hell like hell
Pastor Mike Novotny

I've been to hell. No joke. I ran into the very pit of hell and escaped to tell you the story. I should explain. When Jesus talked about hell in the gospels, the word often used in the original Greek was *Gehenna*. Gehenna is a real place in Jerusalem, a valley that plunges down on the south and west side of the city, which I ran down into and up out of on a recent trip to Israel.

Why would Jesus choose that valley to talk about hell? First, because in the Old Testament, Gehenna was a place of weeping, wailing, and death. Children were sacrificed in that valley to appease the false gods of rain and war, a scene that I shudder to imagine. Perhaps Jesus chose that imagery to remind us that losing God forever is even worse than losing your own child in that fire.

Second, because Gehenna was *outside* the walls of the city. When an army marched toward Jerusalem, the only safe place was inside the city. If you were caught in the valley, you were assaulted, enslaved, or brutally murdered. Perhaps Jesus wanted a picture of what it's like to face judgment without the protection of our King.

"But I will show you whom you should fear: Fear him who, after your body has been killed, has authority to throw you into hell [Gehenna]. **Yes, I tell you, fear him"** (Luke 12:5). The only logical fear is the one that affects your forever. But if your faith is in Jesus, you have nothing to fear.

Cabin fever

Jason Nelson

Winter in the north is hard on machinery and people. Winter stops being crisp really fast. Ice-cold things grind slowly if they grind at all. Loneliness and sadness put winter in the soul. The chill goes deep. It compresses our spirits. We desperately want something to change, and that puts us at risk for changing the wrong things, for finding the wrong remedies for unhappy feelings we don't understand, even for exposing ourselves to something deadly.

When I was a church consultant, I made five trips to Alaska. I hit all the seasons. In the summer, I saw active people launching their kayaks in the Kenai River at 11:00 P.M. because there was plenty of daylight left. I also heard about the negative effects of long, dark winters. In winter the rates of alcohol abuse, drug abuse, and teen pregnancies all went up. People were inclined to find the wrong solutions for their problems.

I also saw how people survived when their snow machines wouldn't start or their truck batteries were lifeless blocks of ice. What do you do? You depend on each other. You rally to each other's rescue. You keep each other going. When God's people were falling apart in the wilderness and were ready to give up, God told Moses to **"gather the people together"** (Numbers 21:16). God would give his people what they needed to survive when they were all together. Getting together is a good way to survive cabin fever.

Commit your spirit to God?

Andrea Delwiche

"Into your hands I commit my spirit; deliver me, LORD, my faithful God" (Psalm 31:5).

What does it mean to "commit my spirit" or give God full oversight over my soul? While these words perhaps are familiar as the last words that Jesus spoke from the cross on Good Friday, in Psalm 31 they are spoken by a person like you and me. So how can these words come from *my* lips in a meaningful way?

As you and I live our lives, God works to train our souls to live in the fullness of reality that God is trustworthy, we are protected, and springs of joy and sustenance abound. With empowerment that comes from the Holy Spirit, we can strive to let God and his ways guide us—in everything. We trust God's wisdom revealed in the pages of Scripture to guide our thoughts and decisions. We trust that the guidelines he gives for us are good because we were created by him. We trust that there are many good options to pursue with our Savior.

As trust becomes our life's breath, we can be untangled from worry, free to follow the path that our heavenly Father offers to us. Jesus suggests, **"Seek first his kingdom and his righteousness, and all these things will be given to you as well"** (Matthew 6:33). As worry departs, it's replaced by wisdom, joy, and curiosity as we discover the beauty and adventure that he intends for us.

Your giants will fall
Pastor Jeremy Mattek

Maybe your giant is stress. A bad habit. A broken heart. A tendency to lose control when life doesn't go the way you want.

David's giant was literally a giant Philistine: **"David said to Saul, 'Let no one lose heart on account of this Philistine; your servant will go and fight him'"** (1 Samuel 17:32).

How did David defeat the giant? By doing two things. He went forward in faith, and he fought with God on his side.

He took one step forward at a time and asked himself, "What's the most godly next step I know how to make?" Once he figured it out, he took that step. Don't let the magnitude of the entire battle keep you from taking your next step. Then David fought, knowing God was with him.

Facing a giant is a really hard thing. It was for David. What has your giant taken from you? Your joy? Your peace of mind? Your confidence? Don't be hard on yourself if it's sometimes hard to believe that you'll be able to snatch those things back again.

But don't forget that God is with you and that your giants have already been defeated. Your living God has promised you a day when, like David, your giants will be dead while you will keep living in heaven, where there is no more struggling or death or pain.

So take your next step in faith—fully confident—as if your undefeated God is right there with you every step of the way. Because he is.

Ready for Christmas?
Pastor Mike Novotny

Are you ready for Christmas? I'm not thinking of the last-minute shopping or the taco dip you have to make before the office party. I'm thinking about focusing on Christ.

Picture a manger placed in the middle of whatever room you happen to be in right now. There are three ways that you could approach this Christmas. First, you could turn your back on that manger entirely, caring little about who Jesus is and what Jesus did. (I'm guessing that's not you.) Second, you could turn your body toward the manger but still be looking back over your shoulder, constantly distracted by all the holiday traditions. Finally, you could turn not just your body but also your eyes toward the manger, thinking often about the blessings that come through the birth of Christ.

"Let us run with perseverance the race marked out for us, fixing our eyes on Jesus" (Hebrews 12:1,2). It takes perseverance to focus on Jesus in the midst of our December to-do lists. Yet that perseverance is richly rewarded as we start to grasp how high and long and wide and deep is the love of God, a love so immense he sent his Son in human flesh for us.

The best way to be ready for Christmas is to block out time to think about those blessings. Can I encourage you to read Matthew 1, Luke 1-2, John 1, and Philippians 2 in the upcoming weeks? These chapters will fix your eyes on the Savior who makes Christmas merry.

God is like my wife

Pastor Mike Novotny

God is like my wife. (Honey, if you're reading this, there has to be a billion brownie points for that line, right?)

My wife, Kim, is one of the most responsible people you'll ever meet. In fact, on the StrengthsFinder personality test, one of her top strengths is Responsibility. So if Kim says she'll do something, she'll do it. She doesn't make flippant promises and then forget about them, like I sometimes do. Rather, she writes them down, makes her list, and works her hardest because she feels morally responsible to get them done.

God is like that. When you cast your anxieties on God, asking him to take care of things you can't control, he doesn't forget about them. Never in his eternal existence has God said, "Oh no! I totally forgot about that one!" Instead, he always replies, "I know. I didn't forget. You haven't seen what I'm up to just yet, but you will. At just the right time, you'll see what I'm doing in your life."

The apostle Paul promised it this way: **"The one who calls you is faithful, and he will do it"** (1 Thessalonians 5:24). He will do it. Not he might do it or he'll try to do it or he'll do his best to get to it. He will do it. So whatever you're worried about, let it go. Throw it onto God's shoulders and get a good night's sleep.

If my wife is good at getting things done, just imagine your God!

How do you stack up?

Andrea Delwiche

"Vindicate me, O Lᴏʀᴅ, for I have walked in my integrity, and I have trusted in the Lᴏʀᴅ without wavering. Prove me, O Lᴏʀᴅ, and try me; test my heart and my mind. For your steadfast love is before my eyes, and I walk in your faithfulness" (Psalm 26:1-3 ESV).

Are you afraid to pray these words? Do you wonder how you would stack up and if the Lord would say to you, "No, you haven't walked in integrity or trusted me without wavering." Do you feel afraid to ask the Lord to test your heart and your mind?

The writer of this psalm, David, says this next: **"For your *steadfast love* is before my eyes, and I walk in *your faithfulness.*"** Do you really know God's unconditional love for you? Do you know that because of Christ's sacrifice, you set out each morning walking on his path?

We experience conditional love from other humans, so it's hard to fathom the unshakeable love of God. His love isn't contingent upon our behavior. We're forgiven. He deeply desires to help us walk in integrity and trust. We can ask him to examine our lives and trust that when he does, he responds in love. He is unflappable. He remembers our sins no more. As he opens our eyes to places where we need to grow, he does this with our best interests in mind: **"I know the plans I have for you, declares the Lᴏʀᴅ, plans for welfare and not for evil, to give you a future and a hope"** (Jeremiah 29:11 ESV).

The weakest link
Christine Wentzel

"A chain is only as strong as its weakest link" is a proverb inspired from an 18th-century book by Thomas Reid.

Ideally, God's visible church is a well-maintained chain formed by his invisible church—the community of people who serve the Lord and the world with their unique gifts. All too often, there's one particular link that tends to be weaker than the rest.

In many Christian communities, there are groups of teens who just finished lengthy biblical basics training. They are energetic, confident, and impressionable. Their link lies between the young children and college groups. They stand on the edge of God's larger kingdom, readying themselves for their adulthood.

It's at this crucial time the link weakens as their priorities tend to shift from linking up to the church to linking up with the rest of the world. To keep their spiritual link strong means to help them transition their heads to their hands and feet as adults in Christ—to prepare them to be future leaders of his church and God-fearing citizens of the world. Without this, Christ's enemies everywhere will break through this link easier than others.

When Jesus sent out his disciples, he said, **"I am sending you out like sheep among wolves. Therefore be as shrewd as snakes and as innocent as doves"** (Matthew 10:16).

Jesus gave his representatives on-the-job training before his ministry on earth was finished. Do we offer the same while our children are still with us?

What life should God give you?

Pastor Mike Novotny

If you were God, what kind of life would you give you? You could give yourself a really good life—stable finances, healthy body, faithful friends. But do you know what often happens when life's that good? We get so caught up in our lives that we forget how desperately we need God. So, you could make life painful. Dysfunctional family, financially broke, friendless, and anxious. But do you know what often happens when life is that hard? We shake our fists. After begging God for a break, we wonder if he cares.

You see God's problem, right? A good life or a bad life might make us miss out on our best life with him.

This is why I love that day on the stormy Sea of Galilee: **"The disciples went and woke him, saying, 'Lord, save us! We're going to drown!' . . . Then** [Jesus] **got up and rebuked the winds and the waves, and it was completely calm"** (Matthew 8:25,26). Jesus' followers couldn't forget about him when they were dying, nor could they claim Jesus didn't care when he saved them from an unthinkable ending.

Maybe Jesus is doing the same for you. He allows storms so you become desperate for his help, despairing of your own ability to control a situation. Then he either calms that storm immediately or promises to do so soon so that you never forget how much he loves you.

How might God be using the good and the bad in your life to keep you close to Jesus?

Blessings, not burdens

Linda Buxa

I was at the grocery store with my three kiddos when the cashier scanned the three bottles of wine I was buying for a dinner party. She looked at me and said, "Oh, three bottles of wine. One because of each kid." Then she chuckled at how funny she was.

It took a while for me to process what she had said, and I missed my opportunity to defend my kids. I was irritated that my kids had heard a perfect stranger suggest they are such burdens that I coped by drinking. Are children a lot of work? You bet. And, because we're all sinful, we all have moments when we make it hard to live with each other.

I'm thankful that my kids get to hear about their worth from a far-more-reliable source—God. In a book called Psalms, he tells us all, **"Children are a heritage from the Lord, offspring a reward from him"** (Psalm 127:3).

There's a whole world out there that will put children down, so today is a good day to remember to say yes more quickly when they ask for attention, to react more gently, and to whisper more words of encouragement. Look for ways to tell them the gospel more, to remind them they have great value because of what Jesus has done for them. They are not burdens but blessings.

Also, a reminder that you too were once a child. That means you were (and are) a reward to your parents. Maybe you needed to hear that.

december 13

Christmas is for shepherds
Pastor Daron Lindemann

Have you considered the high profile of the shepherds in the Christmas story? They were some of the first people God told about the birth of his Son. Why?

Because Jesus comes to the stinky, the sleepless, and the undesirable. He comes to cold nights of loneliness and hopelessness, to those who aren't climbing a career ladder, and to anyone separated from family. He comes to ordinary people in everyday circumstances.

After visiting the baby Jesus lying in a manger, the shepherds headed home to the Monday-morning feel of back to work. On the way, they told the townsfolk all about the birth of Jesus: **"And all who heard it were amazed at what the shepherds said to them"** (Luke 2:18). God had upgraded his spokesperson strategy from angels to shepherds. Yes, upgraded.

People are attentive to and amazed at ordinary, everyday words—even more than an angel's words—because people can relate to ordinary, everyday stories.

So don't wait for an angel to swoop down from the heavens this Christmas and fill the break room or living room or apartment lobby or chat room with *oohs* and *ahs*.

There's an underlying theme of simplicity to Christmas. Some shepherds. A poor, young girl. A carpenter. A sleepy, little town. A manger. A baby. God wants you to know that being right with him and ready for life is not complicated.

Praise God for it. Share it.

The Holy Spirit has your back
Pastor Jeremy Mattek

Zach was about to graduate from high school. It was hard because his mom had died two years previously. And then just a couple days before the graduation service, his dad died unexpectedly. Zach went to his graduation without any parents there to congratulate him.

As he was waiting to receive his diploma, he noticed that when each of his classmates received their diploma, they gave the principal something. They were handing the principal money. So he dug into his pockets, grabbed some cash, and handed it to the principal, only to find out later that his classmates were giving the principal money for him. They wanted Zach to know he wasn't alone as he was grieving. They wanted him to know they had his back.

That's exactly the promise Jesus gave his disciples when he promised them an Advocate: **"Unless I go away, the Advocate will not come to you; but if I go, I will send him to you"** (John 16:7).

The Advocate he's referring to is the Holy Spirit, who filled the hearts of thousands of new believers on Pentecost when the apostle Peter stood up and told the crowd to "listen carefully." Peter went on to tell them of a Savior they had killed but who forgave them and whose resurrection guaranteed all who believe in Jesus will one day overcome every hurt, trouble, and temptation.

The Advocate makes his way to your heart whenever you open the Word of God and listen carefully to the message of God's love you find in it.

You can't, but God can

Pastor Mike Novotny

Have you ever had one of those days when you say to yourself, "I just can't"? Maybe you've been trying to trust God as you wait for the test results, but you just can't do it for another 24 hours. Or you've done your best to love a friend with depression, but you've run out of patience. Or the kids have poked you 162 times with the interruption, "Mom! Mom! Mom!" and you're ready to run and hide in the woods.

We all have moments when we feel like we simply can't. We can't love all these people. We can't keep all these commands. Guess what? You're right. You can't.

But God can! **"And the God of all grace, who called you to his eternal glory in Christ, after you have suffered a little while, will himself restore you and make you strong, firm and steadfast"** (1 Peter 5:10). There's courage in these words! The God who is at your side and in your heart is the God of "all grace," covering you with undeserved, promised love and compelling you to do what's right. Your call to "eternal glory," to spend forever saying, "Wow!" as you look into his face, fires you up to do the good works that God wants in this moment. And his never-ending power will make you strong and firm and steadfast today.

So don't give up and don't give in. It's true that we're so weak, but it's also true that our God is so strong.

Inner strength starts outside
Pastor Daron Lindemann

My trainer explains that physical strength improves only with active exertion past a stress point. You have to reach a place of exhaustion and then keep going.

When the Bible commands, **"Be strong,"** what does that mean? **"Be on your guard; stand firm in the faith; be courageous; be strong"** (1 Corinthians 16:13).

This is talking about spiritual strength. Note the word "faith." In the original Greek language of the New Testament, this verb for the command "Be strong" literally says, *"Be strengthened."* That's a big difference!

Increasing spiritual strength is not like going to the gym. Increasing spiritual strength often means sweating and stressing less. Controlling less.

Spiritual strength starts here: Your own personal strength that you manufacture (your own opinions, ideas, and abilities) is weak, fragile, and vulnerable. But your personal strength that God produces (divine truths accepted by faith, answered prayers, Spirit-led enlightenment about Scripture, salvation, good works of love, carrying the cross of suffering, resisting temptation) is resilient, courageous, and able to stand firm.

Inner, spiritual strength starts from the outside. It is received from God by faith.

What situations fill you with fear? Confess how you have approached them too much with your own manufactured strength. Instead, trust in the spiritual strength promised by your Savior. Ask in prayer to "be strengthened" as he wants you to be.

Then see what God can do. For you. In you. Through you.

december 17

Pain is temporary

Pastor Mike Novotny

According to Jesus, I'm afraid of the wrong things. Like my back. A few years ago, I was a solid 6' and 2.5" tall. But at my last doctor's visit, they measured me at 6'1" and change. I lost an inch in my 30s! I've heard horror stories of degenerative discs, pinched nerves, back surgeries, and pain pills that are hard to give up. So the thought of the pain I might have to live with for years (decades?!) makes me afraid.

But Jesus says that's the wrong thing to fear. And he claims the same about your fears too—getting cancer, going through chemo, enduring arthritis, caring for a loved one with Alzheimer's, breakups, bankruptcy, raising kids, or getting bullied at school. Jesus said, **"I tell you, my friends, do not be afraid of those who kill the body and after that can do no more"** (Luke 12:4). Notice Jesus' logic—While there are situations that can end our lives, "after that" they "can do no more."

Your Savior knows that eternity is a long time, an epic novel compared to the single sentence you call life, and that none of your fears have the authority to change that eternity. Because of his sacrifice on the cross, the worst that can happen to you is that 0.000000000000001 percent of your life is painful (and I'm rounding up!).

So, my friends, don't be afraid. You might feel pain today and tomorrow, but there is only pleasure in your eternal future.

Praise him in the hallway

Sarah Habben

When someone shuts a door in your face, it's unpleasant. Momentum is broken. Communication is shut down. What to do? Pound on the door and protest? Slump in the hallway and sulk? Turn and walk away?

When God closes a door, it isn't pleasant either. When he shuts the door on your careful plans, your carefree assumptions, the dreams you're invested in, the outcomes you're counting on—you feel duped. You thought you had God's understanding and blessing. Instead . . . *slam*. What to do? Protest? Pout? Turn your back on God?

There's some folksy wisdom that offers another choice: *When God closes a door, praise him in the hallway.* The apostle Paul, in prison, said it like this: **"Rejoice in the Lord *always*"** (Philippians 4:4).

But how can we bear the long, dark hallway of disappointment, let alone praise God there? You've been in that hallway. It's not an obvious hangout for joy. Anxiety and loss are there. Grief is in that hallway. But, obvious or not, joy is there too. Because with you in that gloomy waiting area is . . . Jesus. When he closes a door, he doesn't hide behind it. He steps out and stands beside you with his promises and strength. His Word lights up the long, dark corridor before you like aisle lights in a theater. **"The Lord himself goes before you and will be with you; he will never leave you nor forsake you. Do not be afraid; do not be discouraged"** (Deuteronomy 31:8).

Rejoice always. Because when God closes a door, he guides you through the hallway.

The answer to anxiety

Pastor Mike Novotny

I used to really love 1 Peter 5:7. Now I really, really love it. That's the passage where Peter wrote, **"Cast all your anxiety on** [God] **because he cares for you."** The fact that God cares so much that we can talk to him about "all" our anxiety is breathtaking.

But what I didn't realize until recently was the definition of the word *cast*. In Greek, that word only appears twice in the entire New Testament—here and in Luke 19:35. In Luke, on Palm Sunday, the disciples cast/threw their cloaks on a donkey for Jesus to ride. In other words, they didn't share their cloaks with the donkey, keeping an arm in one sleeve as the donkey lumbered toward Jerusalem! No, the disciples threw their entire cloaks off of themselves and onto the donkey. That's what *cast* means.

Get where I'm going? Peter picked the same verb, meaning that God doesn't want you to hold on to any of your anxiety. He doesn't want to go halfsies on your worry or split the bill with your fear. No! He wants you to cast all of it, to throw it off of yourself and onto him. He cares about you that much. So make wise plans, do your best, and say your prayers, but then leave the rest to God. That's what it means to "cast all your anxiety on him."

I told you it was a really, really great passage!

Reminders of God's love

Pastor Clark Schultz

When the end is near, some begin to reflect on life. This journey back in time can take one to the sweet mountaintops of days gone by, or it can be a valley of missed opportunities and regrets. When Paul wrote to Timothy what would be his last letter, Paul was in prison and his head was literally about to be on the chopping block. Paul needed encouragement, so what did he do? He encouraged another. **"For this reason I remind you to fan into flame the gift of God"** (2 Timothy 1:6).

Paul didn't feel sorry for himself, blame God, or complain. He made lemonade out of the lemons of life he endured. Paul knew why he was in jail, he knew who Jesus was, and he knew where his strength came from—it wasn't from within; it wasn't from the outer world; it was entirely the "gift of God," which means the gospel. It's the same gospel that made Paul not reflect on his past as Saul (enemy of Christ) but on Paul the redeemed child of God. This is the same gospel message young Timothy was brought up in by his mother and grandmother. The very same gospel that comforts you, reminds you that we are no longer prisoners to sin but dearly loved and forgiven children of God. When I have one of my valley days, I need to hear this message and remind myself of it. Like Paul, I remind you to take the time to remind someone else today of their Savior's love.

Blind Jesus

Pastor Daron Lindemann

Ask a physically blind person if they're blind and they'll say, "Well, yeah, of course." Ask a spiritually blind person if they're blind, and they'll say, "What? Who do you think you are accusing me of being blind?! You're the blind one, you fool!"

When people are physically blind, they're aware of it, and they address it. The spiritually blind aren't aware that they're blind; therefore, they don't address it.

Jesus once said, **"For judgment I have come into this world, so that the blind will see and those who see will become blind"** (John 9:39).

Jesus has the right and will exercise that right to judge all people. He won't judge you on whether you're blind or not but whether you are aware of it. Whether you see your blindness and seek help and repent.

To make that possible, Jesus himself became blind. The night before he was crucified, the guards **"began to spit at him; they blindfolded him, struck him with their fists, and said, 'Prophesy! Who hit you?' And** [they] **took him and beat him"** (Mark 14:65; Luke 22:64).

Jesus was blinded. He couldn't see the sinners smashing his face. Not because of the blindfold (Jesus can see through anything) but because he closed his eyes and became the curse for spiritual blindness.

So you're not spiritually blind when you see Jesus as your Savior. Your eyes are opened to see his mercy and to see others who need your mercy too.

God is your strength
Andrea Delwiche

"The LORD **is my strength and my shield; my heart trusts in him, and he helps me. My heart leaps for joy, and with my song I praise him"** (Psalm 28:7).

Can you picture David sitting and composing these words? Mighty King David speaks out of the vulnerability and simple joy that is the posture of anyone, man or woman, who has learned to trust God's all-encompassing faithfulness.

David says simply, "He helps me." He doesn't brag or speak about his own implementation of a plan to bring about the end of his problem. He is helped by God, his strength and shield.

David was a privileged person, yet his help was still in the Lord. You may be privileged in the world's eyes. You may feel rightly that the world is against you and your back is to the wall. In the Lord's eyes, you are precious, and he longs to help you.

Sit still. Ask the Holy Spirit to calm your distracted or frantic mind. Take a few moments and picture yourself writing David's words. These are words that are true for you too. God is your strength. God is your shield. You are precious. You are helped.

What's under the wrapping?
Sarah Habben

"I'm telling you, she's the total package. She's funny and beautiful AND smart."

It's a rare guy who wouldn't want a girl like that. And a rare girl who wouldn't want to be described like that.

But what if that "total package" is really just—wrapping? Frugal types know that no matter how carefully they unwrap a gift, the pretty paper won't ever look new again. The Bible says that **"charm is deceptive, and beauty is fleeting"** (Proverbs 31:30). Just like wrapping paper, charm and beauty delight the senses, but they are disposable.

I have four daughters. They can turn on (and off) the charm. They're beautiful when they actually brush their hair. But if that's *all* I'm raising them to be—charming and beautiful—I'm investing a whole lot of time and effort in wrapping paper. I've forgotten the real gift. The Bible tells us what that gift is: **"A woman who *fears the Lord* is to be praised"** (Proverbs 31:30).

The "fear" of God is respect. Awe. Reverence. Obedience. It's a praiseworthy quality in women and men alike. Learning to fear the Lord starts at the cross, where our Savior suffered in our place. It becomes praiseworthy when that astonishing Savior-love seeps under our skin and into our souls and shapes what we do and say and how we act. Women and men who fear the Lord can't help but serve, encourage, forgive, and support others.

Pretty wrapping paper gets *oohs* and *ahs*. But the gift of a soul mate who fears the Lord . . . that's worth a hallelujah!

It's personal this time
Christmas Eve
Jason Nelson

"You are to give him the name Jesus" (Matthew 1:21). It took a while for me to be comfortable calling him by his first name. I've thought about that a lot over the years. Why was it so hard for me to say, "Jesus"? I think part of it was the formalism of my training. We talked about him but never used his name. We wrote about him but never used his name. I read things about him that never mentioned his name. I got the impression it wasn't appropriate to be that chummy with God. I guess we were trying to show respect by addressing him with his titles: the Son of God, the Lord, the Savior, the Messiah, the Christ. We could intone those names with seriousness and keep God at a safe distance. We talked about loving his Word and knowing his Word but not much about knowing Jesus and loving Jesus.

But the phonics of his name draws us to him. The only way to say it is with soft sounds: [ˈjē-zəs]. I can imagine the shepherds entering his birthplace with trepidation. They probably stood at a distance, looked down at the baby, and then looked up at Joseph and asked, "What's his name?" When Joseph said, "It's Jesus," I'm sure they repeated it. "Yes—Jesus—that's a very nice name." And then they approached him and bowed before him because they knew **"he [would] save his people from their sins"** (Matthew 1:21).

Christmas is about Christ
Christmas Day
Pastor Mike Novotny

My family of four has the tradition of eating lunch every Sunday with my parents and my mother-in-law, a meal that we call FamFest. It's our way of prioritizing time together in the midst of our busy lives. However, I all too often inhale my lunch, shovel dessert into my mouth, and jump up to clean the dishes before running out the door to prepare for our afternoon church service. Often, my mom tells me not to worry about the cleanup, a request that I ignore so I don't leave her with extra work. One memorable day, however, she said, "Michael, I would rather have FamFest be about time with . . . my family."

Duh. That should have been obvious, right? After all, it's right there in the name!

I tell you that story because the same thing can happen at Christmas. In the midst of wish lists, mall traffic, tree decoration, cookie baking, card writing, party attending, ugly sweater wearing, interstate traveling, and Elf on the Shelf hiding, we can rush through the season with barely enough time to catch our breath. I wonder, in those moments, if our Father wouldn't say something like my mother—"Child, I would rather have Christmas be about time with . . . Christ."

"Today in the town of David a Savior has been born to you; he is the Messiah, the Lord" (Luke 2:11). Please say no to a few good things this season so you have time to say yes to the best thing—pondering the peace that comes through the Messiah, our Lord.

A little of this . . . a little of that
Pastor David Scharf

My workplace has an amazing cafeteria. There are so many options: the mainline options, a salad bar with anything you could want, rotisserie chicken, Mexican food, a stir-fry line, eight types of ice cream, and on and on. Is your mouth watering yet? The best thing about the cafeteria is that I can pick and choose only my favorite things. I don't have to eat the brussels sprouts if I don't want to. Sorry, Mom!

The cafeteria approach works for food, but not for God's Word. *Every* word counts. *Every* word has your salvation in mind. Maybe you know the Ten Commandments by heart, but is each commandment firmly planted in your heart? Which commands of God have you taken the cafeteria approach to?

Listen to God's will for your life and remember why it's so important. God wants you to take every law word seriously *so that* you will take every gospel word seriously. He says, **"There is now no condemnation for those who are in Christ Jesus"** (Romans 8:1). Jesus has rescued you from every sin, not just some of them. He presented the payment he made for you on the cross to the Father. And the Father declares, "You are not guilty."

There is no condemnation for you because God condemned his own Son in your place. Let the news that we stand before God as innocent because of Jesus motivate you to consume every word he speaks!

Millennials are people too

Jason Nelson

To all of you who graduated high school since 2000, on behalf of Baby Boomers and Gen Xers everywhere, I want to apologize for talking about you like you couldn't hear us. Sorry about the insensitive remarks about tattoos, piercings, self-centeredness, and laziness. You don't need to feel inadequate because you aren't. I like many of your causes and your sass. I believe it's just what the world needs if you can work it right. The fact is, you won. You're the largest age group on the earth, and the rest of us desperately need you. You'll be in charge of the world we grow old in. I'm praying you'll be kinder to us than we have been to you.

Please give Jesus a fair shot in your life. He's a lot like you. He was misunderstood and still is. He's the ingathering of every race and class of people. He was the first millennial. A thousand years is nothing in his sight. He puts the past behind him. Your future now and forever means everything to him. Ask him to bless you so you can show his love to everyone. Jesus is the King of glory. This is his promise to you. You **"will receive blessing from the Lord and righteousness from the God of your salvation. Such is the generation of those who seek him, who seek the face of the God of Jacob"** (Psalm 24:5,6 ESV).

The dress code
Pastor David Scharf

Have you ever been to a restaurant that requires men to wear sport coats? I've never been to one, but I've heard that if you don't have a suit, you can't get in. Now, in the restaurant business, they will often have a closet with various-sized coats in it so you can dine there, but the principle still holds true: You need the right clothes to get in!

Did you know heaven works the same way? You must have Jesus' perfect white robe of righteousness to get in. You can't show up in the jean shorts of your own goodness or the Hawaiian shirt of your best efforts. If you tried that, you would only look foolish and wouldn't fit in. I'm not even sure that you would be "kindly" asked to leave!

The church father Augustine once prayed, "Lord, give me what you demand of me, then demand of me whatever you want." Thankfully, what God demands, he gives. The Bible says, **"All of you who were baptized into Christ have clothed yourselves with Christ"** (Galatians 3:27). In Baptism, God gives us the clothes we need to get into heaven. You are right now wearing the perfection that Jesus lived, died, and rose to win for you. Far from breaking the dress code of heaven, you are wearing the most beautiful clothing ever made. You can look into the mirror today and say, "I look good!"

december 29

Why are you worthy?

Pastor Mike Novotny

The other day I was meditating on these words of Jesus: **"Don't be afraid; you are worth more than many sparrows"** (Luke 12:7). Curious, I opened up Google images (the website that has all the pictures) and typed in "worthy." Instantly, my screen was filled with two very distinct types of images. Want to guess what they were?

The first images were all about how worthy we humans all are. Pinterest posts declared to every reader, "You are strong. You are brave. You are worthy." However, my dictionary says that the word *worthy* means, "good, virtuous, moral, ethical, honest, blameless, guiltless, righteous." Does that really apply to all of us? to any of us? While I appreciate the self-esteem booster, the definition of *worthy* disqualifies me from claiming to be it.

Which is why I loved the other type of image I saw: "God is worthy. Jesus is worthy. Worthy is the Lamb who was slain." These biblical quotes turned my eyes toward Jesus, the only good, virtuous, moral, ethical, honest, blameless, guiltless, righteous person to ever walk this earth. He is the Lamb who laid down his life to prove just how worthy he is.

By God's grace, that worthy Savior has given us worth. By taking away our sins and giving us his worthiness, Christians can dare to say, "I am worthy! Through Jesus, I am worth more than many sparrows to our Father!"

Repeat it. Believe it. In Christ, you are worthy!

Transplant recipients

Linda Buxa

Macey Wright was born with a congenital heart defect. She was 14 when she learned she'd be getting a new heart. Her mom filmed the emotional reaction because she wanted the world to know what getting that call is like. While they struggled with being sad for the donor's family, they were also filled with gratitude for the gift.

We are transplant recipients too. We were sick and dying, facing a future of only pain and suffering because we were separated from God. Then God sent Jesus to make the ultimate sacrifice, and he gave us an unbelievable gift. **"I will give you a new heart and put a new spirit in you; I will remove from you your heart of stone and give you a heart of flesh"** (Ezekiel 36:26).

While we struggle with being sad that Jesus—our donor family—had to die so we could live, we are also filled with gratitude for the gift of life he gave us.

Now we get to celebrate our new heart, our living heart, one that isn't cold and insensitive to the needs of the world but a heart that loves God and looks for the ways he has prepared for us to serve others.

As transplant recipients, we don't keep this news to ourselves. We tell the world that they can have the same surgery and have the same new outlook on life.

Drunk with the devil?
New Year's Eve
Pastor Mike Novotny

Have you ever gotten drunk with the devil? I'm not talking about drinking beers with the prince of darkness. I'm thinking about thoughts served up by the father of lies. Have you ever gotten "thought drunk" with the devil? Just like it only takes a few shots to mess you up physically, it only takes a few thoughts to mess you up mentally and spiritually. Have you ever thought a thought that makes you forget about the love, power, presence, plans, and goodness of God, the kind of thought that makes you anxious, unsettled, and afraid?

Me too. That's why Peter commands us, **"Be alert and of sober mind. Your enemy the devil prowls around like a roaring lion looking for someone to devour"** (1 Peter 5:8). Why stay mentally sober? Because the devil wants to devour you! He wants you to think the kind of thoughts that will take vicious bites out of your joy. So be alert! Stay sober! Don't get drunk with the devil!

How do you do it? By doing what you're doing right now! Since the devil is the father of lies (John 8:44), you stay sober when you think about what is true. When you open your Bible for your daily chapter or check your email for a morning devotion or meditate on a passage while in your garden, you are resisting the devil by thinking the thoughts of God.

Don't let your guard down. Fill up on the Water of Life. That's how you stay sober and avoid getting drunk with the devil.

Devotions for Special Days

Did Jesus have a beard?
Good Friday
Pastor Daron Lindemann

Back in my college days, I wrote love letters to my girlfriend. I tried to be creative and fun. One time I mailed a handful of whiskers. I had shaved off my beard (which she didn't like). It was a vivid, visual reminder that I was thinking of her.

When she opened the envelope, the shavings scattered all over the place like ugly, black glitter. She wasn't impressed. But, two things happened: 1) she married me and 2) of all the love letters we shared, that one still stands out as the most memorable.

Did Jesus have a beard?

As a faithful, law-abiding Jewish man, Jesus likely would have had a beard. Jesus would have carefully taken care of his beard by putting oil on it, and he would have refrained from clipping the corners.

Then, there's this prophecy in Isaiah 50:6 where the servant of the Lord is speaking, and we rightly identify that these words God gave to the prophet Isaiah represent the future Savior, Jesus. He says, **"I offered my back to those who beat me, my cheeks to those who pulled out my beard; I did not hide my face from mocking and spitting."**

Jesus offered himself. All of himself. All of his life. All of his love. All of his pain. All of his body, including his beard.

Forgiving forever all of your sins. Inviting you to give him all of you.

Find a reason to believe
Easter Sunday
Pastor Jeremy Mattek

"On the first day of the week, very early in the morning, the women took the spices they had prepared and went to the tomb. They found the stone rolled away from the tomb, but when they entered, they did not find the body of the Lord Jesus" (Luke 24:1-3).

Sunday morning was difficult for these women. The image of Jesus hanging on a cross was still fresh in their minds. The rapid pace at which it all happened was still so unexpected. Have you ever felt like these women?

Have you ever gone nights without sleep because your sorrow is so deep? Has your heart ever tried to carry a heavy burden you didn't see coming? And have you ever felt like that feeling would never change?

It seems these women did. You wouldn't bring burial spices to a grave if you were looking for the living. They weren't expecting to see life. They were expecting to see death. But what they found was enough to give hope, peace, and joy to anyone who has ever been convinced he or she will never again feel those wonderful things.

They saw proof that Jesus was risen and that his sacrifice for our sins was accepted. They saw God's ability to keep a promise to love us and to give us the greatest victory of all. They saw, just as we do as we consider the empty tomb, the glorious significance of Easter morning.

Moms can do things that Jesus can't
Mother's Day
Pastor Daron Lindemann

Jesus ascended into heaven. He's no longer physically here, but seated at the right hand of the Father, he is ruling all things with his grace.

He doesn't have a physical lap in this world for children to sit on. He doesn't look at us with a physical face that can give that "I've told you a million times" look like Mom can.

So, moms can do things that Jesus can't! Jesus himself isn't a mom. Never will be. Moms make lunches, give hugs, shuttle kids to practices, and plan spectacular birthday parties.

Moms can do things that Jesus can't. But Jesus can do things that moms can't.

Jesus once prayed to God the Father, **"I will remain in the world no longer, but they** [any believers who follow Jesus] **are still in the world, and I am coming to you. Holy Father, protect them by the power of your name"** (John 17:11).

Moms, you can't be the Savior of your children. Only Jesus can. Let that remind you of these three things.

1. Jesus ascended and is doing his job protecting you and your children.
2. Jesus is the Savior of you and your children.
3. Jesus can do things for you and your children that you can't.

Rest and rejoice in those promises from Jesus. While Jesus is doing his job of protecting you and your children with his saving grace, you just keep doing your job of mothering.

A compassionate Father
Father's Day
Sarah Habben

There have been bad parents ever since sin grew roots in the Garden of Eden. Parents who get more pleasure from a private vice than from pitching balls in the backyard. Parents who beat and belittle and serve up guilt.

There have always been loving parents too. Parents who help with homework and chase away bedtime monsters and sit shotgun with new drivers and pray for their children. Those parents aren't perfect. They lose patience. They break promises. They hurt feelings. But they love their children. Rather than burdening their children, they step in when situations exceed their children's physical or emotional limits. That's compassion.

"As a father has compassion on his children, so the Lord has compassion on those who fear him" (Psalm 103:13). God knows our limitations: we're sinful; we're dust. God, who can do anything, does not demand the impossible from us. God, who is powerful, doesn't beat or belittle us. God, who is perfect, doesn't serve up guilt. Instead God chooses to love us with compassion. He sent Jesus to be holy in our place. To lift the heavy suitcase of our sin from our feeble arms. To pay the extravagant price of that overweight baggage with his life. To forgive our parenting fails—the times when our words and actions toward our children don't reflect God's character. To earn for us the joy of addressing our holy God as "Abba."

Lord, thank you for the gift of loving, Christian fathers. Make them ever more like you. Amen.

Slow down your Thanksgiving
Thanksgiving Day
Pastor Daron Lindemann

The rush is on. Get the turkey in the oven. Finalize the cleaning. Make that last-minute trip to the store, pick up Grandma, and get to church. Lots to do.

And Thanksgiving happens. You quickly clean up so that you can score the best Black Friday shopping deals, get back home, decorate the house for Christmas, and start baking snickerdoodles.

Whoa, partner. Just a minute now. Slow down your Thanksgiving.

After the flood, Noah paused and **"built an altar to the Lord and, taking some of all the clean animals and clean birds, he sacrificed burnt offerings on it"** (Genesis 8:20). Noah's behavior at that moment was built upon a patient, trusting faith that he displayed already on the ark.

Water had covered the earth for 150 days. That's 5 months of bad weather! And then it took another 3 months for the murky floodwaters to recede enough that the mountaintops were visible. Then 40 days later Noah opened a window in the ark and sent out a raven and then a dove that returned to him, indicating there was no dry ground. He waited a few more months. Finally, **"God said to Noah, 'Come out of the ark'"** (Genesis 8:15,16).

All total, Noah occupied the ark for one year and ten days.

Take time to thank God. Patiently trust that he may do his divine work over a longer period of time than you might prefer. Slow down your Thanksgiving. The waiting is actually worship too.

About the Writers

Pastor Mike Novotny has served God's people in full-time ministry since 2007 in Madison and, most recently, at The CORE in Appleton, Wisconsin. He also serves as the lead speaker for Time of Grace, where he shares the good news about Jesus through television, print, and online platforms. Mike loves seeing people grasp the depth of God's amazing grace and unstoppable mercy. His wife continues to love him (despite plenty of reasons not to), and his two daughters open his eyes to the love of God for every Christian. When not talking about Jesus or dating his wife/girls, Mike loves playing soccer, running, and reading.

Linda Buxa is a freelance writer and Bible study leader. She is a regular speaker at women's retreats and conferences across the country, as well as a regular blogger and contributing writer for Time of Grace Ministry. Linda is the author of *Dig In! Family Devotions to Feed Your Faith, Parenting by Prayer,* and *Made for Friendship.* She and her husband, Greg, have lived in Alaska, Washington D.C., and California. They now live in Wisconsin, where they are raising their three children.

Andrea Delwiche lives in Wisconsin with her husband, three kids, two dogs, cat, and a goldfish pond full of fish. She enjoys reading, knitting, and road-tripping with her family. Although a lifelong believer, she began to come into a deeper understanding of what it means to follow Christ far into adulthood (always a beginner on that journey!). Andrea has facilitated a Christian discussion group for women at her church for many years.

Pastor Jon Enter served as a pastor in West Palm Beach, Florida, for ten years. He is now a campus pastor and instructor at St. Croix Lutheran Academy in St. Paul, Minnesota. Jon also serves as a regular speaker on Grace Talks video devotions and a contributing writer to the ministry. He once led a tour at his college, and the Lord had him meet his future wife, Debbi. They are now drowning in pink and glitter with their four daughters: Violet, Lydia, Eden, and Maggie.

Pastor Matt Ewart and his wife, Amy, have been blessed with three young children who keep life interesting. Matt is currently a pastor in Lakeville, Minnesota, and has previously served as a pastor in Colorado and Arizona.

Sarah Habben is a pastor's wife and mom of four daughters. She and her family have been blessed to call several beautiful places "home": Alberta, Canada; the Caribbean island of Antigua; and most recently Flagstaff, Arizona. Sarah is the author of *The Mom God Chose: Mothering Like Mary* (2015, Northwestern Publishing House) and the coauthor of *The Bloodstained Path to God* (2012, Northwestern Publishing House).

Ann Jahns and her husband live in Wisconsin as recent empty nesters, having had the joy of raising three boys to young adulthood. She is the director of marketing for a Christian nonprofit agency and a freelance proofreader and copy editor. Ann has been privileged to teach Sunday school and lead Bible studies for women of all ages. One of her passions is supporting women in the "sandwich generation" as they experience the unique joys and challenges of raising children while supporting aging parents.

Pastor Daron Lindemann is pastor at a new mission start in Pflugerville, Texas. Previously, he served in downtown Milwaukee and in Irmo, South Carolina.

Daron has authored articles or series for *Forward in Christ* magazine, *Preach the Word*, and his own weekly Grace MEMO devotions. He lives in Texas with his wife, Cara, and has two adult sons.

Pastor Jeremy Mattek has been married to Karen since 2000. God has blessed them with five children (three girls and two boys). Together, they find great joy in encouraging souls with the gospel of Jesus Christ. Jeremy is currently a pastor in Greenville, Wisconsin, and is a regular speaker for Grace Talks and Evening Encouragements.

Jason Nelson had a career as a teacher, counselor, and leader. He has a bachelor's degree in education, did graduate work in theology, and has a master's degree in counseling psychology. After his career ended in disabling back pain, he wrote the book *Miserable Joy: Chronic Pain in My Christian Life*. He has written and spoken extensively on a variety of topics related to the Christian life. Jason has been a contributing writer for Time of Grace since 2010. He has authored many Grace Moments devotions and several books. Jason lives with his wife, Nancy, in Wisconsin.

Pastor Jared Oldenburg has worked with churches in urban and suburban Milwaukee; Seattle; Denver; and Santa Maria, California. He and his wife, Aimee, and their three children currently live and serve a congregation in Castle Rock, Colorado. Jared is also a speaker on Grace Talks video devotions.

Pastor David Scharf served as a pastor in Greenville, Wisconsin, and now serves as a professor of theology at Martin Luther College in Minnesota. He has presented at numerous leadership, outreach, and missionary conferences across the country. He is a contributing writer for Time of Grace and a speaker for Grace Talks video devotions. Dave and his wife have six children.

Pastor Clark Schultz loves Jesus; his wife, Kristin, and their three boys; the Green Bay Packers; Milwaukee Brewers; Wisconsin Badgers; and—of course—Batman. His ministry stops are all in Wisconsin and include a vicar year in Green Bay, tutoring and recruiting for a Christian ministry at a high school in Watertown, teacher/coach at a Christian high school in Lake Mills, and a pastor in Cedar Grove. He currently serves as a pastor in West Bend. Pastor Clark's favorite quote is, "Find something you love to do and you will never work a day in your life."

Christine Wentzel, a native of Milwaukee, lives in Norfolk, Virginia, with her husband, James, and their fur-child, Piper. After two lost decades as a prodigal, Christine gratefully worships and serves her Salvation Winner at Resurrection in Chesapeake, Virginia. There she discovered latent talents to put to use for the Lord. In 2009 she began to write and create graphic design for an online Christian women's ministry, A Word for Women, and now also joyfully serves as a coadministrator for this ministry. www.awordforwomen.com

About Time of Grace

Time of Grace is an independent, donor-funded ministry that connects people to God's grace—his love, glory,
and power—so they realize the temporary things of life
don't satisfy. What brings satisfaction is knowing that
because Jesus lived, died, and rose for all of us, we have
access to the eternal God—right now and forever.

To discover more, please visit **timeofgrace.org** or call
800.661.3311.

Help share God's message of grace!

Every gift you give helps Time of Grace reach people around the world with the good news of Jesus.
Your generosity and prayer support take the gospel
of grace to others through our ministry outreach and
help them experience a satisfied life as they see God
all around them.

Give today at timeofgrace.org/give or by calling 800.661.3311.

Thank you!